BETTER THAN THE BEST

Black Athletes Speak, 1920–2007

BETTER than the BEST

BLACK ATHLETES SPEAK, 1920–2007

EDITED BY *John C. Walter* AND *Malina Iida*

A V Ethel Willis White Book

UNIVERSITY OF WASHINGTON PRESS
Seattle & London

This book is published with the assistance of a grant from the V Ethel Willis White Endowed Fund, established through the generosity of Deehan Wyman, Virginia Wyman, and the Wyman Youth Trust.

UNIVERSITY OF WASHINGTON PRESS
PO Box 50096
Seattle, WA 98145–5096, USA
www.washington.edu/uwpress

LIBRARY OF CONGRESS CATALOGING-IN-PUBLICATION DATA
Walter, John C. (John Christopher)
Better than the best : Black athletes speak, 1920–2007 /
John C. Walter and Malina Iida.
    p. cm. — (V Ethel Willis White book)
Includes bibliographical references and index.
ISBN 978-0-295-99053-8 (pbk. : alk. paper)
1. African American athletes—Biography. 2. African American athletes—History.
I. Iida, Malina. II. Title.
GV697.A1.W34   2010   796.0922—dc22   2010031726
[B]

The paper used in this publication is acid-free and 90 percent recycled from at least 50 percent post-consumer waste. It meets the minimum requirements of American National Standard for Information Sciences—Permanence of Paper for Printed Library Materials, ANSI Z39.48-1984.

FRONTISPIECE: Wyomia Tyus anchored the U.S. 4 x 100-meter relay team, which won the gold medal in world record time at the 1968 Summer Olympic Games in Mexico City. UPI-Bettman/Corbis.

CONTENTS

ACKNOWLEDGMENTS

WE WISH TO THANK THE FORD FOUNDATION FOR PROVIDING THE funds to interview the thirty-seven athletes in the Blacks in Sports Oral History Project and the athletes whose stories were selected for this book. Thanks also to research assistants, Katherine Bolland and Jennifer L. Dobson, who arranged Dr. Walter's interview schedules, and to Aurelio "Jay" del Rosario, who searched archives for difficult to find photos. A special thanks to Johnnella Butler, who cheerfully edited and shared insights.

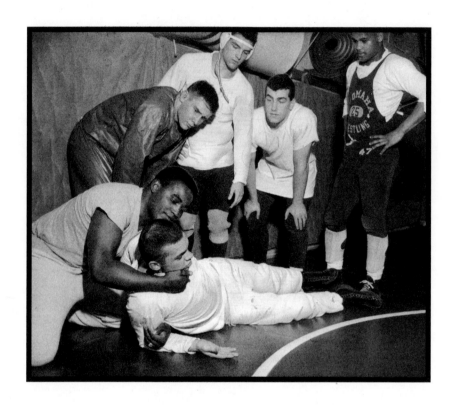

Don Benning teaching a winning strategy, ca. 1965.

INTRODUCTION

THE ORIGINS OF THIS BOOK ARE TWOFOLD. FIRST, I WANTED TO provide a first-person account to demonstrate that black athletes have historically acted with a consciousness of their significance in the struggle against racism. The second is more personal, but part of the same consciousness. In January 1953, I came to the United States from Jamaica on a track scholarship to Philander Smith College, a small, black liberal arts college in Little Rock, Arkansas. For a long time I had wanted to attend college in the United States. This was against the wishes of my mother and father, who wanted me to go to Oxford, Cambridge, or Heidelberg University. I longed for America, however, because in American movies there was so much student enthusiasm at college sporting events, including track and field. One such film, *Crazylegs*, told the story of Wisconsin University football player Elroy Hirsch, called Crazylegs because when he ran with the football his legs would fly in every direction. The students in the stands were cheering for him, and I wanted to be part of that college milieu. I also was fascinated by a number of cowboy movies that, for some reason, I thought were set in the Southwest. When the opportunity came to go to Arkansas—without any knowledge of what went on there—I seized the moment. Furthermore, Les Laing, a graduate of my high school, had attended Fresno State College on a track scholarship and was part of the 1948 Jamaican Olympic team. On a visit to our high school (Dinthill, which was located in Linstead, a major town in the island's interior), he spoke enthusiastically about college life in America and about the superior training afforded by American schools. Anyone aspiring to become an Olympic athlete, he said, would be best served by obtaining a scholarship to an American college. Becoming an Olympic star was not on my agenda; just being in America, and competing and winning for my college, was my dream.

My dream was reinforced in 1952 when I won the schoolboy Jamaican championship in the 800-yard run. Consequently, my coach, Ted Lamont, put me in a race against my two heroes, the Jamaican Arthur Wint and the American Mal Whitfield, silver and gold medalists in the 1948 and 1952 Olympics, respectively. At that time we did not have a national stadium so the race was held on a field that served the high schools in Kingston. The stadium came much later, in the 1960s, and was named after the same Arthur Wint against whom I ran in 1952. As expected, I came in third, but Whitfield remembers that race even today. It occurred two years before he won the coveted James E. Sullivan Award for America's outstanding amateur athlete. Mal tells his story in this book from his boyhood in Texas and Los Angeles, where he first saw his heroes, the Olympians Eddie Tolan and Ralph Metcalfe, at the 1932 Los Angeles Olympic Games.

Luckily for me, a recruiter from America saw me run and, a few weeks later, Philander Smith College offered me a full scholarship. I knew nothing about Philander Smith. All I cared about was that it was an American college in the Southwest and, therefore, it would be a wonderful place to be. To my parents' dismay, I accepted the scholarship. All my dreams had come true! Philander Smith College recruited five of us together to create, as the coach later said, an instant track team: two sprinters, two middle-distance runners, and myself, a multipurpose runner who ran the 440 yards, the 880 yards, and the mile. My teammates were twins Roy and Willy Taylor, the sprinters, and Alan Moore and Oswald Winter, the two middle-distance runners. Before our arrival, Philander Smith did not have enough runners to compete in the various meets of the Southwest Conference and, furthermore, no one at the college had a good enough record to compete in the Penn and Drake Relays, national, integrated meets. The expectation was that with additions to this Jamaican nucleus, Philander Smith would have a winning team. To compete successfully, a school had to have four people who could capably run 100 yards to compete in the 4 x 100-yard relay. Similarly, in competitive times, to get accepted at the integrated big meets a school needed four people who could run 440 yards to compete in the 4 x 440-yard relay. These athletes would also compete in individual events such as the 100 yards, 220 yards, and so on up to the mile run. We did not have four people capable of running 440 yards at good speed, so we improvised. In the 4 x 440 relay, we had two men who ran 440 yards at very good speed, and I would run 440 yards even though my specialty was 880 yards. We would then dragoon one of the 100 meter specialists to run the 440. We usually gave this person the third slot and tried to give him a nice lead. That way, we could compete as a team. Astonishingly, we competed successfully with these jury-rigged relay teams and excelled in our individual events. I usually won the 880 yards and the mile run.

Arriving in America in January 1953, we knew nothing of racism and segregation. The American Olympians I had met had not mentioned it and the concept of segregation was foreign to us, coming from Jamaica. Before reaching Little Rock, however, our introduction to American segregation began. Because of fog, our aircraft landed in Memphis and we were to continue on by bus to Little Rock. We needed to use the bus station restroom before continuing our journey, so all five of us strolled toward the places indicated by the signs. We saw "White" and "Colored" signs, but I thought the "Colored" sign meant a colored tile finishing on the floor— perhaps a beautiful restroom for women—so we entered the nearest one marked "White." In brief, there was an African American janitor in there, who after questioning our origins, suggested that perhaps we should not be in there. Thinking he was mistaken, we ignored him and he said nothing else to us, so we used the facility and boarded our bus to Little Rock. We mentioned the incident to our coach that night.

Stunned by the coach's explanation, we decided to leave for home the next day! We were astounded because in Jamaica segregation did not exist. At the end of slavery in 1833, the majority of people on the island of Jamaica were of African ancestry. These ex-slaves, by the last quarter of the nineteenth century, had made it clear to the so-called white population that since they were freed persons, they would not abide by any laws that hinted at segregation. It would be false to say that there was not some discrimination by former slave owners and later even by those people of African ancestry who rose quickly to the upper and middle classes and became part of a group that discriminated on the basis of class. For this reason, obtaining an education and property became of paramount importance to all people in Jamaica, as in the rest of the Caribbean. Being segregated then on the basis of color was incomprehensible to us when we came to

America in the middle of the twentieth century. By that time, discrimination by class was even beginning to be challenged. This is why Bob Marley later sang, "One love, one heart, let's get together and feel all right."

The coach advised that we should meet the president of the college, Dr. Marquis LaFayette Harris, who was probably named after the great Marquis de Lafayette of the American Revolutionary War, and if we still wanted to leave, then we could. The president, a most persuasive speaker, explained the facts of racial segregation in America, but suggested we stay for the semester and then decide. A huge man, the president always wore a three-piece suit with a vest with piping and a Phi Beta Kappa pin on a gold chain draped prominently across his broad chest. His shoes always gleamed. Everything about him suggested a well-educated Edwardian man of learning. After retelling the story of segregation that we had heard from our coach, he said he thought that we for the most part would not be discriminated against because we were foreigners and because of that we could form a bridge between the school and the surrounding white community.[1] After conferring with each other, we decided to remain until the end of that semester, learn a thing or two, and then leave for home.

As it turned out, we remained for the duration because a few days after our meeting with the president, the president or the coach introduced us to a local black "man of means" who knew the governor of Arkansas, Orval Faubus of Central High School fame. Soon after, this businessman took us to pay a courtesy call on the governor. Mr. Faubus greeted us warmly, welcoming us to Arkansas. He said that we could form a bridge between "us and them," although there was no reference to race, so we wondered what this "us and them" meant. Before long we found out. Our host mentioned that Philander Smith College had no track. Our track was the basketball gym. The governor said he would look into the matter. I do not know how it happened, but by March our team began to practice at Central High School. To the best of my knowledge, this had never happened before. Soon some of the white high school athletes would ask us technical questions and watch as we practiced things like baton passing. We did not race against them—after all we were college athletes—but sometimes their aspiring 880-yards runner would jog along with me.

This was 1953, the year before the 1954 *Brown v. Board of Education* decision. Because of the governor's intervention, we were able to practice at a white, segregated high school on the same track as the white high school athletes. One of my teammates, who remained at Philander Smith, reports that they practiced there until 1956 when he transferred, but there was, indeed, a subtle change. After 1954, the black college runners had to wait until the white high school athletes had totally left the field. I left Philander Smith College after two seasons, in the fall 1954, for Arkansas AM&N, now the University of Arkansas at Pine Bluff.

Graduating cum laude in 1956, the year of the Melbourne Olympics, I had near Olympic times in the 800 meters, but knew I could not make the Jamaican team because I had developed a bad case of asthma. My grades, however, got me through two graduate schools on academic scholarships. I could not have had my education completely paid for were it not for my track scholarships at those first two colleges.

In 1971, as assistant professor of American and African American history at Purdue University, I found myself telling students of the Governor Faubus I knew in 1953, much to their dismay and disbelief. I discussed with them the complex web of relationships among politics, economics, social interaction, race, and sports. What if that black "man of stature" had not taken us to see the governor? Practicing in a basketball gym, we certainly would not have performed as well as we did in our conference.

Ever since becoming a professor, I had thought of doing a book about African American athletes who by dint of very hard work, discipline, and intelligence managed to parley their athletics skills into successful lives. I decided in 1990 to ask The Ford Foundation for a grant to collect the stories of a number of these athletes in their own words. I wanted to start with a representative number of black athletes who began the assault on segregation in sports, and of those who came soon after. Fortunately, The Ford Foundation granted me enough money to interview thirty-seven former athletes who fit that description. After 1995, edited segments of these interviews were made available to researchers on request.

The stories contained in this book represent thirteen selections from those interviewed between 1990 and 2007. I have selected those most representative of the expanse of participation of African Americans in sports from the late 1940s to the present, including outstanding accomplishments in sports where black athletes are a rarity. The selection also reflects the issues and perceptions of the different decades as the color line twisted and turned.

The African American athletes, who were part of the first wave of the integration of white colleges and universities in the twentieth century, experienced, for the most part, a life distinctly different from their white peers. The restrictions in places of higher learning were very similar to those outside the academy. Only with the civil rights gains of the 1950s through the 1970s was there surcease from racial discrimination. Even on the playing fields of colleges, universities, and professional sports racial discrimination ruled.

Any student of sports in the United States will find in the literature, especially between 1960 and the present, long treatises on the practice of "stacking," which is the practice of preventing black athletes from playing in positions that required leadership on any team. Until recently the quarterback position was considered a place for very intelligent athletes. Since blacks were not considered intelligent, they were prevented from playing quarterback even if they had excelled at the position in high school. Instead, coaches relegated black athletes to running backs and wide receivers on the offensive team, and safeties and linebackers on the defensive team.[2] In basketball, the point guard runs the team so, until recently, no blacks were point guards. In Seattle, for example, Warren Moon was a star at the University of Washington as a quarterback, but could find no job in the National Football League, not even with the Seattle Seahawks who hired comparatively much less talented quarterbacks and went nowhere. Moon went to Canada, where he won five championships with the Edmonton Eskimos of the Canadian Football League. Only after that did the Houston Oilers, and later the Seahawks, find it appropriate to offer him a starting job. His case is representative of the topic of Phillip M. Hoose's *Necessities: Racial Barriers in American Sports.*[3] *Necessities'* chapters are not mere cerebral musings; they deal with real-life situations in all sports. Rigorous and evenhanded sociological studies show that even now, particularly in professional football, the preference is still for white quarterbacks, even those with mediocre skills.[4] No second chances were afforded black quarterbacks. Generally, the burden on the black athlete to be always superior existed in all sports, prompting one researcher to exclaim that in baseball, "mediocrity is a white luxury."[5] In baseball, as late as the year 2000, shortstop and first base positions were also sacred, not to be violated by someone of dark skin. The majority of African Americans played outfield positions requiring speed and agility—not brains, it was thought. Sports involve more than players on the playing field. Sports include managers, coaches, coordinators, and owners too. Even now, there are teams in all sports that have yet to employ a black coach, a black athletic director, or a black general manager.[6]

Interestingly, the racial prejudice black athletes experienced during the nineteenth century was less than that experienced during the early years of the twentieth century. Throughout the pre–Civil War era and up to the late 1880s, black Americans played significant roles in many sports of the period. Most of the jockeys of that period were black men, and black boxers abounded. However, soon after the end of Reconstruction, with Southern states bent on reestablishing white supremacy by physical segregation, black people were pushed slowly and unyieldingly out of the sports they once dominated.

Horse racing provides a dramatic example. In the 1870s, black jockeys dominated the sport. In the first Kentucky Derby, held in 1875, fourteen of the fifteen jockeys were black men, including the winner, Oliver Lewis. Isaac Murphy, between 1879 and 1895, won three Kentucky Derbies and 44 percent of his races, an "incredible" success rate.[7] Such successes against the background of creeping Jim Crow laws caused anxiety among race patrons and the general population. By 1894 the newly formed Jockey Club adopted a "whites only" policy.[8] For a while this ban was not enforced. White replacements of similar caliber were hard to find, therefore, despite the ban, black jockeys continued to dominate horse racing until 1911, when the rising tide of racism across the entire American landscape made it easy to rid the sport of black jockeys.[9] Black jockeys disappeared from the Kentucky Derby in 1912 and from the sport entirely by World War I. Edward Hotaling points out, "the Jockey Club gave itself the power to outlaw tracks and stable owners, banning them from club-approved tracks until reinstated."[10] Soon after its founding, it also assumed the job of licensing jockeys and all others it decided needed to be licensed. The Club also published the American Stud Book, designed to keep the provenance of "thoroughbreds pure."[11] The Jockey Club, a product of the New York / New Jersey horse racing entrepreneurs who wanted to impose order and precise rules on the sport, also eventually successfully banned black jockeys.[12]

Cycling was another popular sport among Americans in the last decade of the nineteenth century. Yet from 1896 until 1910, Marshall "Major" Taylor, an African American, reigned as the best cyclist in the world. Soon, some cyclists, rather than meet the challenge of this gifted athlete by competing against him, withdrew from the League of American Wheelmen, forming the American Racing Cyclists Union in 1898, a "whites only" group. Fortunately, the League continued to compete with Taylor until his retirement in 1910, at age thirty-two. He died destitute in 1932, but his old white competitors from the league, embarrassed by Taylor's lowly place in a pauper's grave near Chicago, banded together in 1948, exhumed his body and gave him an honorable burial complete with a bronze plaque that read, "World's champion bicycle racer who came up the hard way without hatred in his heart, an honest, courageous, and god-fearing, clean living, gentlemanly athlete. A credit to his race who always gave out his best. Gone but not forgotten."[13]

Before the Civil War, black people played with whites in Northern baseball clubs, but after the war, in as early as 1867, the National Association of Baseball Players banned all black players. Yet, in some venues, the ban was unenforced. In 1876, the newly formed National League reinforced the ban (although a few African Americans continued to play on minor league teams until 1889).[14] In response, the first all-Negro professional teams were founded beginning in 1884. These were mostly entities of short duration; however, in 1920, a black man, Rube Foster, founded the Negro National League that became an enduring and commercially successful organization.[15]

In sports other than organized team sports, blacks did somewhat better because it was more difficult to segregate athletes, and the taboo of close physical contact was limited by the nature of the sport. By 1880, interracial boxing had gained acceptability. Boxing contests were seen as surrogates of promoters and sponsors, and combatants usually met for an hour or two, and contact was completed. Unlike in a team sport, boxers did not travel together, share facilities, or socialize.

However, as more black men began to win in the various divisions of the sport, complaints arose regarding the so-called undue prominence of black boxers. Sportswriters such as Charles A. Dana, editor for the *New York Sun*, wrote in 1895: "We are in the midst of a growing menace. The black man is rapidly forging to the front ranks in athletics, especially in the field of fisticuffs. We are in the midst of a black rise against white supremacy. . . . What America needs now is another John L. Sullivan."[16] This was indeed a quaint plaint, because John L. Sullivan had beaten no black boxer; he had merely avoided them. Perhaps Dana had been thinking of the convincing victory of George Dixon four years earlier, who defeated Cal McCarthy and earned the bantamweight title, becoming the first black man to hold an American boxing title. Another black boxer, Joe Gans, known as "The Old Master" even though he died at the age of thirty-six, fought from age seventeen until his death in 1910, and compiled a scary record of knockouts on the way to the lightweight championship in the first decade of the twentieth century.

This fluid form of discrimination and segregation in the ranks below the heavyweight division was not to be found in the heavyweight division because it was clearly understood by most in America that a black man becoming heavyweight champion would undermine all the racist theories about blacks being physically inferior. Therefore, white heavyweight champions avoided black challengers at all times until 1908. This segregation in boxing ended when the formidable African American heavyweight boxer Jack Johnson, along with a number of sportswriters looking for a sensational story, goaded the reigning white champion, Tommy Burns, into fighting Johnson for ready cash and the heavyweight championship of the world. Burns, a true miser, fought only for big purses. Interestingly, the bout was held in Australia, for Burns wanted to avoid the possibility of losing on American soil. He lost anyway, and Jack Johnson became heavyweight champion of the world. Tommy, though, was much richer.

The exclusion of black people from competing with whites in any sport continued unabated well into the twentieth century, and indeed it was under freakish circumstances that Johnson had been able to taunt Burns into a fight. So outraged were white Americans that a black man held the heavyweight championship that thousands of people importuned the former white heavyweight champ Jim Jeffries—who like John L. Sullivan, had always refused to fight black boxers—to return after a four-year retirement to fight Johnson, and restore white supremacy. The words "Great White Hope" now entered the national vocabulary. Jeffries fought Johnson in 1910 in Reno, Nevada, and lost. He honestly admitted that even in his prime, he could not have beaten Jack Johnson.

Johnson's career, from 1908 to 1915, is the best example in the history of American sports of the pervasiveness of the color line and the difficulty of African Americans to break and erase it. In fact, Johnson was persecuted throughout his entire life. Harassed for dating and marrying white women, threatened with death from unknown sources, harassed by the FBI and the U.S. Department of Justice for breaking segregationist laws, he eventually left the country, remaining a fugitive until 1915. Fatigued by this constant harassment, he finally lost to Jess Willard in a dubious decision in Cuba in 1915. Subsequent white heavyweights refused to fight black boxers until 1937 when James J. Braddock, expecting an easy win, fought Joe Louis and lost his heavyweight championship. Braddock's decision to fight Louis may have resulted from what had happened the previous year when Louis, with a record of 27–0, lost to the German, Max Schmeling, then touted as a prime example of white supremacy. If this were the case, it proved a disaster for James J. Braddock. He lost badly, remarking after the bout that Louis's punches were "like someone jammed an electric bulb in your face and busted it."[17]

American football resisted segregation until 1934 when the newly formed National Football League capitulated to racist pressure. However, by 1946, professional football, now in its ascendancy, realized the backwardness of its 1934 decision and integrated. That year the Los Angeles Rams hired two African American players, Kenny Washington and Woody Strode, and the Cleveland Browns, playing in the All-American Football Conference, signed two black players, Bill Willis and Marion Motley. Black men could play, but only at certain positions. At the quarterback position, the rule against black men remained. In October 1953, Willie Thrower became the first black quarterback in the professional ranks, starting for the Chicago Bears. But by the end of the season, Thrower was gone. There was no second chance for him. Seventeen years later, James Harris played as a regular quarterback beginning in 1969, but at the end of his career remarked, "[blacks] get two types of opportunities to play QB in the NFL. A chance and a 'nigger' chance."[18]

Throughout the period of rigid racial discrimination in sports, there were many explanations for not allowing black players to play with whites. The most frequent explanation was that black people were an inferior species and, therefore, contact with white people in something as intimate as sports violated natural laws. With time, that reasoning began to lose its potency. New ones had to be found as black athletes continued to perform extraordinary feats, particularly in northern colleges and universities, and in the Olympics. By 1932, the idea of black physical inferiority was a canard. Excuses such as the one by a sportswriter when Joe Louis, on his way to the heavyweight championship, defeated Primo Carnera in 1935 that "Something sly and sinister and perhaps not quite human came out of the African jungle last night to strike down and utterly demolish the huge hulk that had been Primo Carnera, the giant,"[19] became standard fare. Evidence of a change in the excuse formula appeared when Louis defeated Max Schmeling in 1938 and avenged his previous loss to the German. Syndicated newspaper columnist Hugh S. Johnson wrote, "The piteous flash I got of Schmeling, wrecked and out on his feet, was vivid pictorial disproof of this nonsense about Aryan physical supremacy."[20] Turning to the local problem, Johnson finally gave up on the myth of white physical superiority. "The average of white intelligence is above the average of black intelligence probably because the white race is several thousand years farther away from jungle savagery. But, for the same reason, the average of white physical equipment is lower," he decided.[21] Yet if black men had equal opportunity in sport competition, it could result in no "white champions at all."[22] It was now important to embrace America's Negro competitors. "There should be just as much pride," he concluded, "in their progress and prowess under our system as in the triumph of any other American. For all their misfortunes and shortcomings they are our people—Negroes, yes, but our Negroes."[23]

The evidence was clear that after 1936, no sane person could think of Joe Louis and other athletes like him in other sports—including Olympic sports—and claim that African Americans were inferior physical specimens. So the excuses were switched and, as the *New York Sun* noted, "The American Negro is a natural athlete."[24] In the South at the same time, O. B. Keeler, writing for the *Atlanta Journal* about Joe Louis and on Jesse Owens's exploits in the Berlin Olympics, had no need to comment on the intelligence question. That was understood; therefore, all that needed to be emphasized was: "Our fastest runners are colored boys, and our longest jumpers, and highest leapers. And now our champion fighting man with the fists is Joseph Louis Barrow."[25]

At least by the mid-1930s, white sportswriters had arrived at the conclusion that being white did not confer natural physical superiority on white people. A grudging admission that black athletes were at least the equal of whites emerged. Yet, behind all the excuses and obfuscations, fair-thinking white Americans and the black population knew that the record suggested that what was in play was fear held by white athletes and the white population that the concept of white superiority in everything could no longer be sustained.

In the years 1909 and 1910, two progressive interracial organizations were formed: the National Association for the Advancement of Colored People (NAACP) and the National Urban League (NUL). While the NUL worked quietly with institutions, corporations, and governments to improve the lot of black people by removing racial discrimination, particularly in employment and in government services, the NAACP, from its outset, attempted to use all political and legal means possible to rid the United States of racial discrimination. These two soon-to-be-powerful civil rights organizations, appeared coincidently with the drawing of a more rigid color line in every social activity, including sports. The right to vote in primary elections asserted by the NAACP began as a legal matter in 1924, with victory partially achieved by 1944, when in the case of *Smith v. Allwright* the court ruled that African Americans could not be prevented from voting in primary elections in the former Confederate states.[26] There can be no doubt that owners of professional teams, as well as college and university administrators, sensed a change in the nation regarding racial issues and made the changes necessary to avoid criticism.

But there were other forces at work, too. Legal challenges to segregation in housing had begun in the 1920s, resulting in the celebrated 1948 *Shelley v. Kraemer* decision where the Supreme Court essentially ruled that state-involved racial discrimination in housing was unlawful.[27] This did not end segregation in housing, but it marked the beginning of the slow march toward the eventual congressional action in the Fair Housing Act of 1968 that, in great part, outlawed discrimination in housing.[28] Not only in housing and voting, but in equal educational opportunities, the efforts of civil rights organizations resulted in the 1938 *Missouri ex rel. Gaines v. Canada* case that served notice that soon Southern colleges and universities would have to accept blacks into their graduate programs on the same basis as whites.[29] This progressive case, even though it did not reach a Supreme Court ruling, clearly indicated that the attack on segregation in graduate education would intensify. It is significant that this coincided with both the removal of segregation in heavyweight boxing and the politically influential exploits of black athletes at the 1932 Olympics in Los Angeles and the 1936 Olympics in Berlin.

Additional pressure resulted from the work of individuals with an unquenchable desire to see black athletes have equal opportunities. One of the earliest crusaders for the integration of professional baseball was the celebrated sports columnist Sam Lacy of the Baltimore *Afro-American Newspapers*, the first narrator in this book. Lacy played professional baseball from 1920 to 1930, then turned to writing until his death seventy-three years later. He labored tirelessly not only to bring about the initial integration of baseball, but also to rid baseball of its discrimination in housing. Lacy points out that in this endeavor Wendell Smith of the *Pittsburgh Courier* helped a great deal, and he credits Smith with promoting Jackie Robinson to Major League Baseball ahead of his picks, Junior Gilliam and

Joe Black. Both players soon entered the League and played exceedingly well, validating Lacy's assessments of them. Lacy's story, told with great charm and panache, shows how the black national press played a vital role in the desegregation of organized sports in America.

Nearly all the black athletes admitted to professional teams, and those who made the teams at colleges and universities in the North, quickly made themselves stars. This noteworthy development undermined the reigning perception in the general population that black people lacked the discipline to work hard in order to excel and/or the intelligence to master the intricacies of baseball and football. The very swift success of black athletes in baseball and football was not lost upon the owners of basketball teams. It was no accident that within four years of the initial "integration" of professional football and Major League Baseball that the Boston Celtics decided that it was in their best interest to integrate its organization by signing Chuck Cooper in 1950. That same year, the New York Knicks signed Nathaniel Clifton and the Washington Capitols signed Earl Lloyd. Within a few years, black men dominated the playing ranks of professional basketball. Interestingly, that same year the American Bowling Congress, which controlled segregated bowling in the Northern states, responded to pressure from the National Committee for Fair Play in Bowling (NCFPB), led by Hubert H. Humphrey, then-mayor of Minneapolis, Minnesota; Walter Reuther of the United Auto Workers (UAW-CIO); and the NAACP, to get rid of its whites-only clause.[30]

However, the Professional Golfers of America (PGA) appeared blind in the 1940s to the progressive changes taking place. In 1943, the PGA decided that they would have a whites-only policy on their tour. This was an anomalous decision, one that perhaps deserves further study. Pressures by black people, aided by California's Attorney General Stanley Mosk, finally persuaded the PGA in 1961 to rid itself of the line in its bylaws, "of the Caucasian race."[31]

If the PGA was regressive, then the United States National Lawn Tennis Association (USNLTA) was retrogressive. Tennis had always had an unwritten rule of not allowing blacks to play in the USNLTA Championships. In 1929, when two African American players tried to play in the USNLTA Junior Indoor Event in New York City, they were prevented from participating because the USNLTA had an "unwritten rule barring blacks from participation."[32] In response to a complaint by the NAACP, the United States Lawn Tennis Association[33] replied: "The policy of the USLTA has been to decline the entry of colored players in our championships. . . . In pursuing this policy we make no reflection upon the colored race but we believe that as a practical matter, the present method of separate associations . . . should be continued."[34] A breakthrough did not occur for many players until 1952, and it was not by legal action but by a series of thrusts and parries by African Americans against the USLTA. In many instances top-ranked white players, who felt that segregation in tennis was unworthy of this elite sport, assisted. Consequently, tennis segregation came to an end in 1952, two years after Althea Gibson, a black woman, finally broke through and played in a regular tournament sponsored by the USLTA. She then won at Wimbledon in 1956 and 1957.

In 1947, President Harry S. Truman received the report of the Civil Rights Commission, titled "To Secure These Rights." The report came out strongly against lynching and racial discrimination, particularly in employment, housing, and education. Truman knew that supporting these recommendations would be of great assistance to him in 1948 when running for re-election. He therefore announced his support for anti-lynching legislation and the establishment of a permanent Fair Employment Practices Committee. Nonetheless, to black people, without actual legislation these announcements smacked of promises not likely to be kept. Thus, in response to the imposition of the military draft in 1948, A. Philip Randolph, founder of the 1941 March on Washington, formed the League for Nonviolent Civil Disobedience and told the President point-blank that black people would more than likely not go to war or join the draft without desegregation of the armed forces. When, at the 1948 Democratic Convention, the Dixiecrats, led by South Carolina Senator Strom Thurmond, walked out and formed the States' Rights Party, Truman immediately issued Executive Orders 9980 and 9981, banning racial discrimination in federal employment and racial discrimination in the armed forces, respectively. Mal Whitfield was an active athlete at this time, a sergeant in the United States Air Force and an Olympian in 1948 and 1952. He tells his story in this book, from his childhood experience watching the 1932 Olympics in his hometown of Los Angeles to the present.

Nineteen forty-eight marked the beginning of an interesting sub-story of the Tennessee State University Tigerbelles, a group of black women at a historically black university, who under the leadership of Coach Edward Temple, left a legacy in Amateur Athletic Union (AAU) meets and in the Olympics that is unequaled by any school to date. Mae Faggs Starr, who went to the 1948 Olympics while still in high school was trained and supported by the New York City Police Athletic League (PAL). She was only sixteen and did not expect to win any medals when she qualified for the 1948 Olympic team. In order to go to college, this remarkable athlete, who represented the United States in three separate Olympic Games between 1948 and 1956, had to go south for an education. Recruited by Tennessee State University, she was by the 1952 Olympics, a formidable sprinter from 60 yards to 220 yards. About her trip to Nashville to attend Tennessee State University, she recalled:

> I get down to Nashville, and there I stand with my suitcase in my hand. I was standing out there in the middle of this train station looking up at this big sign over this greasy-looking waiting room that said "Colored." I was standing out there staring at that, and then I looked over at the white waiting room and it had oriental rugs on the floor, with nice provincial furniture in there, and it was beautiful. The colored waiting room had hard chairs and an old greasy looking counter, and the windows weren't even clean.

Faggs ended her running career in 1956 with a host of AAU titles, and one gold and one bronze medal in Olympic competition.

The aim of Executive Order 9981 to desegregate the U.S. Armed Forces was not achieved until after the end of the Korean War. Nevertheless, it was not lost on the general population that a deep chasm existed in the Democratic Party, and worse, the Dixiecrats were now likely to coalesce with the Republican Party to form a new North-South divide resembling the political cleavage of the immediate pre–Civil War years. But for black people, President Truman was a hero, and in the fall of 1948 he got their vote. Owners, managers, and coaches in the professional and collegiate ranks must have sensed that the times were "a-changin'."

These changes in American society, though slow paced, placed pressure on all aspects of sports in the United States. Colleges and universities stepped up the recruitment of black players after 1950. By 1956, the University of Oklahoma recruited its first black football player, Prentice Gault. Soon after other southern, white colleges and universities followed suit, though slowly and with trepidation. The famous game between the University of Southern California and Alabama with Southern Cal's Sam "Bam" Cunningham running roughshod over that all-white team in 1970 marked the end of the maintenance of the color line among southern schools. Four years earlier, at the famous National Collegiate Athletic Association Finals basketball game between Texas Western University (now the University of Texas at El Paso) and the University of Kentucky, when a squad of five black young men defeated the formerly unbeatable University of Kentucky team, the walls came tumbling down. A few years later, the University of Kentucky itself decided that in order to compete, it too had to integrate.

The presidential election of 1960 served as a crucible for American politics and sports. It was a referendum on whether the politics of intellectual stagnation, social ennui, status quo-ism, and racial bigotry could coexist with the rising militancy of African Americans and progressive whites, insurgent criticism by the Communist bloc, and the uncertainty of the friendship of the non-aligned nations of the world.

By 1960, sports began to exert a huge influence in American life and culture. The enlarged radio and television audience brought about material and structural influences for change. Even the quadrennial Olympic Games became a supremacy contest between the United States and the Soviet Union, distorting a sporting event into a political struggle for global influence.

The assassination of President Kennedy and the March on Washington in 1963, and the murder of Malcolm X in 1965 just after the passage of the landmark 1964 Civil Rights Act, all led to a political ferment unprecedented in the civil rights struggle since the Civil War. Sit-ins, Freedom Rides, and physical confrontations were the order of the day. As the "Civil Rights Revolution" heated up in the early 1960s, colleges, universities, and corporations, aware that America could indeed lose the propaganda war for the "hearts and minds" of a major part of the world's population, rushed to employ black people in visible positions. Many colleges and universities opened their faculties to black scholars, many of whom came from historically black colleges.

Six athletes, whose stories are recorded here, came into prominence in the 1960s—Arthur Ashe, Don Benning, Ken Hudson, Alan Page, Wyomia Tyus, and Lenny Wilkins. Cognizant that the opportunities now available to them had not been there for their parents, or even for their older sisters and brothers, they realized that failure was not an option.

In Omaha, Nebraska, Don Benning, a fierce former college wrestler, finally got the chance from the enlightened president of the University of Omaha to become head wrestling coach and assistant professor in 1963.

Conscious of tumult and violent racial confrontations in many parts of the country, Benning knew that if not for those turbulences, he perhaps would not have been given a chance to excel. In this book, he reflects that "because of the uniqueness of the situation, and the circumstances, I knew if I failed I was not going to be judged as Don Benning, but as an African American. . . . I was very aware those pressures were on me, and given those challenges I had to perform at the highest level in order to pass all the scrutiny."

Closer to the civil rights wars in Gary, Indiana, and Chicago, but ensconced on a bucolic college campus, Alan Page entered the University of Notre Dame on a football scholarship in 1963. Page recalls his awareness of the battle raging elsewhere, but he had to get his education. When he entered the National Football League, it bothered him that he had not become the lawyer he wanted to be. He finally resolved this conflict when he earned his law degree while playing professional football. After retiring from football, Page ran for a seat on the Minnesota Supreme Court. It was not easy. He recalls, "It was always some variation of 'He's not qualified; he's just a football player.' Alan Page won and is currently serving his third term as a supreme court justice as of 2007.

The United States, between 1960 and 1972, appeared to be in the throes of civil strife at home, even as it found itself in a referendum war against communism in Vietnam. Neither struggle was going well for the American government, but the Olympics provided a highly symbolic international challenge in which we could defeat the Soviets in the Cold War. Much depended on America's black athletes and they were not unaware of their importance.

The passages of the 1964 Civil Rights Act and the 24th Amendment to the Constitution—trumpeted as a forward step in race relations since it eliminated the poll tax—encouraged African American athletes at the 1964 Tokyo Olympics. As it turned out, the Tokyo Games marked an overwhelming victory for Americans, particularly in track and field in which African Americans predominated. In sprinting, for example, African American women distinguished themselves. The two standout performers were Wyomia Tyus, who won the gold medal in the 100 meters, and Edith Maguire Duvall, who won gold in the 200 meters in Olympic record time. The Americans went on to win fourteen track and field events, with African Americans winning ten gold medals.

Four years later in 1968, the hopeful political era had come to an end.

In January 1968, President Lyndon Baines Johnson, always viewed as a supporter of civil rights, decided not to run for re-election. Rumors held that U.S. Supreme Court Chief Justice Earl Warren, who had been scrupulously fair in his judgments, would retire by the next year. The 1964 Civil Rights Act soon showed disheartening flaws, and well-informed African Americans expected that the 1968 Fair Housing Act would be revealed to be just as flawed. Malcolm X was dead and, in early 1968, Dr. Martin Luther King Jr. had been assassinated. Robert Kennedy suffered the same fate in June of that year. For African Americans, the struggle for equality appeared stalemated, with a grim outlook. The Republicans, led by Richard Nixon, seemed bent on a "Southern Strategy," clearly a program to resurrect white supremacy in a different guise.

The athletes who decided to protest at the 1968 Olympics in Mexico City knew the pivotal role black athletes had played in international competition since 1932. But despite racism at home and the economic burden of the Depression, black athletes had excelled at the 1932 Olympics, bringing glory to track and field in the United States. Eddie Tolan won two gold medals for the 100 and 200 meters, and Ralph Metcalfe came in second in the 100 meters and third in the 200 meters.[35] It is an interesting footnote that Louise Stokes (the "Malden [Massachusetts] Meteor") and Tidye Picket, the first two African American women to qualify for the U.S. Olympic track team, were not allowed to compete in the 1932 Games, but were replaced by two white runners, whom they had beaten in time trials.[36] Four years later, Nazism was in place in Germany, and fascism reigned in Italy. Nazi Germans not only were prejudiced against Jews, but they were racist and bigoted against blacks and anyone who was not of the so-called "Aryan race." At the 1936 Berlin Olympics, the exploits of Jesse Owens, Ralph Metcalfe, Mack Robinson, John Woodruff and all the rest, spoke loudly to the world that the Nazi and fascist promulgation of the Aryan epitome of the human race, at least in athletic prowess, was a sorry myth.

Arthur Ashe, also in this volume, notes in his book, A Hard Road to Glory, that the 1952 Olympics in Helsinki, Finland, was:

> significant because it marked the first appearance of a team from the
> Soviet Union. The United States was caught up in the "red scare,"
> brought about in part by Senator Joseph McCarthy, who held accusatory
> hearings and suspected Communist infiltration in every government
> department. Even *Ebony* magazine, the most widely read periodical in

the black community, joined the bandwagon in headlining an article entitled "Can Negro Athletes Stop the Russians?"[37]

There can be no question that the African American athletes, even with inferior training facilities and with a sure knowledge that even brilliant performances in Helsinki would earn little respect back home, performed with dedication and perhaps uncalled-for patriotism, and did indeed stop the Russians. At that Olympics, the American track and field contingent won fourteen gold medals. African Americans won six gold medals, plus a silver medal and a bronze. Allen Guttmann points out in his book, *The Olympics: A History of the Modern Games*, that "The Olympics took on a new political dimension in 1952, one that was destined to grow increasingly important in the decades to follow."[38] He notes also that in 1952 the "Soviet men won not a single gold medal in men's track and field."[39]

Aware of their significance to the image of the United States on the worldwide Olympic stage, some African American athletes decided in 1968 to use their increasing leverage to protest against oppression, racism, and bigotry in the United States. They knew they were mainly responsible for the poor record of the Soviet team. Conditions now seemed propitious for a boycott of the Mexico City Olympic Games. This idea was not really new. Black athletes had considered a boycott in 1960, but could not go forward without a majority of the black contingent in agreement. In 1968, absent a majority, each athlete agreed to protest in his or her own way. Tommie Smith and John Carlos, first and third in the 200 meters, eventually raised black-gloved fists on the victory stand, a gesture that created a political firestorm in the United States. Even though the men hardly consulted the African American women's contingent, Wyomia Tyus, who set a world and Olympic record in the 100 meters, and whose narrative is in this book, contributed significantly to the black athletes' protest by publicly dedicating her win to the protest. She remembers that

> as far as women were concerned, we were never really approached to be a part of that movement. . . . I felt we needed more people to be supportive of it for it to really work. I also thought it was the best thing that could happen, because it definitely exposed the world to what was happening to black people in America, how unfairly we were being treated . . . it was left up to you as the athlete to make your own protest, to make your own statement. I felt that whatever I did, or whatever I could do, it wouldn't make

a big difference; the only thing I could do was speak out anytime I was interviewed, and the only way I would be interviewed a lot was to win.

Mal Whitfield at the time was away, assisting African countries in developing their athletic programs. He notes that

during the 1968 athletic revolution at home and at the Mexico City Olympics, I was in the foreign service. I had mixed emotions at the beginning of the Black Power business. I was trying to keep with the Olympic Code. It says that we are supposed to bring together brotherhood and sisterhood, friendship and respect, for one another and for different countries. . . . The more I thought about it, the more I began to change my whole view. I had to ask myself, "Why did I come home in 1963 for the March on Washington?" Living in Africa at that time, . . . I was seeing things differently, and I became a little bit more radical toward my own country, even as a foreign service officer. There was too much racism at home. Something had to be done . . . I thought, "Here is a chance to really give the racial problem visibility worldwide. . . . " The 1968 Olympics had the biggest impression on me, outside of my first victory in 1948, because it meant more to the world.

As for the competition with the Soviet Union, despite the protest, the 1968 Olympics was a tremendous success for the United States and for black athletes. The men's track and field team won thirteen gold medals. African Americans were one, two, and three in the 400 meters. The winner, Lee Evans, set a world and Olympic record of 43.86 seconds that stood for more than twenty years. African American women also distinguished themselves. Wyomia Tyus won the 100 meters in Olympic and world record time, and Madeline Manning Mims won the 800 meters, the first win in this event by an American woman. In all, the African American women won six gold medals, including the 400-meter relay, all winning in Olympic record time. Bob Beamon set a long jump record of 8.90 meters. The American basketball team also won. George Foreman won the heavyweight division from a Russian and carried a little American flag around the ring in his oversized hand.

The civil rights protests and confrontations of the 1960s accelerated the pace of racial integration—or perhaps the decline in racial discrimination. Jobs, once the province of white people, only now began to be available in limited quantities. By 1968, the number of black players in professional football, baseball, and basketball was impressive. Yet very few African Americans rose to the ranks of referees, umpires, and managers. Basketball had no black refs until the coming of Ken Hudson. An employee of the Coca-Cola Company in Boston and approximately 5'6", he persuaded Bill Russell, who was then playing for the Boston Celtics, that he could be a referee in professional basketball, while keeping his job at Coke. He tells how Russell took him to see Red Auerbach, who engineered Hudson's employment as the first full-time African American referee in professional basketball.

But racism still abounded, and the protest at the Mexico City Olympics by Tommie Smith and John Carlos prompted the head of the International Olympic Committee, Avery Brundage, to banish the two men from the Olympic Village. He later said of the black glove gesture, "The nasty demonstration against the United States flag by negroes [sic] . . . had nothing to do with sport."[40]

The Mexico City Olympics coincided with the presidential campaign of 1968, marking the beginning of the end of an era. Nixon's "Southern Strategy" pandered to the racial fears of Southerners. "Law and order" became the code phrase for northern and southern bigots. By 1968, the moderate aspects of the Civil Rights movement had ended and the Congress of Racial Equality (CORE) and the Student Nonviolent Coordinating Committee (SNCC) had come under the leadership of more confrontational leaders. By 1969, when the Chicago police, without provocation, murdered a number of Black Panthers and brazenly lied that they had been fired upon, it became clear to the black population as well as to progressive whites that even in northern cities, law enforcement departments and their political overseers were not above "legal murder." One year later, in May, on the campus of Kent State University, Ohio National Guardsmen killed, again without provocation, four white students who were protesting the Vietnam War.[41] That same month at Jackson State University in Mississippi, local and state police shot and killed two African American students during a protest.[42] Following a riot at Attica prison in 1971, Governor Nelson Rockefeller, with his eye on a presidential run in 1972, allowed police and state troopers to kill thirty-three prisoners, mostly black and Puerto Rican, and ten guards, all in the name of "law and order."

In this period of Nixon mania, the media abandoned fairness in search of greater newspaper circulation and higher television ratings. Instead of reporting the activities of the restrained but still assertive NAACP and NUL, it pandered to the sensational, such as the invasion of the California Legislature by Huey P. Newton and the Black Panthers, the takeover of churches by James Foreman, and other similar acts. In this hyped up atmosphere, the image of black people, besmirched by carnival barker-like reporting, took a severe beating. Only with Watergate did the orgy of black bashing subside for a while, to begin again in 1980 with the defeat of President Jimmy Carter and the election of Ronald Reagan.

President Carter, due to unwise advice, enraged the large majority of the American Olympic team when he ordered the U.S. Olympic team not to participate in the 1980 Olympic Games to "punish" the Russians who had invaded Afghanistan. One outstanding Olympian rower, Anita DeFrantz, the first African American to represent the United States on the International Olympic Committee (IOC), and the first woman to serve as vice president of the IOC, unsuccessfully sued Carter.[43]

During this period of "Sturm und Drang," sports flourished in America, nurtured in great part by television revenues and perhaps by the American population's desire to forget the trials and tribulations of everyday life and immerse themselves in watching sporting activities on television. A look at the amount of money spent on the Olympics provides a clue. In 1964 for the Tokyo Games, broadcast-television paid the Olympic committee $1.5 million. By 1972, the cost was up to $7.5 million for the Munich Games; and by 1980, $87 million for the broadcast from Moscow even though Americans were not represented. By 1984, for the Olympics in the United States at Los Angeles, television paid a stunning $225 million.[44] "The rights to televise the summer games in Barcelona (1992) and Atlanta (1996) were sold for $636 million and $900 million, respectively."[45] These sums alone are enough to show that sports had become an enormous influence on American life, and neither the black athlete nor black people were exceptions.

The most important person advancing sports to such a powerful entity that it distracted Americans from their usual daily concerns was Roone Arledge. Arledge came to ABC in 1960 as director of sports programming and brought "showbiz" to sports. All kinds of sports activities, formerly below the radar, now were shown in primetime and hyped. "New sports" were televised: Davis Cup matches, the winter sports and winter Olympics, international skating, and, with all that, an hour of ABC's Wide World of Sports with the mantra-like slogan that everyone seems to remember, "Spanning the globe, see the thrill of victory and the agony of defeat."

Monday Night Football and the National Football League Super Bowl became spectacles beyond belief. Amid all of these developments, African American athletes came into their own, much like the white athletes.

By 1980, it appeared that sports had been truly "integrated," because by then the majority of players in football and basketball were African Americans. However, in baseball, where the word "integrated" had been used so often, the number of African Americans began to decline, but few people seemed to notice or care.[46] The decline coincided with Al Campanis's statements on a 1987 broadcast of the "Nightline" show that black people did not have the "necessities" for assuming leadership in management and ownership.[47]

In that ambivalent period in American history, a kind of twilight time when no one could be certain of the outcome of the conflict between progressive liberalism and conservatism, the immediate future of American sports could more easily be predicted. ABC television's "showbiz" initiative was working, and for the moment all was well. Into this new atmosphere two African American athletes achieved prominence in an elite sport known to a few white people, and to even fewer in the black population. Peter Westbrook took up fencing because his mother bribed him to try, hoping he would stay out of trouble as a boy in the projects of Newark, New Jersey. By 1970, he was good enough to win a fencing scholarship to New York University, where he won the NCAA Championship in 1973. The next year he won the men's National Championship in sabre, becoming the first African American male to do so. He recalls that in the same year he won the men's National Championship, he was invited to practice at the New York Athletic Club's fencing club:

> I was the first black kid they allowed in. . . . Every time I walked into
> the club . . . they would always talk. Always! For years and years, when
> I walked into the club I always got that face, but when I went upstairs
> to the showers and the fencing room, everybody said, "Hey, Pete! . . ." It
> wasn't just the fencers, everybody started talking to me: the wrestlers, the
> judo people, the karate people, everybody knew Pete now.

Westbrook eventually became arguably the best sabre fencer in U.S. history. He tells his story here with candor and wry humor.

By wonderful coincidence, Nikki Franke took up fencing while in high school as a way of getting away from mandatory tennis, and soon found herself at Brooklyn College, under the tutelage of an outstanding white coach, Denise O'Connor. In 1975, she became the second African American U.S. Fencing Association National Foil Champion. She recalls the time with a sense of awe and wonder:

> Arthur Ashe won Wimbledon in 1975. We thought, "Oh my God, Arthur Ashe won! . . . " That year, in 1975, we had a black man win the men's foil for the first time, . . . Ed Ballinger. Peter Westbrook also won. . . . For the first time, two out of the three men's events were won by blacks. Then I won the women's, and that year we had three black national fencing champions. . . . What a year!

Now a coach at Temple University, Franke's teams have participated in the NCAA National Championships in thirty-four out of the past thirty-five years. She is the first and only African American woman to coach fencing at a Division I university.

Another African American woman rose to prominence in this era, but in a sport not usually followed by the average sports fan. Jennifer Johnson became a star in 1972 in wheelchair table tennis, holding this status until the 1992 Paralympics. She is now a Paralympics administrator. "It is important for us to demonstrate that we can excel," she concludes her story, "precisely because we are too often told we are no good."

By 1980, although racial discrimination persisted in American traditional sports, it was not as restrictive and pervasive as in the period before the 1960s. Now a new sport entered the American scene without the baggage of racial restriction. Kickboxing arrived without fanfare, the result, most sportswriters agree, of the influence of Bruce Lee, the late movie star. Many African American athletes saw this sport as a new opportunity for them, and by 1980 one person emerged head and shoulders above the rest. Maurice Smith of Seattle, Washington, after a few years as an amateur, turned professional in 1980, and in 1983 became the first black American to win the light-heavyweight championship sanctioned by the World Kickboxing Council, as well as the heavyweight championship sanctioned by the World Kickboxing Association in the same year. His early road to those championships was rocky, but in this book, Maurice tells his story with a kickboxer's customary bravado.

By the 1990s, as Richard Lapchick details, the goal of the racial integration of sports changed to diversity in sports. Sports became big business and the historical expectation that "sport and sportsmanship may have been a force to better society" waned.[48] Yet the men and women athletes in this book attest to several realities during their lifetimes: 1) that second chances were rare; 2) that racial politics shaped their approaches to their careers; and 3) that all felt the responsibility to be better than the best, while carrying the responsibility of their community. As Lenny Wilkens puts it:

> I wanted to be a positive influence on other African Americans, particularly young people, because they need positive images. They need someone they can look up to. That is when I decided how to live my life. And I haven't wavered from that. It was a burning desire, and it motivated me through college and into my career in professional sports.

At present, the African American athlete faces more problems in the struggle for a college athletic scholarship and for work with a professional team. Their numbers are falling in college sports and the professional ranks. Since the early 1990s, the percentage of black players in all professional sports has decreased, and the percentage of black players in Major League Baseball dropped to a ten-year low point in 2000. Division I men's college basketball and baseball, in similar decline, sank to its lowest level since 1991–92. In Major League Baseball in 2000, Latinos comprised 26 percent of the players, with that percentage climbing, while African Americans leveled off at 13 percent.[49] The rise in Latino players indicates a practice in baseball that began in the 1960s where players from Puerto Rico, Cuba, Venezuela, and other places could be obtained cheaper than U.S.-born African Americans. The trend of recruiting foreign players became well-defined in basketball in the 1990s. In the major sports, these imports have served to decrease the numbers of African Americans. Football does not reflect this trend because, apart from Canada, no other country in the world plays American football to the level played in the United States.

In the other sports such as golf, tennis, and hockey, the African American athlete faces problems not primarily due to racial discrimination. Rather, they are victims of what may be called secondary discrimination. The fact is, for a young black athlete who desires to be a golf professional, the odds are stacked against him or her. Such an aspirant would have to at least attend a college with a golf team, or more important, attend a high school or prep school that has a golf program. If not, such an athlete would have to have the money for lessons and practice at public golf courses or have parents who belong to country clubs. Since the majority of African Americans even now remain not far above the poverty line, very few parents can provide such opportunities for their children. It is no mystery then, despite the efforts of the Tiger Woods Foundation and the First Tee organization that no African American other than Tiger Woods has appeared as a serious candidate for inclusion in the Professional Golfers Association or the Ladies Professional Golfers Association.

The case of hockey is self-explanatory. It has had a few black players so far to date, but hockey too is beyond the means of most African American families and, so far, there are no outstanding African American players to serve as role models. Tennis is also out of reach for the prospective African American player. Despite the successes of Arthur Ashe, the Williams sisters, and James Blake, tennis remains perceived as a refuge of elite country club white people.

For the above reasons, black athletes tend to engage in sports in which there have been a plethora of role models for a very long time—basketball, football, baseball, and track and field. Nevertheless, at the present time, the percentage of black players in baseball has dropped to its lowest level in years—8 percent—simply because, as Sam Lacy points out in this volume, the sandlots where young black children used to practice baseball have been cleared away and are now filled with condominiums. Former college players staff the professional baseball teams, and few black men are graduating from the college scene into the majors because there are fewer of them on college campuses in the first place. The black athlete aspiring to play professional basketball, baseball, and even golf, finds it tougher to achieve his or her goal for all the aforementioned reasons, and because of the additional numbers of well-trained foreign competitors who have been recruited by American professional teams.

Perhaps this book will encourage some to continue the struggle for equality and fairness in sports despite the changing sociocultural demands. Hopefully, these athletes' stories will also inspire young athletes, coaches, teachers, and parents to emulate these men and women who successfully strived to be better than the best. The prospect is daunting, and for those black athletes who have the opportunity to compete in high school and college their only chance is to be beyond excellent, otherwise the odds are stacked against them. Their only chance at success is to be better than the best.

John C. Walter

NOTES

1   To maintain good foreign relations an exception to segregation was made that allowed black people of foreign descent to be often treated as whites. Africans in the District of Columbia, for example, could frequent white barber shops, and whites expected those blacks considered foreign to sit in the white section of the movie theater or at the front of the bus.

2   Lapchick, *Smashing Barriers*, 229–30.

3   Hoose, *Necessities*.

4   Ibid., xv–xxvii.

5   James H. Frey and D. Stanley Eitzen, "Sport and Society," *Annual Review of Sociology* 17 (1991): 515.

6   See Lapchick, *Smashing Barriers*, 211–32. On stacking, see Hoose, *Necessities*, xv–xxvii; Benjamin Margolis and Jane Allyn Piliavin, "'Stacking' in Major League Baseball: A Multivariate Analysis," *Sociology of Sport Journal* 16(1) (1999): 16–34; Hartman, *Race, Culture, and the Revolt of the Black Athlete*, 252-53.

7   Hotaling, *Great Black Jockeys*, 272. See also Wiggins, *Glory Bound*, 21–22.

8   Hotaling, *Great Black Jockeys*, 303.

9   For a full discussion of the gradual decline of black jockeys, see Hotaling, *Great Black Jockeys*, 323–40; and Ashe, *Hard Road to Glory*, 68–77. This date is somewhat questionable because many owners at less prominent tracks would use black jockeys.

10 Hotaling, *Great Black Jockeys*, 303.

11 Ibid.

12 Ibid., 302–3.

13 Ritchie, *Major Taylor*, 257–58.

14 Ashe, *Hard Road to Glory*, 76.

15 Wiggins, *Glory Bound*, 205; Riley, *Biographical Encyclopedia of the Negro Baseball Leagues*, xvii.

16 Ashe, *Hard Road to Glory*, 27.

17 Sammons, *Beyond the Ring*, 112.

18 Ashe, *Hard Road to Glory*, 125.

19 Mead, *Champion*, 62.

20 Ibid., 158.

21 Ibid.

22 Ibid.

23 Ibid.

24 Ibid., 64.

25 Ibid., 157–58.

26 Richard Bardolph, ed., *The Civil Rights Record: Black Americans and the Law, 1849-1970* (New York: Thomas Y. Crowell Company, 1970), 266–70. For more on the Texas White Primary cases, see Derrick Bell, *Race, Racism and American Law,* 5th ed. (New York: Aspen Publishers, 2004), 482–84.

27 Bell, *Race, Racism, and American Law,* 257.

28 For more on the Fair Housing Act of 1968, see Bell, *Race, Racism, and American Law,* 315–17; and Bardolph, *Civil Rights Record,* 425–26.

29 Bell, *Race, Racism, and American Law*, 143.

30 Malina Iida and John C. Walter, "More than Sports," *American Studies Online* 16 (February 16, 2009), http://www.americansc.org.uk/Online/More%20than%20sports.htm.

31 Kennedy, *Course of Their Own*, 139; Dawkins and Kinloch, *African American Golfers During the Jim Crow Era*, 159.

32 Ashe, *Hard Road to Glory*, 61.

33 The United States National Lawn Tennis Association was later renamed the United States Lawn Tennis Association (USLTA), and in 1975 became the United States Tennis Association (USTA).

34 Ashe, *Hard Road to Glory*, 61–62.

35 Page, *Black Olympian Medalists*, 133–34. See also Guttmann, *Olympics*, 51.

36 Davis, *Black American Women in Olympic Track and Field*, 1.

37 Ashe, *Hard Road to Glory*, 181.

38 Guttmann, *Olympics*, 97.

39 Ibid., 98.

40 Ibid., 132.

41 Mark Hamilton Lytle, *America's Uncivil Wars: The Sixties Era from Elvis to the Fall of Richard Nixon* (New York: Oxford University Press, 2006), 354–55.

42 Ibid., 355.

43 "Anita Luceete DeFrantz (born 1952)," University of Pennsylvania Archives, http://www.archives.upenn.edu/histy/people/1900s/defrantz_anita_l.html (accessed November 15, 2007).

44 Guttmann, *Olympics*, 163.

45 Ibid., 174.

46 See Debra E. Blum, "It Wasn't All Fun and Games at the NCAA's Premier Basketball Event," *The Chronicle of Higher Education*, April 13, 1994, A34; Charles S. Farrell, "NCAA: Blacks Make the Plays But Call Few of the Shots: Study Finds Plenty of Athletes, Few Sports Administrators," *Black Issues in Higher Education* 11, no. 15 (1994): 34; Craig T. Greenlee, "In Sports, Those Making the Off-the-field Decision Remain Overwhelmingly White," *Black Issues in Higher Education* 15, no. 4 (1998): 23(2); Craig T. Greenlee, "NCAA Report Finds Little Diversity in Sports Administration," *Black Issues in Higher Education* 17, no. 9 (2000): 16. For more information on the current status of African Americans in administrative positions, see the Racial and Gender Report Cards, published by the Institute for Diversity and Ethics in Sport with the DeVos Sport Business Management Program at the University of Central Florida.

47 Hoose, *Necessities*, xv–xvii.

48 Lapchick, *Smashing Barriers*, 207.

49 Ibid., 212.

BETTER THAN THE BEST

Black Athletes Speak, 1920–2007

SAM LACY

SPORTS JOURNALISM

March 21–22, 1994
Washington, D.C.

DURING A STORIED CAREER SPANNING OVER SEVEN DECADES, journalist Sam Lacy was instrumental in the desegregation of sports in America. In 1937, Lacy spearheaded a campaign to integrate baseball by tirelessly arguing the case to baseball owners and administrators. He soon found support in other journalists, most notably Wendell Smith of the *Pittsburgh Courier,* and their collective efforts came to fruition in 1945 when the Brooklyn Dodgers signed Jackie Robinson. The *Afro-American Newspapers* appointed Lacy to the Robinson beat, considered at the time to be the most significant assignment ever given to a black sportswriter. While chronicling Robinson's early career, Lacy continued to work at ending segregation in housing for athletes and for the desegregation of other sports. A pioneer in his field, Lacy was the first black reporter to gain membership to the Baseball Writers Association of America (1948), and the first African American to be inducted into the Maryland Media Hall of Fame (1984). His awards and recognitions also include the J. G. Taylor Spink Award (1997), the Maryland Press Club Lifetime Achievement Award for Journalism (2002), and inductions into the Black Athletes Hall of Fame (1985), and the writers' wing of the Baseball Hall of Fame (1998). Sam Lacy died on May 8, 2003, at the age of ninety-nine.[1]

CHILDHOOD

I was born in Connecticut on October 23, 1903. My mother was a Shinnecock Indian, which is part of the Mohawk Nation. My father was in school up there, and he and my mother's brother were very close friends. He met my mother, they fell in love, and got married. My oldest sister was Evelyn. My next sister, Rosina, was named after my mother whose name was Rose. The name translated from Shinnecock means "morning flower." Next I had an older brother, whose name was Henry Erskine Lacy, named after my father's father. My grandfather was Henry Erskine Lacy, my father was Samuel Erskine Lacy, and I took Samuel from my father. But when they got to me, my mother made my middle name Harold, for what reason I don't know. I was two years old when they moved to Washington, D.C., in 1905. My life has been spent in Washington ever since except for about three years, when I went out to Chicago for a very definite reason, related to my career in sports. I was ninety years old in October. If I don't look it, well, that's the gift of God.

I came from a very ordinary beginning. My father was a notary public. My mother was a hairdresser, and she had a clientele. She would go around to people's homes and fix their hair. She did that all in the morning after we were at school, and my father worked in a downtown office, notarizing the documents that came in. There was always food on the table, hearty food, maybe nothing fancy, no filet mignons or anything like that, but it was food that we could survive on and that kept our bellies full. I can't say that I was at all unhappy with my childhood. It was one that kept me busy, kept me family-bound, and just kept me on an even keel.

When I was six years old, I was working for two dollars a week as a printer's devil. The only reason I was permitted to take that job was that it was after school and on weekends. Also, it had to be not more than three or four hours a day. My mother would not permit that, and the only reason she let me take the job was that the print shop was just two blocks away from the house where I lived, and on the same side of the street. We lived at 10th and S and the print shop was at 10th and Q. Duke Ellington and all those musicians lived down in that area. She said, "Okay, as long as you confine yourself to that. When you get out of there you come right back to your home." And, see, avoiding distractions was one of the things that was instilled in me early.

In those days your father worked and your mother stayed at home, took care of the kids and the family. Even if your father was just making forty dollars a month, that had to satisfy the food and the clothing needs of the children. The youngest child wore the shoes of the older brother. The young girl wore the same dresses and shoes as the older girl so that it wasn't until the shoes wore out that the forty-dollar-a-month father had to provide money for a new pair. Many times I had paper in the soles of my shoes, many times. Why is it not that way today? Credit buying! People pass by stores and see things in the window they don't need, but they're attracted to them, and today they can buy them. Once upon a time they couldn't, because they didn't have the cash. Today they can walk in and put up a piece of pasteboard and take those things out. That means the bills pile up, and then the mother has got to get out and help the father provide money, so that leaves the kids unattended in the afternoon when they come home from school. That is the reason there's an entirely different attitude among children of today. If I didn't get home from school within fifteen minutes, I got a licking. If I said that the teacher kept me back for something I had done, that's another licking! But today, there's nobody there to discipline the kids. There's nobody there to accept them at home, so what do the kids do? They come home and watch violence on TV, or they don't even go home until they think they're going to be beaten by one of their parents. That is one of the reasons that I feel that my early life is not exactly typical of today's youngsters.

At eight years old I was delivering papers and delivering groceries. At ten years old I was selling papers. At fourteen years old I was working as a soda jerk in a black drugstore, old Board's Drugstore in Washington on 14th Street. All these things were a mesh of jobs that I had undertaken with the idea of always moving just a little bit forward. I didn't resent that I had to work, as long as I had some time to myself, to get out and play baseball or stickball or whatever we had and get to the playground.

When I was growing up in Washington we kids used to go out to Griffith Stadium. The old Washington baseball club was known as the Nationals. They later became the Washington Senators. They had people like Clyde Milan, George McBride, Walter Johnson, Chick Gandil, Eddie Foster, and Danny Moeller. In those days they didn't have any night baseball, they played afternoon games. As a consequence, they had batting practice in the morning, so we would go out there and chase batting practice, going after the balls and throwing them back to the pitcher. At that time they allowed black people into the park, but they had a Jim Crow section. The way we got around it, and we didn't do it intentionally, was by going out there and chasing batting practice. Then we got to sell wares at the games in the afternoon. I used to take the players' shoes to be shined, take their suits to be pressed, and run little errands like that. I was the head gofer and, as such, I became a favorite among them, and they would give me the best things to sell. When it was cold, I sold hot consommé and coffee. When the weather was warm, I got to sell the cold drinks, the Cokes and lemonade, etc. When the World Series came to Washington around 1924 and '25, I was the scorecard seller, which was a choice item because in those days people didn't have television, and they needed to know who was on the National League team and who was coming in to play against them. That experience gave me an opportunity to view all of the ballplayers on all the teams in the major leagues, because I saw them when they came to Washington. I was able to compare them to the players I played with later on in my life.

When I went to high school, I started at Dunbar High School but finished at Armstrong High School. At Dunbar I made first sergeant in my second year on the drill team, and that was unusual, to become first sergeant so quickly. One day when drill practice was called it was unbearably hot, something like 94 or 95 degrees in the shade. I went out and called the roll and then I disappeared. When they discovered that I had gone off to play baseball, Principal G. David Houston dishonored me. He tore my chevrons off at an assembly. That was in my second year. Then I transferred to Armstrong.

At seventeen, while I was still in high school, I began playing baseball and writing for the *Washington Tribune*, which was absorbed by the *Afro-American* back in the early 1940s. I played baseball and basketball. I was so obsessed with baseball. I wasn't much of a football player, I was too light at the tail, but I played end on the Armstrong High School football team. I was a three-sport athlete, and they thought this was just fine, as long as I behaved in the classroom. We won the baseball championship and the basketball championship, beating my old school, Dunbar.

COLLEGE AND PROFESSIONAL LIFE

When I came out of Armstrong High School, I went to Howard University, but did not stay. By then I was tied up in baseball; I was just so obsessed. I couldn't focus on my college education. That's when I played baseball for the Bacharach Giants in Atlantic City. I did that for less than two years, and that was the loneliest period of my life. My mother didn't want me to do it, but my father was all for it. He said, "Let him go. He's got to get out on his own. If that's what he wants to do, let him do it." See, my mother had visions of me becoming a teacher because my two older sisters had become schoolteachers. I quickly discovered that playing for the Giants didn't interest me at all. The idea to play in the Black Leagues was fine, but I would've got homesick real quick. They were all older fellows, and when they would go around to fast houses in the evening, I would go to the movies. It became a rather lonely time for me.

I was homesick, so I didn't even finish up my second year with them, I just said, "I'm gonna dump it, I gotta go home." Then I came on back to Washington. I went back and tried to apply myself at Howard, but I didn't finish. I dropped out of there because I was interested in journalism. They had a journalism school at Howard at that time, but I was too involved in sports and too concerned with getting outside. I could not apply myself. That is when I took up the cudgel of getting some blacks into the major leagues.

I had no plans, except to go to the *Washington Tribune* to work as a reporter. Because I had worked for them when I was in high school, they said, "Yes, we can use you." When I first started working at the *Washington Tribune* in 1930, you could stretch out a living with maybe fifteen, eighteen, or twenty dollars a week in pay. I was staying at home with my parents, and I would give my mother maybe five dollars a week. It wasn't what you would call a living wage, but it was a surviving wage.

When I went back to the *Washington Tribune*, like all young black reporters of that time, I covered everything. Everything. In the morning I would go down to the court and cover cases involving fornication, domestic fights, crap shooting, gambling, all that sort of business. At lunch I would cover maybe some kind of luncheon meeting, like the NAACP (National Association for the Advancement of Colored People), or something like that. Later in the afternoon, I'd go to a high school game. Then at night, I had to cover the ministerial alliance meeting. That's a long and a diverse day. That is the reason many of the black reporters who stayed in it are pretty versatile. It's similar to the situation with the black baseball player, when he was playing in the Black Leagues he had to play in the half-lit ballparks. You become very good working under those conditions.

In 1937, I went over to see Clark Griffith, who at that time owned the Washington Nationals and Griffith Stadium. I told him that I had seen the Washington team play and that, for the most part, it was a very poor team. Back then, the way the Black Leagues survived was to play in major league parks when the major league team was out on the road. Griffith was able to see these black teams come in to play in his ballpark on Thursday nights and Sunday afternoons when his team was out of town. He saw teams like the Homestead Grays, Philadelphia Stars, and Kansas City Monarchs; and players like Josh Gibson, Satchel Paige, and Buck Leonard. All these outstanding black teams and players were coming into this stadium. I pointed out that any one or two of those ballplayers could help him change the old adage about Washington: "First in law, first in peace, last in the American League." Griffith told me he didn't feel that the climate was right, that most of the players he had on his team—and most of the players in the major leagues at that time—were from the South. Asking them to intermingle with black players would be a little touchy and could very well lead to disturbances. He didn't use the word "riots," he just used "disturbances" and "confrontations." I said, "It's going to come eventually." He said, "Well, you may be right, but I just don't feel that it's right at this time." He added, "It would destroy the black teams and the Black Leagues." I said, "That may be true, but though the black teams and Black Leagues are an inspiration to people in the black neighborhoods, they're also a symbol of 'separate but equal.'" I was not interested in anything that would perpetuate segregation. He just said, "Well," and left me at that. But I let him know that I knew he was just copping out.

Around 1939, the *Afro-American* lured me away from the *Tribune* with a little bit more money, maybe something like twenty-five or thirty-five dollars a week. I had no problem making out during the Depression because I had a job. It wasn't much of a job, but I was working. The paper didn't falter at that time. Later on the *Afro-American* absorbed the *Washington Tribune*, which is the same thing that happened in Richmond some years later. *The Richmond Planet* merged with the *Afro-American*, and made the *Afro-American* the paper in Baltimore, Washington, Philadelphia, Richmond, and Newark. But now, of course, that strength has diminished considerably because of the economy. When asked the question, "How can the *Afro-American* survive?" the point that I make is that the *Afro-American* is 101 years old, and it has survived where papers in Philadelphia, in New York, in Chicago, all the major cities have lost once-powerful daily papers, but the *Afro-American* has survived. That is something that should be taken into account when you consider the fact that the *Afro-American* is underfunded, in comparison to these other papers. There's a certain amount of dedication that the *Afro-American* persists in showing.

I don't remember my impressions of Jesse Owens when he won the Olympics, but I wrote about him, and in 1938 he came to Washington and stayed with me. Now, there's a story there. He and Joe Louis came to Washington for an Elks convention. Bob Considine wrote for the *Washington Times-Herald*; he worked for the Hearst syndicate. As a matter of fact, he and I played basketball against each other, and we played tennis, too. We were very, very good friends. He called me, at the old *Washington Tribune* office, and said, "Sam, I'd like to do a story on Louis and Owens, and I understand he's staying with you." I said, "Owens is, but Louis isn't." He said, "Would you be able to get me in up there?" This was back in those days when white folks weren't coming up to U Street, so I said, "Sure, but I'll tell you one thing, Bob. You've got to give me assurance it's not going to be one of those Alexander's Ragtime Band stories." He said, "Oh, no, I wouldn't think of that."

I talked to Jesse from time to time, and he was engrossed in the fact that he had made these records at Ohio State and had done all of these various things, but I had to describe Jesse later on as one who wouldn't rock the boat, and I criticized him for it. I knew Jesse, and I lost a little respect for him in his later years. He became sort of a lackey. We talked experiences in Germany, and he said that he would live it again if he could, mainly because that German fellow, Carl Ludwig "Luz" Long, had come up and complimented him and put his arm around him. He said that relieved all the tension he'd had prior.

In 1941, I went out to Chicago because I had still not given up on integrating baseball. I had Bob Considine at the *Washington Times-Herald* and some other people who were in my corner. Though I had the support of these people, it didn't move the owners. Each owner who responded told them—they didn't tell me, they told them—that they would have to deal with Judge Landis, who was the baseball commissioner, and they knew that he wouldn't approve. As a matter of fact, whenever the matter was brought up he would tell them "No," in no uncertain words. He would say, "While I don't run your team, I'm not in favor of that kind of situation." That is when I decided that I was going to get a little closer to Judge Landis, and I went out to Chicago to work for the *Chicago Defender*. When I was at the *Defender*, I sent Judge Landis a telegram telling him—he was on a tour of the spring camps at that time—that I'd like to meet with him, anywhere in the country, any day of the year, any time of day, and asked for a return receipt to my telegram. I got the return receipt, with his signature, but no appointment. I went out there, and I still wasn't able to get anywhere.

Finally, when Judge Landis died in 1944, his administrative assistant Leslie O'Conner stepped up to become chairman of the baseball council, which they established at that time to run baseball. The other two members were the president of the American League and the president of the National League, and they were supposed to be running baseball. In Leslie O'Conner I had a sympathetic ear, and he said, "Okay, we'll let you come and speak to the joint meetings at the Hotel Hollenden in Cleveland." But when the appointment came, the *Defender* decided to send Paul Robeson instead of me. I have no idea why. I suppose they thought that his voice would be stronger than mine, or that he was a more prominent figure than Sam Lacy. But I knew that Robeson was going out there with his communist leanings, and they were going to say, "Don't call us, we'll call you," one of those things. That pissed me off.

During the war years there was a decline in sports activity because many athletes had to go fight. I came of fighting age between the wars; I was too young for World War I and too old for World War II, so I survived because I came along in that period. When the war broke out in 1941, I was in Chicago. I had gone there to try to get closer to this Landis thing, and—I remember it just as distinctly as if it were yesterday—I was walking down State Street, when I heard the boys yelling "FDR! FDR!," because Pearl Harbor had just been attacked. I wondered whether or not it was going to interfere with my career, naturally, and then I began to speculate on whether or not there would be some type of exception made for me as a newspaper man, because there were various classes of exemption at that time. That went through my mind, but I was just riding the waves, taking it as it came. I said, "Well, if it comes, it's comes, that's all." But it never came to a point where I had to go. As a consequence, I went on writing. By this time my mind was all focused on desegregating baseball, and as a result I didn't relate to any wars or depressions.

Now it just so happened that I came down to Washington to see a couple of my old friends, John Murphy III, who was a grandson of the founder of the *Afro-American Newspapers*, and Bill Scott, who was a photographer. These guys were good friends of mine. I came back to visit my family the week before Christmas, and I went down to the office on Christmas weekend. I went in to the Washington office and Dr. Carl Murphy was standing there in the lobby. He turned around and said, "Mr. Lacy?" At that time it was "Mr. Lacy," but up until I had left it was "Sam," and when I came back permanently it became "Sam" again. He said, "Mr. Lacy, what are you doing in Washington?" I said, "I'm looking for a job." I wasn't really, but I just said that, just being a smart aleck. He said, "Are you? Come in." Then I said, "Mr. Carl, I'm not really looking for a job, I have a job. But if there's something available and it appeals to me, I would certainly consider it, because as you know my family's here, and when I want to see them I have to spend the time and money to come down here." He said, "Well, what about a job with us? We'd like for you to come in, I know you like sports." He had heard through the NNPA (National Negro Publishers' Association) that I had been working on desegregating baseball, although he didn't say it at the time. The NNPA had learned about Leslie O'Connor and the acceptance of my request to speak before the commission, and they knew that Paul Robeson had replaced me. He said, "We'd like for you to come on in, take over the sports a while." I said, "Wait a minute now, Mr. Carl. Art Carter is overseas as a war correspondent, and he and I are good friends. I don't want to put him out of a job." He said, "No, don't worry about that. If you are interested in coming back, you come on back, and when Mr. Carter returns, he'll have a job." I said, "Well, if that's an assurance, I'd be happy to take it."

When I left, Dr. Murphy offered me twice the salary I was making at the *Defender* and paid for the move back to Washington. This was in 1944. I think he recognized even then that I was working on a volatile situation, one that could propel the *Afro* into national prominence. I think he wanted me at the *Afro* because he was a man of vision, a great thinker.

That brings me up to the continuation of the deal with Leslie O'Conner and the Baseball Council. In 1944, I got a meeting with them at the Hotel Cadillac in Detroit, and they agreed to organize a committee that was supposed to recognize the Black Leagues as a fourth triple-A league. My proposal was that we take the Black Leagues and set them up as a pool for the major league teams to draw from, similar to the International League, the American Association, and the Pacific Coast League. Those were the three triple-A leagues that were already in existence, and the Black League would be on an equal bearing. This was the proposal that I made on a committee with the American League, the National League, and myself. For an alternate I had Judge Joe Rainey in Philadelphia, who also was black and had been a track star at the University of Pennsylvania. I met twice with Mr. Wrigley of the Chicago Cubs. Finally O'Connor decided, "Sam, it looks as though we're not going to be able to get together, so I guess we're going to have to abandon this idea of a committee consideration." He said, "I guess whatever we're going to do, I'll have to do it independently, and you can see if you can get someone else to go along with it."

In the meantime, Wendell Smith of the *Pittsburgh Courier* was working on desegregating baseball as well. Wendell and I were sort of colleagues, and even though we were working for rival papers, we had a very close relationship. My coverage area included the Baltimore Giants, the Washington Homestead Grays, the Philadelphia Stars, New York Black Yankees, and the New York Cubans. Wendell got Branch Rickey's ear with Jackie Robinson. At the same time, I recommended Rickey should take a look at Junior Gilliam, who I thought was a better ballplayer than Jackie. Rickey sent two vice presidents with the Dodgers, George Sissler and Fresco Thompson, to Baltimore to take a look at Gilliam. When they came down, they saw Gilliam going from first to third on infield hits, hitting second, hitting behind the runners and all that, and they were quite impressed with him. They also decided to take Joe Black, another excellent player.

Jackie Robinson came on and signed a contract with the Brooklyn Dodgers on the 23rd of October 1945, and he went to the Montreal Royals in 1946. I don't want to take credit for the selection of Jackie. Wendell Smith was the one who suggested him. In Jackie's case, he wasn't the best ballplayer, not even on the Kansas City Monarchs, but he was the most suitable. Jackie was a college graduate, and I made that point. He had played in an integrated society at UCLA and understood the commingling process. He also was engaged to be married, and that forestalled any suspicion that he might become involved with some white gal. They were thinking ahead all the time. There were a lot of other players in the Black Leagues who were better than him like Martin Dihigo, Oscar Charleston, Biz Mackie, and Buck Leonard. These fellows, except Biz Mackie, are all in the Hall of Fame.

Only one time did I think that maybe, just maybe, Jackie's temper was going to get the best of him. I don't know whether it was the 4th of July or Labor Day, but it was a holiday. Sal Maglie was pitching for the Giants, and he knocked Jackie down. With the next pitch, Jackie stepped back and laid a bunt down the first base line, to make Sal Maglie field it, and he ran right straight into him. I looked around and I thought, "Oh my God, I'm the only black person in this press box. What is he doing?" But nothing came of it. I said to him afterwards, "Jack, do you realize we were the only black folks in there?" He said, "Sam, I just had to do it. I wouldn't have been able to live with myself if I hadn't done it."

Incidentally, here's a little humorous touch from a particular visit to Louisville. I went down for the Little World Series in 1946. The Montreal Royals played the Louisville team. Jackie, Dan Bankhead, and I were eating together in a little greasy spoon restaurant, and three white girls came to the window and saw us in there. They did something that was unheard of. They rushed in and got Jackie to sign his autograph, and they looked at it and said, "Aw, shucks! We thought you were Nat King Cole!" Then they turned around and went out!

I went to spring training in Cuba with Jackie. In 1946 we were in Florida, thinking that Bethune-Cookman[2] at Daytona Beach would be a good place to set up dormitories for the ballplayers. The city ordinance at Daytona wouldn't allow it, so Branch Rickey had to set up camp at Sanford, Florida. The following year, 1947, he sent the team down to Cuba, thinking that we're going to get away from this segregation, and that we're going to get an opportunity to live together. He was always working toward bringing the team together. But in Cuba we ran into the same situation because the national hotel, which was the headquarters for the main body, was also American owned, and they put the white folks up there. They put us down at the Atlantic Hotel, which was down in the heart of town and a sort of ghetto, but they provided a rental car for us to come out to the stadium. In 1948, Rickey was still working on the same problem. He established a training camp down in the Dominican Republic. We went down there, and everybody lived together at the Hotel Naragua. But they ran into a problem there, because at that time the Dominican players couldn't give them enough competition to prepare them adequately for the opening of the season. That's when Rickey decided that Vero Beach would have to be his training camp. Bud Holman was at that time a vice president of the Dodgers and had been instrumental in the ownership of the Vero Beach airport, an airport of Eastern Airlines. He was also an officer at Eastern Airlines, and they had an airfield there, with barracks and everything, left over from the war. He moved to Vero Beach and established Dodger Town, where they still train now.

I took the lead in integrating sports because I just had a passion to do it. When I talk to journalism classes, I tell them, "If you want to be a journalist, you have to be thorough; you can't be just a reporter. A reporter is not a journalist. A child that comes home from kindergarten and tells his mother what happened in school that day, that child's a reporter. But a journalist pursues, writes, goes into a story, and is never satisfied." The key word to successful journalism is "restlessness." You can never feel that you have completed a story, there's always one thing more. That has been my drive. I've always wanted to get things done all the way.

After we got blacks into baseball, they still lived in separate housing. When they came to Washington, the black players stayed at the Whitelaw and the white visiting team stayed at the Shoreham. When the white teams came to Baltimore, they stayed at the Lord Baltimore or the Emerson. The black players stayed at the Royal. Even in New York, we stayed at the McAlpin and the white players stayed elsewhere. In Chicago they stayed at the Edgewater Beach, we stayed at the LaSalle. When I was at spring training with the San Francisco Giants in Phoenix, the black players stayed in rooming houses and white players stayed at the Phoenix Hotel.

We went to San Francisco in 1952. They put the white players down at the Palace, and the blacks stayed up at the Olympic. I said to Eddie Brannick, "You got Willie Mays, Monte Irvin, Hank Thompson, Ray Nobling, and all these fellows, about three million dollars worth of talent, staying up here unsupervised"—I used that word "unsupervised"—"at the Atlantic Hotel, and you got white ballplayers, some who won't even make class C, but you got them staying downtown. Don't you think that it's time that you were moving these people together?" He said, "There's nothing I can do about it, Sam." I said, "Okay, I'll speak to Chub Feeney when he comes in." Chub Feeney later became president of the National League. At that time he was president of the Giants. He was a fine man. I spoke to him that evening when he came to the ballgame. I said, "Chub, you know you got ballplayers down there who are not going to make class B, class C, who are down there because they're white. But you got Willie Mays, and three million dollars worth of black talent up here, unsupervised, does that make sense?" He says, "You know, come to think about it, Sam, it doesn't. I'll call Horace tonight." Horace Stoneham was the owner, and his uncle. Next morning, everybody moved in together.

They didn't open up the hotels in those first years. When we went to Cincinnati with the Dodgers we all stayed at the Netherland Plaza, but they told the blacks to stay in our rooms. They'd give us room service at no extra cost, but when we went downstairs we were told, "Don't stop in the lobby, just keep going." Jackie, bless his soul, used to go down every morning, stand in the doorway, and make them turn him away. Then he'd charge the Dodgers for it. I had put him up to it. I said, "Jack, if you're going down there doing that why don't you charge the Dodgers for the humiliation?" He said, "I never thought of that!" The same thing occurred at the Schenley in Boston. We had room service, but you had to come down and go right on out. We were asked not to loiter in the lobby.

Again, I'm going to have to put myself into it. I don't exactly like the idea of saying that Sam Lacy did this and Sam Lacy did that, but in order to put focus on this issue, I spoke to one of the black ballplayers. The Yankees and Cardinals were sharing the Al Lang Field in St. Petersburg. That's where the Orioles are now training. We were living at the private home of Bill Williams. He had a shoe-repair shop at a downtown hotel, and he obtained the contract to take care of the black ballplayers when they came in during spring training. His rooming house took care of all the black ballplayers. I spoke to one of the Black Yankee players at breakfast and said, "I'm going out, I want to talk to Jerry Coleman. I'm gonna ask you to come over." Jerry Coleman was the second baseman and player representative of the Yankees. I said, "I'm gonna ask Jerry about this segregation business, and I'd like for you to come over when I talk to him." When we went out there Coleman was warming up and I said, "I'd like have a few minutes with you, if you don't mind." He said, "Sure, Sam." I called this player over and I said, "Jerry, you're the player representative of all the players, the black and the white. Would it be imposing to ask you to suggest at the next meeting that this housing problem be resolved?" This player turned and walked away. Jerry said to me, "Sam, you see, they're satisfied." That was a real setback, but I kept going. I spoke to Sherman Lawlor, a player representative of the Chicago White Sox; Carl Erskine, player representative of the Dodgers; and Eddie Yost, player representative of the Washington Senators. I spoke to them about it during spring training, and each one of them said, "Sure, we'll take it up." They filed a grievance on behalf of all the ballplayers, and it ended.

Of course there were still some pockets of dissent. St. Louis held out against integrated housing for a long time. We stayed down at the Atlas, and the other players stayed at the Chase. When the Chase manager finally got around to agreeing, Jackie and the rest of us went up but Roy Campanella stayed at the Atlas. He said, "They didn't want me then, they don't want me now. And I don't want them now." The rest of the players stayed with Jackie and went on up to the Chase. It's best to get your foot in the door, that's what Jackie wanted to point out to them. The following year everybody went to the Chase. I guess it all ended somewhere around 1952, 1953. Hank Aaron was a very strong voice in it also. Hank Aaron is a very nice fellow. He was one of the few guys who was really active, who was really outspoken, and still is. I admire him greatly. He is vice president for the Atlanta team. I don't know if they'll fire him, it might happen yet. He's been speaking out strongly for about two years. Apparently he doesn't give a damn. Even so, to hold a position like that, you're in a situation where you can have somebody listen to you.

When I started agitating for equality in the leagues and equal rights in housing I had no idea whether I would succeed or not, but I was going to try. This was my determination, and as I have said before, I was going to see it through. I knew that I was going to run into various problems, as I did in New Orleans. At the Pelican Stadium, they wouldn't let me in the press box. I took a chair and went up on the roof to cover a game, and Dick Young, Bill Roeder, and Roscoe McGowan, who was a very sedate gentleman from *The New York Times*, got chairs and came up on the roof with me. This was something that showed that they respected me, and that pleased me no end. I asked, "What're you fellows doing up here?" Bill Roeder said, "Well, we thought we needed some sun." I knew that was just B.S. because they'd just come from a month in Florida. They didn't need any more sun than I did!

Sports set the example for desegregation for the rest of the country. It occurred in sports before it occurred in the general population. Take boxing, for example. Jack Johnson was whipping everybody, but they cooked up all kinds of charges against him, and he gave them ammunition by marrying a white woman. As a result, from 1915 on, when he was defeated by Jess Willard, there were no blacks to hold the top positions in boxing. Joe Louis came along in 1937 and restored the reluctant respect for black boxers. Again, I think that sports had an awful lot to do with desegregation. Joe Louis and Jackie Robinson, in my judgment, were the mainstays in the whole process.

I first got in the press box in 1948. I got my Baseball Writers' Association card, but getting that card didn't solve my problems all together. I became the first black member of the Baseball Writers' Association in the New York Chapter, but the first time I went to New York in 1949, to cover the Yankees in the World Series, I presented my credentials at the press gate and the white gatekeeper wouldn't recognize it. The implication was, "I don't know where you got that from, but you can't come in here." Just about that moment, someone from the UPI (United Press International) came up and said, "What's wrong, Sam?" I said, "This fellow tells me I can't come in here." He said, "What are you talking about, he has the same card I have! Go on in there, Sam." So you can see I also had an awful lot of help from white colleagues, white writers, and white people who understood my cause and my situation.

Cincinnati, however, stood fast. I went in with the Dodgers, and the chairman of the Cincinnati chapter of the Baseball Writers' Association said, "No, you cannot come in here." Because I'm black, that's an actual fact. He had them set aside an entire field box for me. Nobody else could come in there. There were other journalists coming around, looking, and they wanted to join me in there to show their support, but the ushers wouldn't let them in.

That has been true also of the Washington Redskins. Let me tell you what happens here. Today if you're able to get any tickets, you can get them wherever seats are vacant. In the early days, if the white section was not sold out, they would sell to us. So, if you went to the Redskins' games, you had white folks all around you. The ticket sellers didn't recognize it until their attention was called to it. The question was, "Why do you want to go to see the Redskins when you know they'll segregate you, when you know what their attitude is toward race?" But we'd go to see the other team. That was the kind of response that you got when you asked them for statements: "We want to see the other team come in, we want to see Marion Motley," or "We want to see Buddy Young, we want to see Willie Davis." That was the old cop-out.

Joe King of the *New York Herald, Telegram,* and *World-Telegram,* and Kenny Smith of the *New York Mirror* were the president and secretary-treasurer of the New York chapter of the Baseball Writers' Association and they sponsored my membership. I became a member of the New York chapter of the Baseball Writers' Association, then when I came off the road and came back home, my membership was transferred to Baltimore. But never have I been a member of the Washington chapter.

I was traveling with the New York teams at that time. Baltimore did not have a team then, they didn't get one until 1953. I don't know the process, but I do know that they presented my name. I did not ask them. They knew that I had been having problems getting into press boxes, so they said, "There's really no reason for you to do that, you're traveling with us, with all these other fellows from the *New York Mirror, New York Times, Herald-*

Tribune, World Telegram, Journal American, Long Island Press." All these fellows said, "You're traveling with us, you're a member of the group." They were in New Orleans at the Pelican Stadium. I had a lot of support from so many different writers. Desegregation didn't occur by my efforts alone. I had an awful lot of support from white journalists whose respect, somehow or another, I had gotten.

You can see that I've had both good experiences and bad when it comes to racism and desegregation. My wife Barbara was extremely fair, and we used to get kidded from time to time, but there were also times when it became exasperating. I did a little basketball officiating, and sometime in the early 1960s, I was officiating a national basketball tournament down at Hampton. I said to my wife, "Barbara, let's take the boat down overnight, it'll be an opportunity for us to get a night on the river. We can eat dinner and then get off in Portsmouth," because that's where the boat let you out. We went and got on the boat, went to our stateroom, and I said, "Well, let's go get something to eat." We went into the salon, and the head waiter met us at the door and asked, "May I help you?" I said, "Yes, we'd like to have dinner." He said, "I'm sorry, but we can't serve you." He was a white guy. Barbara asked, "Why?" He said, "We can serve you, lady, but we can't serve him." She said, "What the hell do you mean, you can serve me but you can't serve him? That's my husband!" She was mad, she was furious! He said, "Well, that's your problem, lady." Finally, he ended up putting us in a corner with a curtain around us.

I'll tell you a story about Monte Irvin. Monte Irvin was a fine baseball player with the Giants. In 1971, I was a member of the original selection committee for the Negro Hall of Fame. Monte was working in the office of Bowie Kuhn, the commissioner, and they organized this committee. They asked me to become a member of it and I joined along with Dick Young, Alex Pompez, Eddie Gottlieb, Roy Campanella, Bill Yancey, Wendell Smith, and several others. We had the first meeting and were trying to decide who to choose for the Hall of Fame, to break the ice. There was a question of whether or not it would be Satchel Paige or Josh Gibson, because both of them were famous at the time. I held out for Satchel Paige because Josh was dead, and you didn't want to say you were putting somebody in the Hall of Fame posthumously. That suggestion won out and Satchel was inducted. Gibson was inducted the second year. We had meetings from time to time after that, and we always held them in New York at the commissioner's office. At that time, I was working at the *Afro* and with

WBAL-TV. I was the only one who lived any real distance away from New York; all the rest of them lived right around that area.

In 1973, when time came for a meeting, I asked Monte to let me know when it was going to be held, so I could make arrangements to come up. Monte was the liaison. I needed to make arrangements ahead of time because of my positions with the *Afro* and WBAL-TV. The meeting was set for Thursday, and I told Monte I couldn't make it because that was the night I had to go on TV. I asked him to see if he could set it up for any other time. He said, "All right, I'll see if we can get it moved to Monday." Friday went, Saturday went, Sunday went, and no call. Monte had my home phone, he had my phone at WBAL, and he had my phone at the *Afro*. No call. On Monday morning at 8:30, my phone rings. "Sam, this is Monte. I did what you asked, and we set the meeting up for twelve o'clock today." I said, "Well, in view of the fact that it's impossible for me to get there, you vote my proxy for me."

On Tuesday morning, I called him and asked, "Who did we elect?" He said, "I guess you can congratulate me." I said, "Congratulate you?" He said, "Yeah, they voted me and Buck Leonard." I said, "You and Buck? Monte, your name wasn't even on the list of twelve that we had under consideration." He said, "Well, they voted me in." I turned right around to my typewriter and wrote a letter of resignation, saying there was no way possible that I, in good conscience, could vote Monte Irvin into the Hall of Fame as the fourth-best black ballplayer. I sent that letter off and forthwith I became nonexistent as far as that committee was concerned.

A lot of things have changed since I became a journalist. Every year I hear that the attendance of black people at baseball games has fallen. I get it from the Orioles every year. Take this picture into consideration: the black man is a working man, especially the sports fan. The black man goes home from work, picks up his family, maybe wife and one child, takes them to the ballgame, where by the time he pays for tickets to get in, pays parking, and pays for a couple of hot dogs for his son (you know you're gonna have to get the son something), he's spent thirty-five dollars. Then he gets home at one o'clock in the morning and gets up at five the same morning to go back to work. How can you expect him to go to the games? When more blacks came to the games, the prices weren't that high. They weren't paying four to six million dollars to a ballplayer. The highest-paid ballplayer at that time maybe had $100,000. As a consequence, where you spend twenty-seven dollars for a ticket now, you were spending twelve or ten back then. In those days, you could go to a ballgame and spend a dollar and a half and sit in the bleachers. But now if you want to sit in the bleachers, you got to pay something like seven dollars. You have to take into consideration that these guys are working people. They want to go, but they just can't afford it.

There are still quite a few American blacks—I don't like that term African Americans—in baseball, but of course these Caribbeans are superior ballplayers. They play year-round. They think nothing but baseball. They don't permit any distractions. Baseball is their life, it's their one chance. It might be a combination of two things that account for the influx of Caribbean baseball players in the United States: they might be better players, and they might be cheaper. Very few of them complain. George Bell, for example, he complained because he's not making what he thinks he should make and as a result he's become quite unpopular. But George Bell's playing has deteriorated and he's not anything like the ballplayer he once was. Of course that's just one example, but the quality of baseball has improved. They're playing better baseball now.

I think blacks seem to be less interested in baseball because of the disappearance of places to play, like playgrounds and vacant lots. Now you got high-rises. In my neighborhood, when I was coming up, there were three vacant lots. One of them is now occupied by a hotel, another is a church, and the third is a YMCA. They can play basketball in the YMCA. There's still a lot of interest in basketball among blacks. I see them playing on a little lot up here on Pennsylvania Avenue at eleven o'clock at night. They got lights out there. That touched me again. Way back, they used to call baseball the national pastime, and I said, "How the hell can you call it the national pastime when you got thirteen million people who have no place to play?"

As far as the future of black people in sports goes, it all depends on how many of us can get into ownership and promotion. Not promotion in the image of Don King, but I think it would be very healthy if we could get people like Calvin Hill and Gene Fugate into ownership, because these are people who have business sense, and really know the games and know management.

When I was a young man I can't say that I reduced the inequities of segregation to a personal thing. This brings up a new area of responsibility on my part. I suppose that I recognized the importance of education, which is reflected in the fact that I made sure I sent my two kids to college, but I suppose I violated that principle of being dissatisfied. I think that I was just traveling on. I think that I was satisfied. I was content if I wasn't an intellectual. It's rather difficult for me to place it on a personal level. It wasn't until I began to recognize the unfairness in the baseball situation that I became determined to try to do something to correct it. But even then I was more concerned about the discrimination against other people than myself.

Looking back, I've thought about those who say, "Integration is good, but I wish that had not happened," and I can see what they mean. But at the same time, even though the programs at black colleges suffer, we still have to make this one society. We just cannot operate on "separate but equal." It's not to our ultimate advantage. On a daily basis, on a yearly basis, it really hurt, just like it hurt the Black Leagues when the integration of baseball came along. But you see, the Black Leagues were still limited, they didn't have proper support. When would a black ballplayer sign for forty-six million dollars in the Black Leagues? And although that's just one person, that gives incentive to other young people to pursue bigger goals, not necessarily in baseball, but in any endeavor that can give them a better living. That's why I fought for it.

NOTES

1   For more on Sam Lacy, see his autobiography, *Fighting for Fairness.*
2   Bethune-Cookman College is a historically black college founded by Mary McLeod-Bethune in 1904.

Mal Whitfield with John C. Walter.

MAL WHITFIELD

TRACK AND FIELD

March 23–24, 1994
Washington, D.C.

"Marvelous Mal" Whitfield was the first African American to win the prestigious James E. Sullivan Award (1954), an honor bestowed on the top amateur athlete in America by the United States Amateur Athletic Union. At the 1948 Olympics, Sgt. Whitfield of the U.S. Air Force won the gold medal in the 800 meters, setting an Olympic record, and earned another gold medal in the 4 x 400-meter relay. He was the first American ever to win a gold medal for the U.S. Armed Forces while on active duty. Whitfield repeated his performance in the 800 meters at the 1952 Olympics, ending his Olympic career with a third gold medal. His athletic achievements also included an Olympic silver medal, an Olympic bronze medal, three Pan American gold medals, six world records, and eight National Amateur Athletic Union titles. He was inducted into the U.S.A. Track and Field Hall of Fame in 1974 and into the U.S. Olympic Hall of Fame in 1988.

Mal Whitfield joined the air force in 1943 and became a member of the prestigious Tuskegee airmen squad, the first African American flyers to serve in a war. In 1947, Whitfield was invited to participate in the newly formed Cultural Exchange Program by the United States Information Agency. The program was designed to incorporate sports in America's international initiatives. During his decades-long career for the U.S. Foreign Service, he traveled to over a hundred countries and trained some of Africa's greatest athletes, including Olympic gold medalists Mamo Wolde and Meruts Yifter. He served on the Youth Advisory Committee during

President Eisenhower's administration, and represented President Nixon at the 1972 Olympics. Whitfield retired from the U.S. Foreign Service in 1989. He continues to promote international harmony through sports, academics, and culture with his nonprofit organization, the Mal Whitfield Foundation.[1]

CHILDHOOD

I was born in Texas on October 11, 1924, on a ranch owned and operated by my family. It was near Wharton, and had been handed down for generations. I left there when I was four years old after my father died in a truck accident. My sister sent for my mother and me to come to California. My mother died when I was eleven, and my sister raised me after that. I grew up in Los Angeles, and I did all my schooling in southern California.

As a child and young adult, I was not really aware of racial limitations. I attended Thomas Jefferson High School, which was mixed. There were Chinese and Japanese students until we entered the war. We had whites of many nationalities and ethnicities. And of course we also had lots of Mexicans, blacks, and Filipinos. It was a multiracial school, and the teachers were black and white. We had harmony, and everybody was supportive of one another.

I spoke Spanish at a very young age because I associated with Mexicans. I can still see Papacita out there in the field in his little local garden, cutting cantaloupes from the vine and selling watermelons on the Imperial Highway. I remember working for him one summer. He gave me twenty-five cents a week, and all the watermelon, cantaloupe, tomatoes, and corn I could eat. I ate so much corn, I got sick!

There was, however, one racist incident I experienced when I lived down in Watts, California. I went to a store and asked for a job. The white shopkeeper lived in Fairfax, way over on the other side of town, and he owned this store down on 103rd Street. I went in and asked for a job when I was around thirteen years old, and he told me to sweep the sun off the sidewalk. I didn't understand what he meant at first. I grabbed the broom he gave me and went outside. I came back in and said, "Mister, I can't sweep the sun off the sidewalk." He said," Well, I don't have any jobs for niggers." I hadn't heard that word much up to that point. Coming from a mixed family, that word was just never used.

By the time I entered high school, I was good in almost every sport.

I was good at playing baseball and softball. I had good hands for playing football. On the track team I could pole vault, run the hurdles, long jump, and run 100, 220, 440, and 880 yards. I was a naturally gifted athlete. I had the size and height. I was tall and skinny, but strong. I was pretty much an all-around athlete, so when the track coach saw me in gym class, he said, "You're gonna run the half mile." I had a nice long running stride, like a gazelle, and I had speed, too. My coach figured I could run a good fast pace in the 880, and that became my specialty.

High school championships in those days were in categories: district, city, county, and state. I won the first three, but we didn't have enough money to go to state. We were in a Negro neighborhood, in a low-income bracket, and we just didn't have the resources to pay for it. The Depression really had a lot to do with the decline of athletic programs in those days. Everything was cut back. Meals were short, only one-half a day, or one a day, and we were satisfied with that. We relied a lot on victory gardens, which were popular then because it helped the war effort.

My sister had always said, "You are going to college, so you can get yourself a good job," but when I graduated from high school in 1943 the war was on and I was drafted. Right after graduation I received a letter, saying Uncle Sam needed me. The crisis was on then, so I said to myself, "I know I'm going, but when I come back I want to go to Ohio State."

COLLEGE

I stayed in the military until 1952, but I also attended college. When I was younger, I wanted to be another Ralph Bunche, because he went to my high school. He was my idol. I still had that dream when I went to Ohio State University. There were very few blacks on campus, and that dream helped me to get by. It was tough for a black person to get in.

There weren't many freebies on campus. I had a check coming in from the service for thirty-five dollars a month because I was an air force student. That helped me a lot and I had more money than the average student. Thirty-five dollars was a lot of money in those days. I also had a meal job on campus. I served meals for a girl's dormitory, and I was given free food and a car on the weekends. This was a white women's sorority, and these girls came from rich homes.

Because I was in such a good position, I fed a lot of the black student football players living in the dormitory under the stadium. The house mother who ran the sorority where I worked liked me very much because I was always nice and courteous to her. She would fry up some extra steaks for me to take back to the boys in the dormitories. She'd give me steaks, chops, and chicken and put them in a bag. I'd wrap them up, walk on out the back door, and go visit with the football players. They would salute me when I came in! Today, those guys are educators, judges, state assemblymen, and congressmen. We always tried to help each other, no matter what. Nobody tried to show off, and we were all proud of one another's achievements.

The air force gave me the opportunity to go to Ohio State so that I could receive proper training. I was the first in a pilot program that allowed servicemen to attend a university while still in the service. Because I was successful, the air force soon saw the benefits of allowing others to attend a university while in service and the program was approved by the Commanding General of the Air Force.

My time with the 477th Bomber Group was a good experience. For a black person to fly in those days was a big thing. Being an air force man in those days gave you pride. There were no black navy flyers then. We had another group called the "Spook Wafflers," I think they were flying fighter bombers.

It was when I entered the military that I began to realize there was such a thing as racial separatism. My awareness of race became acute when I was based at Godman Field, Kentucky, in 1944. There were German prisoners of war based at Fort Knox, and they were street sweepers, assigned to clean up the place. They were allowed into the white military PX, while black members of the American military could not go in. These were prisoners! I said, "What is this? This is unbelievable! These are the people we're fighting against!" That really hit me hard. This is the kind of thing that most people don't know about. But that was the United States government at the time.

We were segregated into different military units. It wasn't until President Truman forced the issue in 1948 that desegregation began. It did change, but that didn't mean racism was going to be wiped out completely. I went to Korea in 1950, and there were still some segregated units. I was the only non-white in my outfit, and they had no idea what I was. I am of mixed race, but back then those words were not used. You were either black or white. Although, it is a different thing when you are in a war and you're on the front line. Racism is usually left out of the foxhole or way back in Mississippi. You don't have time for racism when you are under fire and facing death.

When I entered the military I took my athletic skills with me, because I still had Ralph Metcalfe, Eddie Tolan, and Jesse Owens as my heroes. When the air force sent me to Ohio State University, I had the perfect opportunity to train and represent my college at track meets. By 1946, I was an air force sergeant and the best 800-meter runner in the United States. I was not slow in the 400 meters either. I won all my 800-meter events for the air force and Ohio State, which is what I aspired to do. I realized a boyhood dream when I competed in the Los Angeles Coliseum Relays in 1947 and 1948, in the same stadium where I watched Eddie Tolan and Ralph Metcalfe set world records. I also represented Ohio State at the Penn and Drake Relays.

In 1948 I went to the Summer Olympic Games. I won a gold medal in the 800 meters, a gold medal in the 4 x 400 relay, and a bronze in the 400 meters. I set an Olympic record of 1:49.2 in the 800 meters, breaking the previous record of 1:49.8. The Olympics were held in London, and the track was rain-soaked, with typical misty English rain from start to finish.

Becoming an Olympic champion had been my childhood ambition. When I lecture to school kids now, I always like to tell them how I snuck in to see the 1932 Los Angeles Olympic Games when I was a child. My friend Fernandis and I went in with a crowd of people. In those days the gates were big and open, not narrow like they are now. And the crowds were more orderly. We went up to the south side of the stadium, and that's where we stood and watched. We saw Eddie Tolan beat Ralph Metcalfe. That was the thing that stood out most in my mind. This little bitty guy beat this big giant of a fellow, Ralph Metcalfe. We tried to imitate them. I was tall and fast so I had to be Ralph Metcalfe, and Fernandis had to be Eddie Tolan. He was no match for me running back to the food stand, where we had parked our bikes. That race stood in my mind for a long time.

When I came back from the Olympics, it made me feel good, world-class, and I did it because it's what I wanted to do. But I wasn't going to let this one achievement be the end of me. I was going to be even better the next time around. When I told that to a friend, he said, "You'll be too old." I did not subscribe to that kind of thinking. You are as old as you think you are, and I thought I would always be able to compete if I kept to the same formula I had the first time around. Achievements come only when you work hard, train hard, and challenge your own performance.

My greatest competitor has always been myself. Competitors didn't make a difference to me, I didn't even care whether they won the race or not. I had trained down to the finer points. Psychologically and spiritually I knew I was ready and the 1952 Olympics weren't any more difficult than the first time around. After I had finished the 1948 Games, I didn't let up on training. In fact I increased the pace, and built upon the knowledge that I'd gained as an athlete and as a person.

I left Ohio State in 1950, and I was honored to do my regular air force combat missions in North Korea. In 1950–51, I was called back to America from the frontline to join the U.S. team for the first western hemisphere Pan American Games, which were held in Buenos Aires, Argentina. To train for the 1952 Olympic Games, I went to a lot of invitationals, such as the Amateur Athletic Union championships at Berkeley; St. Louis, Missouri; and Nebraska.

I entered the foreign service in 1947 with the Cultural Exchange Program, a preparatory program created with the idea of integrating sports into the U.S. State Department and U.S. Information Service's international initiatives. I toured six continents while conducting workshops and athletic clinics in developing countries during the summer and fall in the years between 1947 and 1952. This program marked the beginning of the intercultural exchange and aid to African countries. By 1963, it had full-fledged involvement in practically all African countries.

PROFESSIONAL LIFE

After I was honorably discharged from the military in the fall of 1952, I was appointed a commissioner for parks and recreation for the county of Los Angeles. There were five commissioners for the whole county. I wanted to be the best. I could have gone to college and gotten a degree and settled in, but I was restless. I've always been a nomadic person, an individual, and I was still competing in track.

By 1953 I had established nine world records, and then broke and set new ones. In Finland in 1953, I was determined to defend my championship. I knew I could beat all these guys. I wasn't over-confident, but I had the ability to psych out everybody. I knew their objectives were to beat the former champion. I was old by then, twenty-eight, and I was just running free. I had a good record, two-time Olympic champion, five Olympic medals. I was ready. I was running on a golden high and it was a great feeling.

The people came to the stadium to meet me. Europeans who spoke a little English would come up and say, "Mr. Whitfield, you great runner." One white guy said, "I want you to marry my daughter." But there was also an incident in Sweden, when a guy wrote me a letter. It said, "You better be careful with your black ass, because we will run you out of town." They were members of the Ku Klux Klan in Sweden! I said, "Well, I'm going to kick their butts while I'm here anyway, and leave town before sundown." And I did kick their butts. That was just more fuel to the furnace. Because I know what it's like to be of mixed race and to be thought of as a nigger, anywhere in the world, even more so than in America. That is why my attitude in America is, "Don't wait for the opportunity. Seize it, take it."

In 1954, two years after my second Olympic victory, I won the James E. Sullivan Award. I was the first black man to do so, but that is not to say there were no outstanding black athletes before me. Jessie Owens, Harrison Dillard, and Barney Ewell were all great athletes who never won the award. Why was this? It was racism. After the Sullivan Award, I became very involved in my overseas programs. I devoted my services very quietly to my programs in international sports education. That took me to many countries in Europe, Asia, the Middle East, Southeast Asia, and Africa.

I took a job as a coach in 1955 at Los Angeles State College. Ohio State was a great university, but to show some allegiance, I studied for a degree from L.A. State College in my hometown. I still had another year of eligibility, which I hadn't used at Ohio State because I went to the Korean War. L.A. State College had good facilities, so I thought, "I'll take advantage of this and try to make a third Olympic team in 1956." They offered me a job as assistant track and field coach. I accepted because I wanted to have something on record to say I was connected with a major university in America. I was back, I was serious, and I was here to stay in the community. Even when I went overseas, I was still connected with Los Angeles. It served as a good base.

When I retired from competition for good in 1956, I gave away about forty trophies and watches to all the people who had been a help to me. That had never been done before. I gave them to churches, YMCAs, YWCAs, even a variety of Boys Clubs, throughout the whole city and county of Los Angeles. Schools like Willowbrook Junior High School, 111th Street School, and down in Watts, Jefferson High School. I even gave a watch to a policeman who had arrested me. I had won 125 watches, how could I wear them all? I wanted to motivate the community by giving them recognition.

I did it out of sincere feeling, because everybody helped me; they fed me, got me jobs, gave me encouragement, and all that goes a long way.

The first African country I went to was Egypt in 1954 for an organization called Education Cultural Exchange. Then Libya, Kenya, Sudan, South and North Rhodesia, back up through Malawi, and back to Kenya, and out of there on to Sudan, Egypt, then back to Europe and on down on the other side. I went on down to Ghana, Senegal, and Nigeria, then back up through Ghana, Ivory Coast, and Liberia. From there I went over to Asia. On average I spent maybe six weeks to two months in each of these places. My job was to conduct a series of athletic training programs, talking about its importance in everyday life. I invited young people to participate in school programs. We emphasized why training is so important, what benefits you receive from training and personal hygiene, on being able to concentrate on your life quests, and what it means to represent your country in international competition. I talked about the Olympic Games and loyalty to your country and community. It was an educational, panoramic view of what sports are all about in society.

They had never heard that stuff before, especially from a black person. They had only heard the words of a colonial director. They had then in each colonial country one man, usually white, who was the sports officer. He was supposed to be the organizer, the coach, the trainer who went around from school to school, but it was in name only. My program was trying to open African eyes and give them some vision and imagination, to let them see the possibility of becoming great Olympic champions. I took an Olympic gold medal with me on all these trips. This medal has been seen by over two million people around the world. They never dreamt in their lifetime they would ever see an Olympic gold medal. That experience was a knockout. I had them standing in line as far as you could see. They felt it, and you can tell this medal has been felt by hundreds of people, because it's worn and I didn't wear it. Many people remember that in Africa, and all over the world. Even later in LaGrange, Georgia, U.S.A., they had never seen an Olympic gold medal in their life, and I gave them the chance to hold one. There were white and black schoolteachers standing in line to see what an Olympic gold medal looked like. It shook them up. But I said, "I'm not giving it to you, you've got to win yourself one."

In 1956 I said, "Well that is the end of my show. I have nothing to regret because I didn't make the team." I had just missed out making it to the Olympics for a third time. I didn't really have the time to train for it, because I was working hard in my favorite part of the world, Africa. I was in Kenya, between my tours of North and South Rhodesia. At the two Olympics Games I attended, I was there for one purpose: to win gold medals, for my childhood dreams and for my country. I had accomplished that. The Olympic Games provided me with many opportunities, and I took advantage of them.

After 1956, I continued to work throughout Africa as sports affairs officer. I did a number of training camps in Africa, and I received monies from the private sector to conduct these camps. I received a million dollars from the Mobil Oil Company to hold a training camp for seventeen African states in west Africa, which was staged in Lagos, Nigeria. Most of them were west and central African states. In west Africa we had people from Guinea, Congo, Zaire, Gabon, Ghana, Togo, Cameroon, Mali, Madagascar, Upper Volta, and Chad, among others. I had another training program of a similar nature in Zimbabwe, and another one in Zambia, in east Africa. These were pre-Olympic training programs. They put the final touches on athletes, to get them ready for the Olympic Games. They lasted from four to six weeks. It stacked on top of what they already knew, sharpening them up with American techniques. I had American technical assistants, and I made it very clear that my technicians were American Indians, Puerto Ricans, whites, blacks, and any other mixture who happened to be an American.

In 1957, I accepted a post in Liberia, as a sports advisor to the President of the Assembly. I spent a couple of years there. It was a difficult job because I was there longer, not like the two months deal when I was with Education Cultural Exchange. Soon I was perceived as bucking the system when I talked about sports as an integral part of education. People didn't want to accept this kind of program, because it was an aspect of education they knew nothing about. But I trained the athletes as best I could.

The other problem in Liberia was money. Some people working with me never received a salary. It wasn't a good experience to hear a government officer say you are going to receive a salary of fifty dollars a month when you finish the course, and then to be told after graduation that there is no money. They'd say to me, "Mr. Whitfield, but you promised us." It was all politics and, of course, everything depended on the tribal relationships.

I went from Liberia to Nigeria to head up the Department of Physical Education at the newly formed University of Nigeria in 1960. I got on fine, knowing that I was not going to stay there long. I have always been the type of guy to speak my mind, and the contractors putting in the sports facilities were making short cuts, which I objected to. They were stealing from the budget and I reported it. They didn't like me because of that and they didn't want me out in the field to see what was going on. The American principal of the university was playing politics himself. I was too much competition for him and he didn't want me around. I had already made my decision to leave, because I had been offered a chance to rejoin the U.S. Foreign Service.

I left in early 1963. The university had become very popular because I had a good sports program going. In just three months' time the university had won all the championships in Nigeria. The students appreciated my presence, but the people stealing money did not, and the principal was trying to make it look as though everything was all right. When I left I told him, "You're a liar. I don't owe you anything, you don't owe me anything. You have no business being in Africa."

Before I went on a new assignment I wanted to go home and join the March on Washington in 1963. I flew out of Africa as fast as I could. I flew into Los Angeles, picked up a car, left my family in L.A., and drove across the country to Washington, D.C. That's when I met the great A. Philip Randolph, who was the initiator of the March. I felt that I had to do this, because I had seen all these positive changes in the governments of Africa when they became independent. I expected similar progress here at home.

My next assignment was in Laos, which was a dangerous place back then. Then I went on to India and Pakistan. I was running the same kind of programs in those countries as I had in Africa. Next I went to Thailand, Hong Kong, China, and Japan. I had run programs in Japan when I was based there, under General Matthew Ridgeway, in 1950.

During the 1968 athletic revolution at home and at the Mexico City Olympics, I was in the foreign service. I had mixed emotions at the beginning of the Black Power business. I was trying to keep with the Olympic Code. It says that we are supposed to bring together brotherhood and sisterhood, friendship and respect for one another and for different countries. That was my understanding. But the more I thought about it, the more I began to change my whole view. I had to ask myself, "Why did I go home in 1963 for the March on Washington?" Living in Africa at that time, I was becoming more Africanized. I was seeing things differently, and I became a little bit more radical toward my own country, even as a foreign service officer. There was too much racism at home. Something had to be done. I began to side with the Black Power athletes. I thought, "Here is a chance to really give the racial problem visibility worldwide." I had to see it from that angle, because we had some serious problems in America. I thought that there had to be more than one way to bring the racial problems forward to be reckoned with. I had to think of it at the very beginning, as a follow up to the 1963 March on Washington. I was still loyal and dedicated to my country, but I was upset, because there had not been equality, even before and during my time of being a popular personality while waving the red, white, and blue flag around the world. I waved that flag, because I believed in the principles of democracy. I did not represent the Ku Klux Klan or the Nazis, or the White Citizens Council. I tried very hard to represent the best of America.

In 1968, I was supposed to go to the Mexico City Olympic Games with the Ethiopians. There was, however, jealousy of my success as a black man in the foreign service, so at the last minute it was decided that I should not go because I shouldn't be too identified with any one country. After all, I was the "Sports Affairs Officer for the whole of Africa." That was the rubbish excuse they gave me. It was an insult to the Ethiopians because they had gotten my uniform, had pictures taken, and had given me an identification card.

The 1968 Olympic Games had the biggest impression on me, outside of my first victory in 1948, because it meant more to the world. This is a very vital point for people who were not around in 1948. How were the 1948 Olympic Games different from those of 1968? In 1948 we had closed out the war, and we needed to find some form of social structure that would be acceptable worldwide. The principle of the Olympic Games is to develop friendship, a brotherly world relationship. Why not let the Games be a tool to bring people together from the fields of strife? It was necessary, because this was the only certain instrument that would be acceptable for nearly all the people who had been in World War II. They got the bulk of the countries together for the first Olympic Games since 1936. The purpose of having the Games in London in 1948 was to unify the world as fast as possible. Peace, harmony, tranquility, and respect for one another. That was the great objective.

I taught programs in the Gulf States as well. Qatar, for example, has great athletes. They've won third and fourth place in the 400 meters in the 1984 and 1988 Olympic Games, respectively. My Somalian coach was a boy I raised and sent to America to get his master's degree. He became a world-class middle-distance runner. When he went to America, he knew very little English, and six months later he was an honor roll student. I sent him from Somalia, paid his way, put the clothes on his back, and he just made me feel proud. When I started track and field in Somalia, they laughed at me, they said, "Tell that American he's crazy." My high jumper in Somalia won the All-Africa High Jump Championship in 1973 in Lagos, Nigeria. That was the first time a Somalian ever won anything, anywhere. He became an army captain and later a major. When we got back to Mogadishu, Somalia, the "sand dunes country," there were so many people at the airport to meet the plane it could hardly taxi. People were all over the runway while the plane was coming in at sixty miles an hour. That was a hell of a sight! The people on the plane were looking down and all they could see were the people on the runway, waving their flags. We could hardly park the plane. That is how sensitive and wonderful they are.

RETIREMENT

I was born a natural athlete, and what a natural athlete needs is coaching and training. That is what I try to bring to young budding athletes. Even though they are good, they still need coaching and training. But I also try to teach them that if they accomplish something, they can't think things are going to be rosy just because they did one great thing. That's just the primer. As a minority in America, you cannot be satisfied with one achievement when there is so much else out there. You cannot stop because you've excelled at one thing. You should have a good sound record of performance. When you have the opportunity, take advantage of it. I've done a lot, but I don't believe in resting on my laurels, because life comes around only once.

We know that role models are parents at home, but we know also that young people can be influenced by athletes of high standards. I keep going back to Eddie Tolan, Ralph Metcalfe, and Jesse Owens, because that's all I knew in my day. I was heavily influenced by them, because they were the only ones around to give us minorities some kind of stimulation. Jesse Owens didn't know a thing about drugs. There was no thought of drugs in those days. He was just a high-powered proficient athlete who could run faster than anybody else. He was the master, and he won four gold medals.

I met Jesse Owens for the first time when he came to a track and field meet in Chicago, Illinois, in 1947. I ran in the *Chicago Daily News* meet indoors. That night they took me over to Ralph Metcalfe's house for the after-meet party, since I, like Jesse, was from Ohio State University. We all were together and we talked about Ohio State. Dave Albritton, a high jumper named Mel Walker, Jesse, myself, and their wives. We had dinner, and that's when I met Jesse. He used to say to me, "All I can say, champ, is you've got what it takes." Boy that was adrenalin! I was fired up when Jesse Owens said to me, "Back at Ohio State, I left everything I could for you."

I just happened to be lucky enough that God put things in the right perspective for me. You see, in my day we had a fraternity of respect for one another and we didn't care where you were from, Africa, South America, Central or Latin America, Jamaica, or America. We knew even though we were from different societies, we had to stick together, because nobody else was accepting us non-whites. I once took Ralph Metcalfe to a Jesse Owens Memorial Trophy Award ceremony at the Waldorf Astoria, one of the finest, biggest award presentations of all time anywhere in the world. But back in 1936 when they had a function for Jesse Owens, he came up in the elevator. What kind of elevator? A service elevator!

I think the statement that black athletes have inherent or genetic skills is a lie. I think black athletes have been stimulated by sports when they were allowed, because of racism in the prime games. If blacks were permitted to play football, that's where they went. They played the game. If they were permitted to run track and field, that's where they went. It was a long time before a black person could be a quarterback. That spot was for the blue-eyed, blonde white boys. All a black player could do was to be on the defense, blocking out, to keep people from hurting that white boy. When coaches saw that a black player was faster than a white player, they put him in as a receiver. The wide receiver was so far, near off the field, all you saw out there was a uniform but no face. For the longest time no black person could play on the PGA (Professional Golfers of America) tour. No admittance! We had to sue the PGA to get in.

Let me tell you what happened in Africa. When colonial countries received their independence Africans didn't want to play tennis, they didn't want to play golf, they didn't want to swim. Why? These were sports for white people and they reminded them too much of colonialism. It took a long time to get out of that spell. Now they are playing tennis in Africa: Nigeria, Ghana, Sierra Leone, Senegal, Ivory Coast, Kenya, Zimbabwe, and Zambia. There are tennis clubs all over Africa today.

There are a lot more black Olympic champions in track and field now than white. Olympic champions are not ordinary people, they are exceptional. They have to be, in order to be achievers. Not everybody can win an Olympic medal. Even some of the best, who thought they could, couldn't. To get to that point, you first have to condition yourself to withstand all the elements that you will face on that day, because it's all uncertain. Clouds can come and there might be freezing rain. What you do when you are in training is to train under adverse conditions. Snow, ice, sleet, hail, blowing and freezing winds, freezing temperatures, hot, humid, dry weather, everything. You get a little taste of it all, and on the day of the competition the conditions won't make any difference to you. Both times I won gold medals in the 800 meters the weather was not conducive to establishing a world record. In London, there was a misty, chill rain, and the track was heavy. In Helsinki, it was cold, Scandinavian weather I just knew how to comfort myself to ward off the chills. I believed in myself. One has to believe in oneself to make yourself go beyond what is normal, and as powerful as you are in the beginning, you must be the same at the finish.

I respected my opponents, but I couldn't care less about them during the race. I could pick up on anyone, anywhere in the race. That's what I trained for, nothing else mattered. As Jesse Owens used to say, "You train for years for a ten-second time." When you are competing, you need to be able to relax with controlled tension. How do you get yourself in that frame of mind? If you are physically sound and ready mentally, then your mind puts all this stuff together, knowing you can do it. "I am ready; I'm at peace."

Looking back over my years in all kinds of athletic activities, I see the black athlete in America as different from the white athlete. The black athlete has encountered the ills of a sick society for so long that their determination is far greater than any white athlete. I say that with the greatest sincerity. Only non-whites who have struggled under discriminatory and hostile conditions and ascended to the level of Olympic champions truly understand this. Former colonized people in Africa understand this as well.

I think I had the greatest impact on the continent of Africa, in the countries where I gave clinics, workshops, and ran programs for the United States and local governments. I would say that as a result, all of those countries eventually excelled at athletics. The whole of Africa! It gave me such joy to see them catch on to the American system of preparatory training, and to see them use that training in major events. What happened in Africa was significant because, for the first time in the history of sports, track and field helped in the rapprochement of African countries. You can see that in the establishment of the first All-African Games, which involved a number of African states such Nigeria, Algiers, Egypt, Kenya, Zimbabwe, and South Africa. That was a magnificent achievement. It is one of the great joys of my life to have been in Africa when these states gained their independence, starting back with Ghana in 1957. I had technicians working with me who came to Africa from the United States, Canada, Germany, and Cuba, and we were part of the history of Africa. I'm very proud of my country's involvement.

My greatest "victory" was to witness the people of Africa accept sports as an international language. Sports are brave, penetrating, and capable of surpassing politics in world affairs. Take soccer, for example. The World Cup has millions of viewers worldwide, all watching one soccer match. You can see the aggregation of manpower it takes to get an event like this together, and it is done by countries that are not united on anything. It is my view, then, that athletes play a wonderful part in keeping the world together. In the span of my career, I've seen countries go from fighting against one another to organizing around a sporting event in joyous amity. I call it "Input for Impact." If you have positive input like sport competitions, it will, in most instances, result in a positive impact. There will be less likelihood of wars and violence. Sports bring unity, peace, and goodwill throughout the world. This I believe.

I say this to young people all over the world when I talk to them about excelling in sports: Yes, any boy or girl can, too! All you need is a dream, a plan, belief in yourself, and hard work. If you let yourself down, you become a "nobody," surely not a winner!

NOTES

1   For more on the Mal Whitfield Foundation, visit the official Web site at http://www. whitfieldfoundation.org. For more on Mal Whitfield, see his autobiography, *Beyond the Finish Line.*

MAE FAGGS STARR

TRACK AND FIELD

October 21, 1994
Cincinnati, Ohio

MAE FAGGS STARR WAS THE FIRST AMERICAN WOMAN TO PAR-
ticipate in three separate Olympic Games. From 1948 to 1956, she represented the United States in all important national and international track
and field competitions, setting a number of world records in the process.
She began her brilliant track career with the New York City Police Athletic
League (PAL), and under the tutelage of NYPD Sergeant John Brennan,
made the 1948 Olympic team when she was just sixteen years old. In 1952,
Faggs became the first athlete ever recruited by legendary Coach Edward
Temple for his Tennessee State University women's track team and her
emergence at the top of her sport coincided with the rise of the renowned
Tigerbelles. Her career highlights include eleven National Amateur Ath-
letic Union titles, a gold medal in the 400-meter relay at the 1952 Helsinki
Olympics, a bronze medal in the 400-meter relay at the 1956 Melbourne
Olympics, and gold and silver medals at the 1955 Pan American Games.
Mae Faggs Starr was inducted into the Helms Hall of Fame in 1965, and
the U.S.A. Track and Field Hall of Fame in 1976. She died on January 27,
2000, at the age of seventy-seven.

CHILDHOOD

I was born in Mays Landing, New Jersey, on April 10, 1932. My grandpar-
ents lived in Bayside, Long Island. When my grandfather died we were living in Newark, New Jersey. Newark was a ghetto. Mom and Dad knew that

it was not a good place to live, so my grandmother invited us to live with her. She told my parents, "Newark, New Jersey, is not good for the kids. You should bring them out here to Bayside." We had a place there at her house. During the 1960s when there was rioting in Newark, they burned down the very apartment that I had lived in as a child.

My parents moved from Mays Landing to Newark because they thought they could earn a better living there. My mother worked days and my father worked nights at the Newark shipyard. Mother had finished the eighth grade. My father was illiterate, but he was a very down-to-earth, intelligent man. He could come to the heart of the matter very quickly and he never raised his voice. He didn't believe in hitting us because he thought he was the only man in the world that had children. He loved us very dearly. I am successful because of my parents. They instilled in me that I must do better. "You must do better than what we're doing. This is not good enough. You are too good to do domestic work." My parents told me that I was somebody. They let me know that they loved me very much.

When I was about fourteen or fifteen years old I was yelling, being smart-mouthed to my father. My father grabbed me and shook me. The shaking didn't hurt me, but the idea that he shook me hurt my feelings. I walked behind him and I cried and cried for fifteen to twenty minutes, and finally he said to me, "Daddy is sorry that he shook you, but you must not speak to me that way." And I said, "I'm sorry, Daddy," and I never did it again. My mother said, "Why don't he get a switch and just tear her off. Look at that, look at him, look at her." My grandmother said, "Leave them alone. It's just between the two of them." My father was a very wise man.

I was such a tomboy. "Always into something," as my mother would say, leading my brothers into things they had no business doing, because I was the oldest. My dad would get very upset because he'd ask, "When is she going to act like a lady? Look at her going down the street! Which one is the girl?" Mom would say, "She's going to be all right as she grows older."

The way I got into track was through PAL (Police Athletic League). A patrolman named Dykes came over to P.S. 162, an elementary school, asking for kids to run track for him. He was looking for kids to run for the 111th Precinct in Queens. He said they were going to have trials after school. During an assembly program he spoke to us about the different dashes and different weight classes in which you could compete. I ran for that precinct. Each barrio would have their top three runners, and then they'd have a citywide meet. They were having indoor track meets in January. I was about thirteen going on fourteen years old when they came looking for me.

We were out there in the school yard running the 50-yard dash. I could beat the girls, so I said, "I can beat those guys running." He said, "Can you?" I said, "Yes!" He lined us up for the 50-yard dash. I bust out there and I was running in front of boys my own age. I beat them by three or four yards. I had my gym shoes on and my little legs were just churning! Patrolman Dykes sort of looked at me real funny, like, "Wow! She's something!" Soon after, he gathered up his kids and we had the 220-dash relay for the 110-pound class. I ran in the 50 meters for that class. I think I also ran in the 100 meters. I wasn't getting any training; I'd just go and run. Indoor I didn't get any training either. I just knew that I had to go someplace for track practice, an outdoor track, and then an indoor track at an armory. He told us where to go, and we caught the bus and we got there.

There was a man named Sergeant John Brennan, who worked for the police force at the time. He oversaw the citywide meets, and he decided to form an AAU team with all the talent he had seen there. He'd seen me running in the 50 meters, and he saw talent. After he formed the AAU team, we had practice three times a week: Tuesday, Thursday, and Saturday. My life from the time I was fifteen, it was Tuesday, Thursday, and Saturday training. Then in the summer of 1947 he told me, "Next year is the Olympic year, and you can make the team." By that time, I was a fifteen-year-old freshman in junior high. I looked at him and asked, "What is an Olympic team?" He explained what it was. He said, "You remember Jesse Owens in Germany?" I said, "Yes." He said, "That was the Olympic team!" Then it began to sink in. I knew about Jesse Owens, everybody knew about him. I knew he was a fast runner and all that, and Mom knew and Dad did, too. But I didn't have a track hero, I was just running.

I found my heroes after I began to run, especially after the 1948 Olympics. They were people I wanted to pattern my goals after because I saw them up close. I wanted to be just as good as they were, if not better. That was my incentive and drive. Plus I had my mom, who encouraged me. We were very poor, but she was the type who would say, "This life that we're living is not good enough. You must do better than your dad and I are doing. We're just existing. I don't know how you're going to do it, but you've got to do better." My grandmother would say, "You have too little education to demand the type of job you want, but you know too much to take these meager jobs." She would say, "I don't know how you're going to get to college, but you get there somehow."

In 1947, when Sergeant Brennan told me that I could make the Olympic team, I just looked at him. He said, "These are the times you should be running next year." In the month of July, we had mini-track meets and he'd say, "Now when it comes down to the indoor season, you should be running this time." And amazingly, I'd run that time. Any time he'd say I was supposed to run, I ran it. I don't know how I did it. I was confident he knew what he was doing.

There were times when I thought I had an awful big gap to make up. For instance, we knew that in order to make the Olympic team you had to run a 26.2 in the 220-yard dash. If you didn't run that time, regardless of whether you won first, second, or third place, you didn't make the team. You had times to run and my coach encouraged me to do it. I believed in him. If he said I could do it, I could do it. This Irish cop just believed in things, and I did, too. He used to tape my instep and I asked him, "Well Coach, why are you taping my instep?" He said, "I just tape it." I'd be at a track meet, I'd walk up to him with my sock off and hang my foot out there and he would just tape it. I don't know what the idea was because my instep is normal. I guess he didn't want my arch to fall. I was the only one he'd tape.

In 1948 I ran in the outdoor nationals. I'd never run in them before, but I showed up. They were held just before the Olympics, in June or the first part of July, in Grand Rapids, Michigan. You had to run the nationals before the Olympic trials. At the outdoor nationals I got fourth place in the 200 meters. It was near Olympic time. When we got back the coach said, "We're going to the Olympic trials." I said, "We're going, Coach?" He said, "Yes." Well of course being a sixteen-year-old, I asked, "Can I make the Olympic team?" He said, "Yes, you can." I said, "Okay, if you say so." When we got ready to go to the Olympic trials I was the only one from the team to go. The trials were held in Providence, Rhode Island. They were a blur except when I was running. Here I am five feet two inches tall, weighing about 107 pounds soaking wet, and everyone is taller than me. I made it to the finals, and Coach was happy. He said, "You're doing fine." I said, "Okay."

The coach thought I would do better in the 200 meters than the 100 meters because my start was not very good. The 200 meters was my cup of tea. We got down to the finals of the Olympic trials and the 200 meters, and I'm thinking, there's Audrey Patterson from Tennessee State and Nell Jackson from Tuskegee. Tuskegee had the dominant sprint team for girls during the 1940s and early '50s. I'm thinking, "These tall girls, I don't know how I'm going to get them." We were down to the final. They shot the gun and like a house on fire I tore out into the 200 meters! I got a good start. I was running hard, the coach was yelling, and I looked up and finished third! But the best part was that you had to run it in 26.2. I ran it in 25.9, so I was well under the time. When I finished my coach was hugging me and all the way home on the train I kept saying, "Have I really made it?" He'd say, "Yes." They had to take my measurements for a uniform. Everyone else already had their uniforms. I was a last-minute addition. They didn't expect me. The uniform was a little too big, but that was okay. When I got home my grandmother took up the skirt. I wore the skirt very well.

When I got home from the trials, my mom and dad were elated and they kept kissing me. Mom and I would be carrying on and Daddy would say, "Shut up and explain it to me, explain the race to me," and I'd explain it to him. All he wanted to know was, "What place did you get? What was your time?" Dad would want to know how I ran the race from beginning to end. "So you're really on the Olympic team?" he asked. I said, "Yes, Daddy, I'm on the Olympic team." They were both bursting with pride because I was so young. After I explained to my grandmother what the Olympic team was all about, she was elated, too.

Before I got ready to leave my coach, Sergeant Brennan, had to help me get my passport. Because he worked for the police department it took just two to three hours to get it. We were leaving that Saturday or Sunday for London, and we were going by ship. It would take seven days. The girls went first class and the boys went second class. As we got ready to leave my grandmother said, "You're going to need some money. You're going to Europe." My grandmother had saved up $7.50, which she gave to me. Mom didn't have any money, she had to get us down to the pier and to get back home to go to work, but grandma had saved $7.50. I had that much and I was happy! In 1948, you know what that meant? When I got down to the ship Sergeant Brennan had a check for me from the PAL for $25. Now I'm rich! I have $32.50 and I'm going to London, to Europe. I have lots of money! I couldn't remember ever having $5 in my pocket and now I had $32.50. Isn't that funny! Whenever I give speeches to kids I tell them about my grandmother. I always ask the elementary kids, "How much money did I have?" I ask the first and second graders and they count on their fingers and raise their hands and tell me. The older kids, the sixth and seventh graders, they laugh, and I tell them that was a lot of money back then.

In London, I met Alice Coachman, Audrey Patterson, Nell Jackson, Theresa Manuel, and Frances Kaszubski. They were the important people for me on that trip. The first person that I think left an indelible impression on me was Alice Coachman. She was such a young lady then, at the age of twenty-six. She was a lady but she persevered and she competed. I liked her very much. I liked the way she did things. As a competitor she was tough. She did the high jump, and she competed in some other events, and she was good. I also admired Babe Didrikson very much. I never met her, but she was my hero.

Alice was my roommate when we went to Paris on a tour, and she would say, "You know you're only sixteen years old, you have time to make the 1952 Olympic team; you'll be twenty. Then in 1956 you'll just be twenty-four, and you might be able to make the 1960 Olympic team and you'll only be twenty-eight." She says, "I'm twenty-six now, it's just about over for me. I'll go home, get married, have children, and that's it." She was the first black woman to win a gold medal. Alice and I still keep in touch.

In 1948, I was in the London Olympics. I was in the 200-meter heat with Fanny Blankers-Koen. She was such a gracious lady. I came in third in my heat. Only the first two in the heat made the semi-finals, so I didn't make it. She walked over to me and patted me on the shoulder and said, "It's going to be all right. You will do better next time." She didn't have to do that; she didn't have to remember a little sixteen-year-old running in her heat. When I finished running, I wasn't too disappointed. I looked at the stadium and looked at the people out there and said, "I'll be back." Then I went back to the dressing room and picked up my bags. They had a stand where you could get Ovaltine and cookies. I loved that. All the girls on the track team ran back there to check me out because they thought I'd be someplace crying. I wasn't crying. I was sitting drinking Ovaltine and eating cookies. I'd say, "No, I'm okay. I'm only sixteen, I'll be back." I was the only one that young in track and field. I wasn't crying. They asked, "You okay?" and I said, "Yes, fine."

I wasn't on the relay team, because I wasn't fast enough. Nell Jackson, Audrey Patterson, Lillian Young, and another person were on the relay team. There was no 400-meter relay team in 1948, just the 100. They didn't have anything over the 200-meter distance for women. They had tried the 800 back during the '30s and I think they did so badly, they took it out.

They didn't think women were strong enough. Now we're doing everything. Coach Brennan could not come, so our coach for the meet was Catherine Meyer. She was from upstate New York. We had a coach, a chaperone, and a manager.

After the '48 Olympics I ran indoor and outdoor track meets. I attended Bayside High School in Queens, which at that time was the elite city high school in New York. I was written up in the school newspaper. I was a big deal. The local papers did really good write-ups when I was over there. Mom and Dad were so excited when I got back. I had to hurry up and put the write-ups in a scrapbook for Mama to show. She wore it out showing it to everyone. People would come to interview me and, when I wasn't telling them enough, Mama would do all the talking. They would interview my mother! Mom didn't understand that in Europe at the Olympic Games, you had people asking for your autograph all the time. You couldn't go anywhere without someone seeing that you were an American on the U.S. Olympic team, and they'd want your autograph. You'd be on the bus going someplace and you got people crowding around you with their autograph books in your face. You were pressed by people all the time, so when you got home all you wanted was peace and quiet.

It was difficult to come back to being poor after the Olympics. I was living middle class at the Olympics. There we stayed at this mansion house, quite different from home. You went out to the garden and it was well kept. There were walls around the property and you came through a gate. Then I came home and I was a poor, black person again. I've heard so many blacks say, "Well, I was poor growing up, but I didn't know I was poor." I knew I was poor! I don't see how you missed it. I knew I lived out in Long Island and we lived in a house and all that, but I knew we were poor. We would have qualified for welfare if they'd had it. Mom and Dad were grubbing to make ends meet. So when I got back home I'm poor and I did not like it.

Brennan asked me how I liked the Olympics and I said, "I liked it and I want to go back again," and he said, "That's it. You will go back again. You will run faster, you will break the indoor record for the 220." It was August when I got back, and he started telling me what I was going to do indoors. Sure enough, I broke the indoor record. I beat Audrey Patterson, Nell Jackson, all of them. I ran away from them. I set an indoor record in the 220 that lasted until Wyomia Tyus broke it. Wyomia or Wilma Rudolph, one of the two, but Wilma just took great delight in wiping out all my records.

I never told anyone I had the indoor record for the 60 meters, so Wilma, after she got the 200 and the 100, she asked about the 60-meter record I had. I said, "Watch your tongue!" She said, "Oh yeah, you didn't tell me about that but I got that one too!" I said, "I didn't intend to tell you about that because I didn't want you all to get it." She said, "Well, I got them all, I got all your records Mae, every one."

I met Wilma when she was fourteen years old. She came to Tennessee State that summer to run. It was in June and before her fifteenth birthday. We were on our way to Compton, Oklahoma. Coach Temple had a summer team there. They were having a high school track meet, and he told me, "You watch that little thing there, that tall one and tell me what you think about her when she finishes running." I saw this little girl and she was running! She was all arms, legs, and feet, and they were going all over the place. She was running the 200 meters. When she finished he asked, "So, tell me, what do you think about her, Faggs?" I said, "Ain't she just the cutest thing." And he said, "I didn't ask you whether or not she was cute, I want to know can she run?" I said, "Oh, she's going to be something!" You could tell she had the talent. At the 1956 Olympic trials, some of the others began to see the potential in her and said, "Well, you can do this, that, and the other." I tried to tell them not to put that pressure on her, because she was only sixteen years old, and she would not beat anyone. You don't get a sixteen-year-old sprinter beating a twenty-three- or twenty-four-year-old sprinter. She couldn't do it. I said, "Just let her enjoy the competition and being here." She was upset when she felt that she didn't do as well as she should have done in the 200 meters. I told her, "No, don't you cry, don't you do that. You're going to come back and you'll have your chance."

I ran in the 1949 Indoor Nationals in New York City. It was an AAU event. My mom said, "Mae, how do you feel?" She's was up in the balcony looking down on us. I said, "I'm okay," because she made me nervous when she was talking to me. She always wanted to see how I was doing. Daddy would always say, "Leave her alone, she's going to do alright." Audrey Patterson looked up at Mama and said, "Oh, she'll do alright. She may not win it, but she'll do alright." Audrey was like that. So Mama said, "Come over here a minute." I went over and she said, "If you don't beat anybody else, you beat that long tall one over there." She was a competitor. At the shot I was gone, running out front so far from everyone I couldn't hear them. I was getting ready to turn to look to see where everybody was, but my coach said, "No Toots, no, don't do that!" and then I went back to running real hard. When I finished, they found out I had broken a record. This was in the 220. I ran it in 25.9 indoors, on a wooden floor! I think that if I hadn't tried to turn to look around, the time would have been faster. Everybody went crazy after that. The coach was happy because I ran the time he said I would be running. Audrey Patterson came in second and Nell Jackson was third. Three black women won in 1949.

At that time, college still hadn't crossed my mind. I was just thinking about running. In high school my grades were very poor, because I met with prejudice. Bayside was an elite high school of about two thousand kids and there were only twenty-five blacks in the whole school. The teachers didn't expect much from me grade-wise, and in order to get a B you had to go for an A. Knowing that I was a star did not help. My counselor put me in the remedial English class. Why I don't know. I was in the Regents class at the time because you had to take so many points of Regents in New York in order to take the Regents Exam that is used as criteria for acceptance into New York State colleges and universities.

Being in the remedial English class was great for me, because I could read the books I wanted. The class would sit over on the side, and I would do the little work the teacher would give us. Everyone else took all period long to do it, but I would do it in fifteen minutes and turn that in, and then the teacher just kept watching me, so I'd go over to the library and get a book. I read the whole Lorna Doone series and *Gone with the Wind*. Then finally we had a test. I kept finishing the tests she was giving us before anyone else, and then sit there and wait. Then some of the teachers said, "No, you don't belong here." So I went back down to my counselor's office, and she said, "Well, you're going back to your regular class, to your Regents class." And I said, "No, no! Leave me in here. There's no homework, I'm happy." But I went back to the Regents class and the teacher said, "I tried to tell them not to take you out of here because you had no trouble reading, you had no problem whatsoever."

At the Olympic trials in 1952, I was battling Ms. Hardy.[1] She was awesome! There we were in the finals of the 100 and 200 meters. Catherine beat me in the 200 meters, and we're battling it out. She'd get me on the lean. I didn't lean soon enough. Now we get down to the 100 meters, where she came in second and I came in first. I was a step ahead of her, I was really moving because I thought, "You may have got me in the 200 meters, but now let's see what we can do in this 100 meters." I was off and running because I was really upset. She was angry after the 100 meters because it was her favorite. The 200 was my favorite and I got taken in and she won it. Barbara Jones from Chicago, who was fifteen years old at the time, came in third or fourth place in the 100 meters. Janet Moreau was also in the 100-meter final; the four of us became the 400-meter relay team.

You have to go to the nationals before you can go to the Olympic trials. It's still the same today. After the nationals we had a chance to go home. That's when Mama said, "Oh, boy she got you in the 200 and 100. What do you think you're going to do at the Olympic trials?" I said, "I'm going to get her." I would practice every day, that's all I had on my mind. We were on each other's mind. I was concentrating on the 200 meters because that was closest to my heart.

But when I got to the Olympic trials, it was not for me to get. She got it again, but I won the 100 meters. By this time we had a telephone so I called home. That year the Olympic trials were in Harrisburg, Pennsylvania. I called Mama to tell her that I'd made the team. "This is the second time you made it!" She was yelling it out. You could hear my father in the background, "Let me have the phone and shut up. You're giving me a headache." And she'd say, "Here, talk to your father." He said, "Did you make the Olympic team?" I said, "Yes, Daddy," and Daddy's very proud of me. Then Mama wants the telephone back so she can get the whole story and then she'd go out to tell the neighbors. I think it was the July 4th weekend and they were going to a picnic. She got to the picnic and told them, "She made it again!" It was the week before we flew to Helsinki, Finland. Things went very well. I made the final of the 100 meters. Catherine didn't, although she was running fast at the time, because they weren't picking times in 1952. They were picking wins, first and second place. My performance was much better in the 200 than it was in the 100, but because I was a national champion from the United States, I had easy heats all the way. Catherine, because she came in second in the 100 meters, had tough heats. If she had been in one of my heats she would have made it to the finals and would have done better than I did in the final, because at the time she was running faster times in the 100 meters than I was. But in the 200 meters, I was running faster. She got to the semi-finals in the 200 meters, but I didn't. I got to the finals of the 100 meters. The German papers said I came in sixth, but I say I was fifth and the German girl was sixth.

The American girls were a big surprise in the relays because it was supposed to be Australia, Germany, and England. We were supposed to be in fourth place the way they were calculating. When it was our heat, we broke the record. Three other teams broke the record in that heat and Australia was ahead of us on time. Now for the finals; it was me, Barbara Jones, Janet Moreau, and Catherine Hardy on the team, in that order. We had a fifteen-year-old on the second leg. I had to pamper and baby her, because she was acting like a typical fifteen-year-old.

We're down to the finals, and there was this German girl. (I ran against her again in 1956.) She was a little taller than me, about five-foot-five. I knew I ran a good leg on that relay because I was running well. When I passed the baton off to Barbara Jones we were in the top three. I think we almost lost it, but then Janet caught it up some, so we were in the pack. We were in the top four running, but then Australia dropped the baton, and by the time they got it again, three teams were out in front of them: the American team, German team, and the British team. We were in third place and this is the last leg. We come up on the turn, so I'm standing there looking and I'm saying, "Oh, I got a bronze medal!" Then Catherine caught the English girl so now we're in second. She was running and I said, "Oh! We got a silver medal!" I was just jumping and yelling, "Come on Catherine!" Then Catherine caught the German girl who was in first place! That was a magnificent race. They haven't talked about that race, about how she came from behind. No one has ever said anything about it or given it any publicity.

You see, Catherine wasn't a flashy runner. Some runners or sprinters are flashy and people notice them right away. Then you get the quiet type of runner who, although they're doing just what you're doing, never gets the publicity that a flashy one gets. I was a flashy runner, therefore I got a lot of publicity. You should have seen me in 1956 after I did the nationals. Everyone was over there, running around, being nervous, and I was walking across the field with my starting blocks in my hand, cruising along. I was very confident. I had to be. I was smaller than everyone else and shorter than everyone else. You have to have confidence in yourself to know, regardless of how tall you are that these legs are going to be turning over.

After the relay, we met in the middle field, and we did the jig, we hugged each other, jumped up and down, and the photographers were all around us and they were taking pictures. We were just so elated. We weren't supposed to win! Now, the feeling hasn't got to us yet. They gave us flowers and we put on our sweats and straightened things out and combed our hair, so we could stand on the top step. That is a feeling that you always remember. When you see athletes standing up there, and they're smiling and some of them are teary, you know exactly what they're feeling inside. My thing was, "You raise that flag for me and you play the 'Star Spangled Banner' and don't you miss a note." You're standing there really tall with your gold medal. It was awesome.

I saw Wilma before she went off in 1960 and I said, "Wilma, are you going to do it?" She said, "Mae, I'm going to do it. I'll bust a gut if I don't do it. They're just going to have to bring me back on a stretcher." I said, "That's the way to go." When she won the 100 meters, I jumped up and down. I yelled, "She did it! She did it!" Now she's got the 200 meters to go and then she won it! I said, "She can get three!" And when the relay team got first place I was elated.

When I got back in 1952 from the Olympic Games the Kiwanis had a special tea for me. I got a $100 gift certificate and two war bonds. I spent the $100 gift certificate to buy a train ticket to Tennessee State and get a few other things that I needed. The Kiwanis launched me to Tennessee State because Mom and Dad didn't have any money. When I went, Mama gave me fifteen dollars. I had my train ticket and my suitcase that I bought at the pawn shop at a 50 percent discount. Those were tough times for us but it made me strong, and by the same token sometimes I think that maybe because we had it so difficult, we make it too easy for our children, and they do not have the drive that we had. Back then, if you didn't have money, you went to work to get it, and if the door shut over here, you went to another door. You go back and fight them.

COLLEGE

I was offered work-aid scholarships for college. I had my choice of either going to Tuskegee or Tennessee State. If I had gone to Tuskegee it would have taken me five years on that work-aid scholarship to finish, whereas at Tennessee State it was four. And I thought that Tuskegee in Alabama was an awful long way away from home, but Tennessee State was not as far. Going to college was a trauma for me because all the way down to the train station my dad kept telling me about what I was going to see when I got to the South, about where I was to go and where I was not to go. I was to do as the people told me to do, and not get myself into trouble because he didn't want to come down there and shoot up some crackers. He just could not impress upon me enough that I was not to lose my temper, and to keep my mouth closed. I kept saying, "Daddy, I'm not there to change things, I'm there to get an education. I'm going to be that schoolteacher you said I was going to be when I was born." When I was born my father said, "I have a schoolteacher." And I had that vision in my mind that I was going to be the schoolteacher my daddy wanted.

I had people coming around to my room because they wanted to see the girl that got the gold medal. There was no one around who had gone to the Olympics. Audrey was not there, Theresa wasn't there. Audrey transferred to a school in Louisiana, so the only one that was there was Jean Patton and she was a senior, due to graduate in 1953. I was the big star on campus. Coach Temple was named coach the year I arrived, in 1952. My years at Tennessee State were beautiful. Of course driving from Tennessee State to the Northern cities, you couldn't stop anywhere. If we had to spend the night, it was at some black college campus. I remember Bill Cosby talking about when he went to Temple, and how he went down South for a track meet. They could not eat out in the front of a restaurant, so they ate back in the kitchen with the cooks. When they got on the bus they'd have more food because the cooks had bagged it up and put it in there. Then on the way back the coach arranged it so that they could eat out front with them, but they didn't want to. They'd say, "No, send us back to the kitchen!" They wanted to go back because when they got on the bus they'd have these extra sandwiches and everything. That's what would happen when we pulled into a restaurant where we had to go round the back, and the cook would look out and see that there was a team traveling. We always had extra in that bag that was never charged to us.

I was almost struck dumb by the situation in the South. I could not believe it. My girlfriend had come the year before and she told me, "Now when we get to Cincinnati we have to change trains because we're getting ready to cross the Mason-Dixon. We're going over the high river and we're going to be in Kentucky, and we're going to be in the South." We had to go where the engine was. I got down to Nashville, and there I stand with my suitcase in my hand. I was standing out there in the middle of this train station looking up at this big sign over a greasy looking waiting room that said "Colored." I was standing out there staring at that, and then I looked over at the white waiting room and it had oriental rugs on the floor, with nice provincial furniture in there, and it was beautiful. The colored waiting room had hard chairs and an old counter, and the windows weren't even clean. When I went outside, looking for a cab to campus, I was told,

"No, you don't use the white cab drivers, you have to wait for the black cab drivers to get back." Here are all these white cab drivers and they're just standing there looking at you, but you have to wait until a black one got back. Then my friend Pat said, "Let's take the bus." There were white and colored signs, and we had to go to the back of the bus.

I enjoyed Tennessee State tremendously. Those four years were the most wonderful experience I've ever had. My grades in college were beautiful, because whatever grade I deserved, I got. When I was in high school there were times when I felt that I deserved an A, but I did not get it.

At times I did question Coach Temple, and I'd challenge him. He would tell you himself, "Yes, she did." As a matter of fact, he would say, "No, I didn't coach her. She just went along and did what I told her to do." But if I felt there was a suggestion to be made, I made it, because this man was only five years older than I am. I was twenty years old and he was twenty-five. Over the years he became like a brother to me. The first year went well. I was not sent to the indoor nationals because they didn't feel I should go to defend the indoor championship. I asked to go, but they said no. So there was a break in my indoor record and that was in 1953, but from then on I ran the indoor and outdoor national championships.

During the four years at Tennessee State there was talk of the Olympics. It was prevalent in my mind that I could go a third time. Every year we won the outdoor national championship. From then on Coach Temple's career was linked with the Tigerbelles. We began to get national recognition, and began to be a power to be reckoned with at the nationals. At Tennessee State I concentrated on the 200 meters. It was my favorite. The 100 meters was something I could win, maybe this time, maybe not. If I got out of the blocks I could win it. Sometimes I could win it anyway, but it didn't bother me. We had good 100-meter runners come along at that time that enjoyed beating me in any race they could. Any girl in the United States that ran past me in the 100 meters or ran by me in the 200 meters knew that they were the best in the United States, because I was the best at the time.

During the summers I went home, back to Bayside. A couple of times I went to work and a couple of times I stayed home during the summer, because I had a younger brother, and Mom and Dad worked. They were just happy to have me home during the summer. I kept house for my mom and cooked. I couldn't cook well, but I could get it half done, and she'd finish it and she was just elated I helped her out so much. She didn't have to pay a babysitter for my younger brother, so she was happy.

During the summer I thought heavy thoughts. I was bitter. When I went home the first Christmas I did not see any of my friends. Half of my friends were white and the other half were black. There were some that I'd gone to elementary school and high school with and we had been close friends. We'd call each other, sit down and eat in each other's houses, but I did not see them the first Christmas I was home, because I was so bitter about the South, about white people. My mother would say, "No, all white people are not like that and you're not to think that way." It took time for me to recover.

At age twenty-three, people began to say I was getting slower because I was running indoor and I was beaten in the 100 meters. I said to Coach Brennan, "May I talk with you a minute?" He always took great delight in watching me run, and I asked him, "What do you think about me? I'm twenty-three, could I be getting slower? Because of the 100 meters?" And he said, "No, you have not peaked yet, not until you are twenty-five or twenty-six years old." So I said, "You don't think I'm getting slower?" and he said, "No, if anything you'll get faster."

I was very excited about the 1956 Olympic Games because for the first time, I had teammates who had the potential to make the Olympic team. I could have some really close friends with me. My teammates were Wilma Rudolph, Isabel Daniels, Lucinda Williams, Willye White, and Margaret Matthews. I am extremely close with the women who made the 1956 Olympic team. When we got ready to go on a track trip I would do everyone's hair. Coach Temple bought the curlers and straightening comb for me because he wanted our hair to look just so. They knew with me doing their hair, I wasn't getting my clothes ironed, so they ironed my clothes. We would share each other's clothes, because we had to have our clothes just right. We are still very close. We enjoy each other and sit around and talk and just have a great time together. We were all poor girls from Mississippi, Georgia, Tennessee, and New York.

The teams from Tennessee State were the best in the country. Coach Temple put three in the race and we came in one, two, three, and if somebody came in between that one, two, three, we'd say, "How did she get in there?" Every day when I went to practice I was in competition with my teammates. I could not let them run by me in a race during practice because if they did they would jump up and down and be elated, so I had a tough time. Every time I went down the track it was like I was going through a full meet. They didn't have respect at all for a two-time Olympian. They'd run by you any chance they got. Buddy, you'd better be running! They gave it to you good. They didn't cut you any slack at all.

We had a habit of talking to each other during a race. At the 1956 Olympic trials, I knew on this side of me was Isabel Daniels, and there was somebody next to me here, and then it was Lucinda Williams. I'm running the 100 meters, and I don't see Lucinda out of the corner of my eye. I turn just a little bit and say, "Come on Lu!" This took place at about the 50-meter line. And she says, "I'm coming!" By that time, when I turn my head Isabel Daniels is in front of me, and she's a power runner, very strong. She beats me. But yours truly had beaten her a week before in the 100 meters at the nationals. I won the 100 and the 200 at the nationals.

Now we got to the 200 meters, and it's just me and Wilma Rudolph in the finals. I'm coming round the turn and I don't see her. I'm in the second lane; she's in the first lane. I turn my head and say, "Come on!" And she says, "I'm coming Mae!" She had a good stride and almost beat me in that 200 meters. I just barely got her. It shocked her that she had pulled up so quick next to me, but she had to realize that she was on the inside and I was on the outside. Later I told her, "Why did you hesitate? You don't ever do that!" I fussed at her for doing it. "You saw your chance, you should have blown past me!" She was sixteen then, still in high school.

At the Olympics in Melbourne, we were in the 400-meter relay finals. Our team got third place. We had a good team, but the Australians had a good team, too. They weren't going to drop the stick this time. They were the primo sprinters in '52 and '56, and they had a very good relay team. I think two of them made it to the finals of the 100 meters. I was the starter again for our team. The second leg was Margaret Matthews, third leg was Wilma Rudolph, and fourth leg was Isabel Daniels. Isabel was running the 100 meters very well. I think if she had leaned at the tape, like I told her to, she would have won. At the last minute I had said, "You got to lean in to take the win, get yourself on one of those steps Isabel." I think she stayed up. It was a photo finish. Nell Jackson was our coach at the time. She had to go back and look at the film. Photo finish, it was so close. It was one hell of a race.

I make no excuses for that 200, because I should have realized I had over trained. If I had just discovered it just a couple weeks ahead of time, I could have checked it, because I felt that I should have been in the finals of the 200. The final 100 didn't matter to me, but I could have been in the final of the 200. I ran very well, but when I discovered that I was over trained, the 200 was upon me. I tried to do something about it; I felt good but not the way I should have. I was just so interested in my teammates, and helping them, and I was running so hard because I wanted us to get a medal. This shouldn't bother me but it still does even after all these years.

PROFESSIONAL LIFE

I always said that I wanted to teach, so I got a job in Lockland, Ohio, teaching high school physical education because the P.E. teacher of the school was going on maternity leave. I was getting back from overseas and Lockland had sent a letter requesting a P.E. teacher from Tennessee State. I was coming back to go to grad school to work on my master's degree, but since there was this job, Mrs. Temple and the coach helped me fill out the application. When I got back from Australia in December I got the job and, in January 1957, I began teaching. Now my aim was to teach, get married, and have children, in that order. I had a double major in health and P.E. It was a good job; the starting salary was $4,000 a year. Everyone was really excited about me coming because they had heard about me being on the Olympic team, and that I'd won a bronze medal and a gold medal. I got a write-up in the papers and the teachers were awed by it. I gave up track and athletics when I left Tennessee State to teach. I knew it was over.

Lockland, Ohio, is a suburb of Cincinnati. Lockland was like any other town because they had segregated themselves. They had built a school for all blacks to go to, but before they built the school, blacks and whites went to the same school. It was segregated when I got there. I only worked in Lockland for a year and a half because they were closing the school and integrating it. In 1958 my job was over.

I got married in July 1958. I met my husband when I first began teaching. He was doing his student teaching and had just gotten out of the army. He went to Miami University in Oxford and got his BA degree, and then he got his master's degree from Xavier University. He went back to Miami University to get his doctorate.

After Lockland I taught at Lincoln Heights. I taught health and P.E. for a while up until 1962, and then I wanted to teach slow learners. I taught them for about seven or eight years. I wanted to teach slow learners because I got tired of the gym. I went back to graduate school in 1960 to get certified to teach slow learners, and I got my certification in 1962 or '63. It was before my daughter was born in 1964. I got my master's degree in 1971. The students knew who I was because the teachers would tell them that we have an Olympic champion here. The kids knew, especially the kids from the black neighborhood because my name would be among the black history people. They would ask me questions and they were very proud.

RETIREMENT

I retired from teaching in 1989. Afterward I got a part-time job at Xavier University and I worked with the study tables for the freshman athletes. I also worked in the College Opportunity Program at Xavier University for two and a half years. I am fully retired now. All I do is run around and play golf two or three times a week.

Looking back on my life as an athlete, I always think, "What if we hadn't moved to Long Island, and we had stayed in Newark, in the ghetto? Where would I be now?" It just happened that my life patterned out, that my life should be in athletics since I was such a tomboy and loved sports. This was probably the best possible course for me to excel in, because there was nothing else. I guess God knew what was best. He knew my parents didn't have money, and I had desire and talent, so these two legs have put me through college.

My reflections on Coach Temple are that he was a tremendous man. He had a dream and he pursued that dream. He built the dynasty. It was not by chance that he did this. He knew what he was doing, even at the age of twenty-five, and he pursued it. Some people think that he just sort of fell into it, but no, this was a bright man who knew what he wanted and proceeded to build it. I appreciate Tennessee State University because at the time they had people who were farsighted enough to see this girls track team and what it could do. Of course you're going to have someone who's going to put stumbling blocks in your path, but in spite of that, he pursued and persevered. Coach Temple was able to get the top sprinters because Tennessee State was giving scholarships. Coach Temple used to say, "First you're a lady, second a scholar, and third a Tigerbelle," and he meant it in that order. We all got our degrees. He saw to it that you got your degree. It was a tough time when grades came out. He got your grades ahead of you, and then there was a meeting. He could not understand if there was another Tigerbelle in the classroom with you, and this Tigerbelle gots an A, and you have a C. How did you get that C? You had to explain that, you had to make good grades. I will always be forever grateful to Tennessee State and to Edward Temple because they really put the icing on the cake.

Reflecting on my life, I think black athletes have excelled when we've been given opportunities that we were not given before. Now you give us a chance to get in there, and you see the drive that we have, that we've always had. It's always been there. We didn't just get to be superior athletes overnight. We had fine athletes during a time when we had very little opportunity. Now we have this opportunity, and we have taken advantage of it. This "superiority" in sports has come because we've not had opportunities, and we've wanted it so bad that we work harder than white folks to get it. Some people say that we've excelled only because of some physical superiority, suggesting we're not as bright as white people. We're just as bright. Just give us the chance and you will see.

NOTES

1   Catherine Hardy Lavender was an American gold medalist in the 400-meter relay at the 1952 Olympics. The U.S. team set a world and Olympic record of 45.9 seconds. She was inducted into the Georgia Hall of Fame in 1999.

DON BENNING, ED.D.

WRESTLING

June 3–4, 1994
Omaha, Nebraska

IN 1963, DR. DON BENNING BROKE TWO COLOR LINES SIMULTA-
neously when he was hired as head wrestling coach and assistant professor
at Omaha University,[1] becoming the first African American head wrestling
coach at a predominantly white university, and the first African American
full-time faculty member at Omaha University. In addition to these positions, Benning also served as assistant football coach and athletic counselor. In 1969 he became the first African American coach to be a member
of the U.S. Olympic Wrestling Committee. He led the Omaha University
wrestling team to a National Championship in 1970. That same year, he
was awarded Wrestling Coach of the Year by the National Association of
Intercollegiate Athletics. In 1971, while still coaching, Benning became
the first African American in the state to receive a doctoral degree from the
College of Education at the University of Nebraska at Lincoln. After his
years of coaching and teaching at Omaha University, Benning went on to
become assistant principal at Central High School (1971–1976), director of
the Department of Human Community Relations Services (1976–1979),
consultant for the U.S. Navy (1979), and assistant superintendant of the
Omaha Public School District (1979–1997). Don Benning's other distinc-
tions include a *Sports Illustrated* Award of Merit (1969), a Nebraska High
School Athletic Director of the Year Award (1974), induction into the University of Nebraska at Omaha Hall of Fame (1982), a Viking of Distinction Award (1986), and induction into the Nebraska High School Hall of
Fame—Sports (2000). Don Benning retired from his position as assistant

superintendent in 1997, and is now coordinator of urban education and part-time senior lecturer of educational administration at the University of Nebraska at Lincoln.

CHILDHOOD

I was born in Omaha, Nebraska, on October 10, 1936. My parents' names were Erdie and Mary Benning. They were married for fifty-three years. Both of my parents were middle-aged when I was born. My father was forty-nine and my mother was forty-eight. I knew my parents as middle-aged and elderly individuals, but the way they carried themselves never did fall into the stereotypical category of invalids or the deteriorating elderly. I was the youngest of five children. My oldest brother, William Philip, was twenty-three or twenty-four years older than me. The next oldest was Earl; then my sister Francis, and finally my sister Phyllis, who was four years older than me.

Earl played sports in high school, but neither of my sisters played sports. I was the first in my family to play any sport extensively. None of the others in my family went to college. At that time there were open discrimination and segregation laws on the books, even here in the northern cities. The circumstances in which I was raised were somewhat unusual. I wasn't raised in the black community. I was raised in a very poor segment of the white community in northeastern Omaha, which was nearly as bad as what you would find in white Appalachia. I never did get the straight story of how my family ended up there. We had very limited resources at that time in 1936. It was during the WPA (Works Progress Administration) and the Depression. One thing I remember about my dad was that he always was working at something, even if it was hauling garbage. He ended up retiring from the Union Pacific Railroad as a chair car porter. Even though I had a two-parent family, we were very poor. If it were today, I would say we would certainly have qualified for welfare.

When I was in elementary school the *Brown v. Topeka Board of Education* decision wasn't in place. That came in 1954. I went to Sherman Elementary School in the 1940s, which was a predominantly white school. At that time it was K–8. The Bennings were pretty much the only blacks that attended. It was a situation where I definitely was the minority. It was interesting because it taught me a few important survival skills early on in life: that I still had to deal with prejudice, racism, and discrimination. I had to learn how to take care of myself. You learn how to survive or perish in those situations. You either become submissive or you become aggressive, stand up for what you believe, and learn how to protect yourself. I chose the latter. It was not unusual for me to have two or three fights a day. You establish your turf and you let it be known that "nigger" wasn't your name. By the time I was in the sixth grade I started playing sports.

At that time I started to attend an African American church. That was a very important part of my history, and very educational and comforting. I am still a member of that church, St. Johns African American Episcopal Church. I used to walk six miles to get there.

As I grew up, I came to understand better the plight we experience as African American males, especially among those who are uneducated. I believe my father was forced to quit school when he was in the seventh grade, and my mother was forced to quit school in the sixth grade. But that also taught me that being educated and uneducated had nothing to do with intelligence. Both my parents were very intelligent individuals even though they didn't have the educational background. My mother was very sensitive, caring, and demonstrative in showing affection. My dad was the opposite. The support came from my mother not my father.

One of the things I learned at a very early age was that I internalize, and I became very comfortable with who I was. I developed strong self-esteem and independence. I could take things or leave them. I didn't need, nor did I have, peer support to steer me in a particular direction, although I did have the support of my mother. I developed a pretty good sense of what was right and wrong, and I knew I had some God-given ability.

Sixth grade was the turning point in my life. I had a physical education instructor and coach who taught me a great lesson. Some people at that time might have said that I had a chip on my shoulder, and I don't know if I did or didn't. Some of that opinion could be that any time you look at an African American who is assertive, that person is considered to have a problem. I don't know how much of that was fact or fiction, but I would fight quite easily for what I believed was right. As a sixth grader, I developed into a pretty good athlete. My physical education teacher was also my coach. He coached football, soccer, and basketball. He was white. We had a square dancing unit, and there was absolutely no way that I was going to square dance. It wasn't because I had only white partners. I had the attitude that I could do what I wanted to do, and because I was an athletic star I thought should be exempt from dancing. I flunked!

I learned a very important lesson. No matter who you think you are or what you think you bring to the table, there are consequences for your actions, and there are rules that everyone has to follow. I am ever grateful to him, and glad that I was at least half way smart enough to understand the message.

My coach at Sherman Elementary School left to become principal in another school district, but he took a personal interest in me. He realized what was ahead of me, being isolated somewhat from the black community. He also ran the city's recreation program. When I was thirteen years old, and in ninth grade, I went to work for him at the Kellon Community Center, which had predominantly black participants. It was a summer program that turned into a year-round full-time job. Aside from needing the money, I was also interested in participating in athletics and developed a relationship with the coach that helped me assess my potential.

It would not be unusual for me to walk to school five or six miles one way. Some people would make fun of me because of the shoes or clothes I wore. If I had two pairs of Levis for the year, that would be substantial. My mother would wash them every day. Even though I was teased and taunted about my clothing, I had enough self-confidence not to be bothered to any great extent. I walked everywhere. I became known because I fought because of the teasing and taunting, but was also a very good student, and a success in athletics.

There was only one individual in my life that I ever was scared of and ran from. He was three years older than me, and a bully. I was in the seventh grade and he was a sophomore in high school. He saw me as I was walking down the dirt road, and I started to run. Somehow he caught me, but that was his mistake. He ended up very much on the losing end. Because of where I lived I got it from both ends. In the black community they asked, "What are you doing with all those white people?" In the white community I was discriminated against because of my race, and in the black community I was looked at as not being black enough because I was raised in a predominantly white community. So I had to fight.

From about the age of thirteen I was in very good physical condition because I walked most places. I worked from the age of twelve. Because my father worked odd jobs and my mother was a maid for a wealthy family, most of my earnings helped to take care of the bare necessities at home. I helped my dad pick corn and feed pigs and chickens on a plot of land that the Union Pacific Railroad rented to us for one dollar per year. This land was near the railroad tracks and what they wanted from this arrangement was us to keep the lot free of weeds and debris.

My dad was a very proud person, and he really resented the fact that people referred to him as "boy." He couldn't hold his anger and would lash out. He had to take a lot of garbage relating to his manhood and the subordination of African American males. I don't remember what I earned on my first jobs, it was nickels and dimes. But it was important to me. The money and the contact meant I didn't have to depend on anyone. It helped relieve the stress for my parents and helped me grow as a person.

In high school I played football and baseball, and wrestled. Practice was usually over around 6:00 p.m. and then I would take the street car to the community center and arrive about 6:45 p.m. If I didn't have the money, or because of the time, I might miss my connection and would have to walk home.

After I graduated from the eighth grade, I went to Omaha North High School. By the time I reached high school I had already shown some proficiency in academics and sports. The year I graduated from grade school, I was selected by school officials as the number one academic male student in the eighth grade. I was supposed to be honored at a service club and given an award. This did not happen. The award was given to another student in my class because the service club refused to recognize a black student.

It was a continual fight in my mind not to become bitter and angry. Even though I played football and baseball, and wrestled, baseball was probably my best sport. Later in life individuals told me that if I'd had someone to champion me I probably could have been drafted and played professionally. In fact, I did play some semi-pro baseball with Bob Gibson, who is now in the Professional Baseball Hall of Fame. The name of our team was the Woodbine Iowa Whiz Kids.

No man is an island. At a very early age, kids in the neighborhood would come to me to start a game, or what have you. My love for sports just evolved. Even though I fought frequently with boys in the neighborhood, they seemed to seek me out as a leader. An example of this is when we decided to play Little League baseball. I went out and solicited money from the local grocery store to buy T-shirts.

I only had one new baseball glove in my life, and that was when I played college ball in Woodbine, Iowa. I was kind of a sports nut, reading the paper, listening to the radio, and following Jackie Robinson and other black sports heroes of the time. Even though I played Little League football, Little League baseball, sports in high school and in college, my parents never saw me play. In retrospect, my mother and father not seeing me play bothered me later on in life.

During my first year in high school I did quite well. I took college preparatory courses, and at that time you had to test into them. I did well, and I made the varsity wrestling team as a freshman. In fact, I probably would have won the state championship as a freshman, but I got a serious staphylococcus infection from the mat. I had probably fourteen matches a year. At that time I was wrestling at 105 pounds. Here again my stubbornness showed. I should have been wrestling at 95 pounds, because I weighed probably 101 or 102, but I didn't want to cut any weight. I still did well and, in fact, I beat the state champion. I would have been favored going into the state meet. Winning that match both did and did not help my confidence. There were a lot of things that I was very confident in, but on the other hand, I guess I always felt I was alone. When you start out really early in life feeling that all you have to rely on is yourself, you don't get overexcited about a lot of things.

As far as my popularity and acceptance was concerned, you might have thought I was a god or something. Really I wasn't much of anything. In grade school I fought every day, but in high school I probably had two fights. I played halfback on the freshman football team, and in college I played halfback and fullback. In my high school freshman year, our Legion baseball team was runner-up in the state. In fact, in 1949–50 Omaha North High was the national runner-up. During my sophomore year, I wrestled and played junior varsity football and baseball. The four years I was in high school we were city champions, state runners-up in football and baseball, and in my freshman year we won the state wrestling title. We were an excellent all-around team and we had quality athletes. You couldn't do anything average or you wouldn't be playing, especially if you were black, because this was a predominantly white high school.

In my sophomore year I was a really good wrestler, and my coach and teammates expected me to win everything, but I did not. I lost the second match of the year to a kid over in Iowa, who really was a pretty good wrestler. The coach jumped all over me, saying, "You let us down." I thought that was unfair, and I quit the team. That decision still haunts me, because I had never quit anything before and I have not quit anything since.

As a senior in high school I was participating in wrestling, football, and baseball. I got more honors in wrestling, but I was also a regular in football. Probably my best talent was in baseball, with wrestling a close second. But no one offered me a scholarship in football or baseball. They came looking for me in wrestling. Iowa State, the best wrestling school at that time, indicated that if I walked on and made the squad I would get a full scholarship. They recruited only the best in the country. There was no way I could pay that initial money to get to Iowa State, so I went to a small college, Dana. But even though I had shown signs I was better than average in wrestling, I still wanted to play baseball. The summer going into my senior year, I batted .440 and our team was runner-up in the State Legion Baseball Tournament. At Omaha University, I could play baseball as well as football and wrestling. In 1953–54 the University of Omaha and the University of Nebraska at Lincoln had racial problems similar to other universities in the midlands. In fact, the Big Seven in general didn't recruit black athletes.

When I told my parents that I was contemplating going to college, my father didn't say much. My mother said, "I'm very proud and excited for you. You know financially there's nothing we can do, but I'm really proud of what you are doing, and I'm going to support you." My priorities probably weren't what they should have been because I was more interested in prolonging my sports participation than my academic career, even though I never had any problems academically. In one sense, I think, I short-changed myself in not achieving my maximum potential in academics, but I did reasonably well.

College was an adventure and a journey that no one in my family had taken. My best friend was the son of a black attorney. I found something very interesting when I visited his home. Even though his mother and father were great to me, their friends and associates looked down at me, because I was poor. After a while it wasn't an issue with me, because I didn't really see young people with money doing anything I wasn't capable of doing. And I was able to graduate from a university in four years in spite of limited resources.

COLLEGE

I went to Dana College for the fall semester in 1954. It was a good liberal arts school and they recruited me hard. It's a Lutheran college. It was too small, not what I was used to, and I felt that it was not challenging enough, especially in regard to my athletic ability. I decided to leave Dana after the first semester and transferred to Omaha University. This was a difficult decision because I liked the student body, and the freshman class thought enough of me to elect me treasurer. At that time Omaha University had an undefeated football season and had won the championship at the racially segregated Tangerine Bowl in Florida. The Omaha University football team was all white and really didn't want blacks participating, because they felt that having blacks on the team would hinder their chance of being selected for a bowl game. Blacks had participated on the team before in a very minimal way and the coaches weren't happy about it. They felt blacks should not play in the backfield because they didn't have "intestinal fortitude." Those were the kind of conditions I faced. I felt that I had to fight both my teammates and the coaching staff in order to accomplish anything.

It's very interesting that during all three years at the university I got hurt. In my sophomore year, I worked my way into the starting line-up on the football team, in spite of attempts to the contrary. I got blindsided and tore my knee up and I was done for the year. In my junior year, by the sixth game I was the leading ground gainer on the team, but I broke my wrist in the first quarter of the game against Northern Illinois. Because of comments made about blacks in the past my attitude was, "I'll show you." I did not tell the coaches about my wrist and went to dinner that evening with the team, threw up my food, and the doctor had to take me to the hospital.

I remember one of the black leaders in the community wrote me a very nice letter. It was really reassuring and supportive and complimented me on my mental toughness and for not giving up. Nevertheless, it was very discouraging not to be able to finish the season. Then in my senior year, on a fluke after the whistle, a defensive player blindsided me and reinjured the same knee I hurt as a sophomore. At that time it was kind of a gamble whether you operate or not, and they left it up to me. I rehabbed, and to everyone's surprise I came back and played in the last game of the year.

At that time racism showed its ugly head. In the last game we played New Mexico State and we stayed in El Paso, Texas. By this time we had three other black players on the team. The coach came to me and said, "The hotel that we are staying at in El Paso would not allow blacks, so we're going to have to find a place for you and the other blacks on the team in the black area of the city." He gave a number of unacceptable reasons and I said, "I will talk to the others and see what we want to do about this situation." Ironically, I was looked at as a leader by both the whites and blacks on the team. I talked about what the coach said with my three black teammates. This discussion lasted at least a couple of hours. The initial response was that we would stay home and not participate and/or take this to the news media and have them question why Omaha University didn't cancel the contest with New Mexico State. The final decision was not to go public but to bring our dismay to the athletic director and have him promise that this would never happen again, and that Omaha University athletic teams would never participate again if all student athletes were not treated equally. We did get to see another part of the country regardless of the implication. So we went and played. In one sense it probably was a mistake, but in another sense it taught all of us a few lessons. After the game the team was going to a restaurant and nightclub in Juarez, Mexico. The coaches and the team expected the black members to attend. I went to the head coach and indicated that we would not participate in the dinner. The coach said "We expect you to go to the dinner as part of the team." I said, "That was not the decision process you used when we had to stay in a very poor section of the black community. We choose not to attend. Give us our money and we'll see you tomorrow when you come to pick us up."

That was 1958, my senior year. And there were similar types of questionable experiences in football and in wrestling. When Omaha University decided in 1958 to reinstitute wrestling, I competed and I was undefeated. I did have one tie, and that was against the defending national champion. Even with my record, the school wouldn't send me to the Nationals. I questioned their reason for not sending me but it was to no avail. I guess they had never sent wrestlers to the Nationals before, but they had also never had any one that had qualified before. The defending national champion went on to win his second national championship and his team, Mankato State, won the team championship. In those years I endured a lot of hardships and a lot of bad luck. I was relatively small at that time for the positions I played in football. I played both offensively and defensively, and I was about 175 pounds. Each year I played at Omaha University, I got hurt and was not able to finish the season. It was extremely frustrating.

PROFESSIONAL LIFE

I graduated in May 1958 with majors in history and physical education. The draft was still in effect so I had a military obligation after graduation. I went on active duty in July in the Marine Corps Reserve. At that time the Omaha Public Schools did not hire blacks in secondary schools (9–12), but they would hire you in elementary schools that were primarily African American. The assumption was that the schools were primarily in all black communities.

I went to Chicago and took a competency test to go to work for the Chicago Public Schools. I passed and was given a contract. I went back to the university just to say goodbye to a couple of people, and I saw the president of the university, Milo Bail, who during the course of my experience there always seemed to go out of his way to talk to me. It seemed he saw something he liked. He wasn't that way with everyone else, but he was very personal with me. He said, "What are you doing?" I said, "I'm getting ready to go to Chicago Public Schools to teach." He said something to the effect of, "No, you are not. How would you like to continue your education? I would like to offer you a graduate fellowship in secondary education." He added, "Would you like to do some coaching?" I said, "Yes!" My assignment was that I would answer to the chair of the Department of Secondary Education (who later became the Dean) and that I would also assist in wrestling and football.

The graduate fellowship was like being out on an island alone. My first responsibility was to do well academically. Aside from the academic schedule I had to do some things in the secondary education department that I had absolutely no experience with. The biggest problem was that some faculty and staff didn't like the decision made by President Bail. This wasn't a position that you saw an African American holding. On the coaching side of the equation, some people, and a lot of coaches, felt that I didn't have the experience and I didn't deserve to hold those positions. Some were against this for what they might have perceived as legitimate concerns, but most of the criticisms were for racist reasons. It's interesting to look at some of the attitudes.

But then the coach said, "Don, why don't you work it so you go through two years and then we will try and get you on full time." I was suspicious. I talked to Dr. Bail, and he said, "I think that's a good idea." After my two years were up—this was 1959 through 1961—I went to talk to the president. He said, "Well, there aren't any openings now, but the first opening that we get I'll hire you back." I said to myself, "Yeah."

I did all the scouting; at that time you didn't have the sophistication of videotaping and other technical equipment that is used now. If you were right, you were right, and if you were wrong, you were wrong. You couldn't point to film exchanges or anything like that to verify what was said. There was a tremendous amount of pressure in being the sole individual responsible for scouting, having no experience and having to learn on the job and realizing that you weren't allowed the luxury of any mistakes. Coupled with that was the fact that when traveling to Kansas, Missouri, and other places, you had racial barriers at all levels. Plus, with a graduate fellowship, I could not get behind in my academic work. If I failed in either one of these areas, it had larger implications than just me failing. Being the first African American, failure wasn't an option. Academically you were expected to get a minimum of a B and there was an expectation of all As. A C would drop you from the program. After finishing my two years as an assistant, I received my master's degree with a major in secondary education and a minor in counseling.

My evaluations by the head coaches in wrestling and football were excellent. I was disappointed that I wasn't offered a full-time position after finishing my degree, but before I left I met with President Bail to discuss whether or not I still had a chance to be hired if an opening occurred. His answer was brief but firmly stated, "I definitely want to hire you, but there is no position at this particular time." Even though the job did not materialize at that time, my mother and father were still alive to see me receive my master's degree and become the first child, not only to graduate from college, but to also receive an advanced degree.

Even though I'm basically an introvert, I've always been in the public arena. It hasn't been easy for me, but I'm good at it when I choose to be. I can be persuasive and articulate and get my point across. I can talk my way into things and I can be pretty convincing if I need to be. That was a very, very rewarding two years. I met a lot of challenges, but I really didn't know how good I was until I left the university and went to the YMCA. About six months later, at the age of twenty-three, I became the acting director of the North Branch YMCA.

I went to the YMCA for a job because John Butler was the executive director. I thought he was a pillar in the community; he had a lot of empathy and understanding, and worked with youth extremely well. That job provided me with an opportunity to work with the youth in the black community, to maybe give something back to them, while I was waiting to see if I had a real chance at working for the university. Whether you want to call it pride or arrogance, I wasn't interested in the Omaha Public Schools at that time. In about six months John Butler died and I became the acting director. I really didn't know if a lot of things were real. I really didn't know that the coaching staff at the university thought I was pretty good until the year I left, and they went for the championship. To get to the championship they had to play a team that was undefeated, and they got a hold of me and asked if I could get away from the Y and scout the team for them. Since I was the only scout they were going to send, they said that I knew my stuff and they had confidence in my abilities, and really kind of put the frosting on it. Then I knew and they also knew it. They weren't doing anything special for me. They thought I had something that was going to help them get to where they needed to go, and they had something that was going to help me get to where I needed to go.

In 1963, President Bail gave me, at the age of twenty-six, the chance to become America's first black head coach at a predominately white university. I was also Omaha University's first full-time black faculty member and assistant football coach. I took over the reins of the school's fledging wrestling program knowing full well I would be closely watched. Because of the uniqueness of the situation, and the circumstances, I knew if I failed I was not going to be judged as Don Benning, but as an African American. Those old stereotypes were out there. "Why give African Americans a chance when they don't really have the ability to achieve in higher education?" I was very aware those pressures were on me, and given those challenges I had to perform at the highest level in order to pass all the scrutiny.

My life experiences prepared me for proving my worth and dealing with adversity. The fact of the matter is that minorities have more difficult roads to travel to achieve the American dream than the majority in our society. We never experienced a level playing field. It's always been crooked, uphill or downhill. To achieve your best you have to know what the barriers and pitfalls are, and how to navigate them.

African Americans know the difficulty of reaping the full benefits of our society, but the absolute key is recognizing that and saying, "I'm not going to allow that to deter me from achieving my goals." That has always been my belief and practice. I knew "good enough" wasn't good enough, that I had to be better. In my eight seasons at Omaha University, the wrestling teams compiled an 87–24–4 dual mark, including a dominating 55–3–2 record the last four years. Competing at the National Association of Intercollegiate Athletics level, UNO won one national team title. The year we won the U.S. National Championship, Iowa finished fifth in the NCAA Division I tournament. We beat them soundly in their own tournament. *The Amateur Wrestler News*, which was the wrestling bible, said of us, "Regardless of any classification you want to put UNO in, they are in the top three or four teams in the country." We finished second twice and third once, earning eight individual national championships along the way. In 1970, I was the first black coach to win a collegiate national championship from a predominantly white university in the United States. I was also National Wrestling Coach of the Year, NAIA (National Association of Intercollegiate Athletics), in 1970. Some of my other wrestling recognitions were Nebraska Coach of the Year honors from the *Omaha World Herald* (1969) and the *Lincoln Journal Star* (1970).

I could name a number of incidents where we were treated poorly or where there was an attempt to humiliate us, but it's enough just to say it happened. One of my biggest supporters was Bob Devaney, the great football coach at the University of Nebraska in Lincoln. At one program where we were both scheduled to talk, Bob Devaney stood up and said, "The best coach in the state is right here." I was sitting there when he said that and he was pointing right at me. That was quite an endorsement if you have any knowledge of how Nebraskans love football! I felt a real honor for the hall of fame football coach to recognize my achievements.

One of the things that I liked to do when I was coaching was to give back to the community, socially and professionally. Professionally I gave clinics across the state to help develop high school wrestling in Nebraska. Socially, I was active in the community, talking and working with young people. Another interesting challenge was that I've had a number of great wrestlers. I believe I had eight national champions, even though I had wrestling scholarships only in the last two years of coaching.

In my coaching years at UNO, I had job offers from ten to fifteen Division I universities both in football and wrestling. Some of the schools offering me positions were Arizona, Wisconsin, Colorado, and Cincinnati. These were quality athletic programs. I had many opportunities to leave Omaha but for various reasons I chose not to.

As far as coaching football, I felt I had a great deal of ability, and a lot of other individuals thought likewise. I had however, three major concerns. One, student athletes seemed to control the coaches, rather than the other way around. Two, my perception was that there were some serious questions regarding money and student athletes as it related to boosters. And three, I had a great deal of success as a wrestling coach, and I didn't want to spend five to six years assisting someone else to build a football program, nor did I want to spend my career as an assistant football coach. But having mentioned those three, a fourth was probably the biggest factor: I wanted to spend more time with my children and help my wife more in the parenting aspect of our children's lives.

I was able to establish a number of firsts at the university and in the state. I was the first African American in the state to receive a Ph.D. from the College of Education at the University of Nebraska in Lincoln in 1971. I was working on getting my doctorate while I was coaching at UNO. A doctorate wasn't required for coaching or teaching.

I'm a long way from being perfect, and I don't want to give anyone that impression, but I've always tried to teach and coach, and say that you need to strive to be the best that you can be. I don't like to be hypocritical about anything, and since athletics never were my only focus, I also wanted to broaden my service to society. Aside from having a heavy teaching and coaching load, I was enhancing my own education.

In our society you are rewarded more for a doctorate degree than for not having one. It was very difficult for me in the sense that, with recruiting and teaching, I had one course every semester, and I had to drive sixty miles down the road to the University of Nebraska in Lincoln for it. In the summer I would have nine hours. At that time the interstate wasn't completed and the University of Nebraska in Omaha did not have a doctorate degree program.

One of the things that made wrestling so popular at the university and in the state was our winning record. We were outdrawing football! In fact, we were so successful it caused some problems internally. People who used to be my friends became distant. We could beat, and we did beat, the University of Nebraska in wrestling. Faculty and staff, I don't care whether it was the English professor or whoever, would say, "Hey, we're number one." People didn't understand when I said it was more important for us to be number one in the state of Nebraska than in the country. That's the only thing that was indisputable. It helped me build some very good relationships.

I should have received my doctorate degree in June of 1971, but I missed the deadline. I earned it in December of 1971. That December I left the University of Nebraska at Omaha. The Omaha Public Schools were heavily recruiting me. When they were recruiting me, they said, "We respect what you have done and you have tremendous skills. We need you, and we have some great challenges ahead of us." They even said, "We feel that you certainly could assist us in achieving those goals. You had so many successful cross-cultural experiences." They sent some feelers out. I said, "I'm not closing my mind on anything." I didn't know what the opportunities were or what my interests would be. They said, "We're looking to place you at our central office but we would like for you to get a couple of years of experience in secondary education. We would like to place you in our best senior high school so that you get a better understanding of what's going on in a school, and when you have an opportunity to go up the ladder your perspective will be broadened." They were offering to make me the assistant principal at Central High School, which was the most prestigious high school in the state. At the time it was a very elitist high school that had a relatively large African American population. They were of the more upwardly mobile class. The job was quite a drop in status since I was used to national recognition, but that's not what turns me on or off.

As assistant principal I would be doing no coaching at all. I talked to the superintendent and the principal. In one sense the principal was enthused, but in another sense it was, "Here's a guy that's never had any actual public school experience." That was ironic, because one of my responsibilities at the university was to teach "Introduction to Teaching," the foundation course for teachers to be trained.

As assistant principal I had a multitude of duties. I was the athletic director and I was the activities director. I had aspects of activities with drama and fine arts, and I also had some curriculum developed. I helped develop the first multicultural class at Central High School. In our school district I had advocated changing our curriculum to be more pluralistic in nature, and so I started doing that in the early 1970s. The state of Nebraska decided to honor, for the first time, the outstanding athletic administrator at the high school level in 1974. With the emergence of gender equity and women's athletics, and the added types of pressures that were put on schools, it was becoming more and more important to identify the need for quality of administration in this particular area of the curriculum. I had shown initiative in this area, and as a reward I received the first Nebraska High School Athletic Director Award for Exemplary Administration in High School Athletics in 1974. I was still an assistant principal at the time.

I moved up to the central office and things went pretty much as they anticipated. We had the most successful desegregation program in the United States! Why? Because our academic achievement had gone up every year, and if you look at minimal disruption as it relates to violence and community acceptance, ours was a model. The reason we desegregated was that the federal government found that the school district was in violation of the 14th Amendment. The court ordered the school district to develop a desegregation plan. Implementing the court order was done with a great deal of inclusiveness, which was not the norm, by bringing grass roots people together to discuss and formulate a plan that would be acceptable. One of the primary components of that plan was that it would include two-way busing, which was somewhat unique. In fact, we are no longer under court order to bus. The order was lifted in 1984, but we still run our desegregation plan by the edict of the Board of Education, which is voluntary. This is commendable, to remain a unitary school system.

There was another black administrator at the central office and he was the assistant superintendent. I became the director of human community relations. My responsibilities were training; staff development, linking with businesses and other external publics of the community, and crisis management. My duties were what I made them. The director's job was enjoyable. Let me qualify this. I really operate to the beat of my own drum on one end, but I'm very respectful of line staff and relationships. Sounds somewhat contradictory, but I refused to let anyone put me in box. When the black assistant superintendent retired, I took the position. Is there a situation where individuals are slotted in the school district? Yes, there is. It's my experience that you make of situations what you make of situations. What has happened in the past has no bearing on what is going to happen in the future if you take charge and control of your own destiny.

The superintendent, who was there for another fifteen years after I came in, and I didn't really have a good relationship. I was too aggressive for him. But he knew that from the very beginning. He had to make all the decisions. He was very much under the gun, as it related to whether desegregation was going to be a success or failure. And I was the individual that had the most credibility, whether you are talking about the black or white community. I knew that and he knew that. I walked a tight line. With things I didn't like, I voiced oppositions. There are certain things that I'm not going to give up for anyone. I'm also realistic enough to know that sometimes you have to jump ten feet before you can jump twenty feet.

I was the director from 1975–79. I feel that I was very helpful and supportive to this superintendent, so that he could move forward. One of the reasons we haven't been successful to the extent that we should have been is because of jealousy and finger pointing at each other. The superintendent didn't want to promote me to assistant superintendent. After 1979 things were pretty solid and going in a good direction. It's like a lot of us have experienced. We haven't survived this long because we're stupid. I had too many people, both white and black, who didn't give him a choice in the matter. He did not want to make that decision, but I was appointed assistant superintendent.

In 1963, when I got a full-time position, both my parents had the opportunity to see me do some things that they could only dream about. It was very satisfying to me. That's the good part of the scenario, but both my mother and father died in November of that year, just two weeks apart. My father died first of emphysema, and then my mother died of cancer. Even though they got to see history being made, they never got to see the fruits of my labor like I wanted. I really felt I earned what I deserved. But I look at it and say, it's really sad that in the long history of the Omaha Public Schools there have been only two black assistant superintendents.

I've always thought that I am just as capable as the next person, and one of the reasons I stay in Omaha is that I like the community. I felt that Omaha was, and is, a very good place to raise children. I turned down at least two superintendent positions and an associate commissioner of education position because of those reasons. There have been many times in my life where I've faced extremely adverse situations. I have talked about quitting or hanging it up, but something just would not allow me to do that. It sounds corny and trite, but I said that adversity is a tremendous teacher if you can survive it. You develop a confidence that, "I'm going to work through this or I'm going to beat it; I'm going to turn this thing into a positive." It almost becomes a value.

I think the assumption that blacks are not intelligent, or that we excel at sports because we have physical capabilities that white people do not have, is inaccurate. I think if you look at the fact that a disproportionate number of black people are poor, and you look at the means in which they survive, and the types of food that they have eaten to survive, and what they have to do for transportation, that a lot of things that they do are physical. The other part of that is there have been more opportunities in the areas of athletics, so a lot of blacks have chosen to go in an area where there's relatively easy access. They work very hard to achieve in these particular areas and you get disproportionate results. If you look at what has happened to our immigrants in our society from the Italians to the Jewish population, sixty years ago you saw a lot of outstanding Jewish fighters. You look at the lifestyle from which they came, the ghettos, and the hunger that they brought with them. Now you name me a Jewish fighter. It's the same with the Italians. The thing that we haven't been able to transcend in our society in the United States is the color barrier. That has kept us in a status quo position; we haven't been able to step over that last hurdle to have ready access to any direction we want to go.

My life bridges a very important time in American history. It extends from a time when laws still supported overt segregation and racism to an era where constitutional amendments and federal legislation outlaw the same behavior. You have to understand what was going on in society at the time that made life and social progress extremely difficult. The country was having a social revolution, authority was being threatened, race riots were a reality, and we as blacks were rebelling for equal rights. The experiences we learned bridging and surviving this segregation and racism is lost to most of our young people.

Young athletes today are being deluded into thinking that things might come easy for them, because we are desegregated. That's one of the biggest arguments, I think, as it relates to desegregation, and the value of neighborhood schools. A lot of individuals that are role models aren't there to nurture these young people. They don't get the nurturing in the oral history that they used to get. That's why I think this oral history project is so great, in that it ensures our history isn't lost or stolen.

I think that if racism didn't still exist we would do even better than we have done. That's a factor, but I think it's two-edged, in that we have to work to eliminate racism. On the other hand we have to tell our black brothers and sisters that "you may not be responsible for being down, but you are responsible for moving up." And at the same time give them a helping hand to get there. Too often we use bigotry as a convenient excuse: "because of racism I can't accomplish this," or "I may as well not do that, because the 'man' is not going to let me do it anyhow," so we don't even try. We have to get past that. I'd say that you have an obligation to be the best that you can be. Not only for yourself, but for your significant others and for those that look to you as some type of role model, even though you might not want to be. So, along with the ability that you have, you need to develop the responsibility that goes along with it. I told my children, and many other young people, that no matter what the hardships are that the only one that can stop you from being the best that you can be is yourself.

NOTES

1   Omaha University is now the University of Nebraska at Omaha (UNO).

LENNY WILKENS

BASKETBALL

September 3, 1990
Cleveland, Ohio

THROUGHOUT A NATIONAL BASKETBALL ASSOCIATION (NBA) career spanning over four decades, Lenny Wilkens distinguished himself as a successful player, coach, and administrator. Wilkens began in the NBA as a first-round draft pick out of Providence College in 1960. He played a combined fifteen years for the St. Louis Hawks, Seattle SuperSonics, Cleveland Cavaliers, and Portland Trail Blazers. Wilkens became one of the first three African American player-coaches in the NBA in the 1960s era.[1] He became head coach of the Seattle SuperSonics in 1977 and the next year (1978–79) led that team to its only championship. Included among his numerous awards and accolades are an All-Star Game MVP trophy (1971), a Coach of the Year award (1994), and two Olympic gold medals (as assistant coach and head coach for the 1992 and 1996 games, respectively). In 1995, he surpassed the legendary Red Auerbach as the winningest coach in NBA history. His outstanding success as both a player and coach is reflected in his election as one of the Ten Greatest Coaches in NBA History, as well as one of the league's Fifty Greatest Players, on the NBA's fiftieth anniversary. He is the first African American to be inducted into the Basketball Hall of Fame as both a player (1989) and as a coach (1998). Most recently, he served as vice chairman for the Seattle SuperSonics, a position from which he resigned in July of 2007.[2]

CHILDHOOD AND COLLEGE YEARS

I was born on October 28, 1937, in the Bedford Stuyvesant section of Brooklyn, New York. I grew up in a mixed neighborhood. My dad was a chauffeur and my mother was a housewife. She took care of the family. My dad died when I was five, and at that point my mother had to get part-time work and assistance from welfare to raise her four children. I have two sisters and a brother, and I later gained a stepbrother as well. I guess we were poor in that we didn't have a lot of things, but we had each other. The one thing my mother stressed constantly was staying in school and getting an education, so we would be able to function in society. She felt that without an education, we would not get anywhere. There were a lot of things to distract from education, because there were gangs where we lived, and if you went from one neighborhood to the next, you might have to fight your way back. That was part of growing up and it was something we accepted.

After my dad died, there were a lot of times when we just didn't have things. It was important that my sisters dressed halfway decent. My brother would wear whatever was leftover from me. There were times when we didn't have the nicest clothes, and I remember people would comment about it, both black and white. I can remember going to a cotillion that was put on by the Girlfriends, a black group out of New York, and they always seemed to look at me strangely as though they were thinking, "Who's your father? What's your background? Where are you from?" As if any of those things are the measure of a human being. I resented that very much. From that point on I made a pact with myself. One, I would never want for anything; and two, I was going to be successful, because I would have that drive. I wanted to be a positive influence on other African Americans, particularly young people, because they need positive images. They need someone they can look up to. That is when I decided how to live my life. And I haven't wavered from that. It was a burning desire, and it motivated me through college and into my career in professional sports.

I graduated from high school mid-year in January 1956, and I worked from January to September at Montgomery Ward. I played in some post-season tournaments for high school kids and based on that, and a letter written by Father Thomas Mannion from my parish, I was eventually given a scholarship to Providence College. I was very fortunate to get an athletic scholarship, because I couldn't have afforded to go to college otherwise.

Growing up in Brooklyn and attending Holy Rosary, a boys' high school, I didn't notice a lot of prejudice, although I knew it existed. I was with a lot of my peers, a lot of black kids, so I didn't think about things like that. I began to notice it for the first time when I began college. During my years at Providence there were only six blacks in the whole school, and in my class there were just two of us. On Friday evenings the school would have dances, and all the students were invited. Of course, there weren't any black girls there. I danced with a couple of the white girls, which some people did not like. In fact a good friend of mine, a white guy from New York, almost got into a fight because he heard someone make a comment about it. But overall Providence was a great experience. I met people from all walks of life and they left lasting impressions that shaped my idea of what kind of person I wanted to be.

I always felt the need to excel in everything, not just athletics. I wanted to show that I was just as good in the classroom as anyone else, and I had always been told as a youngster that we as African Americans had to be twice as good as other people. I hadn't had to work hard at doing well in high school, because things came easily. When I went to Providence College there were a lot of things that motivated me. I knew people would accept my athletic ability, but I wanted to show them that I could think as well as they could. In my freshman year, they used to post everyone's grades publicly, and I wanted to be sure I was in the upper third and on the Dean's List. I had a B+ average, and I know that surprised people. I majored in economics. I remember in my freshman year economic theory class, we sat alphabetically and all the Ws were way in the back. The professor was asking a question, and he was skipping over certain students, some of them white. I looked to see who these people were, two of them were hockey players and one was a baseball player. I knew what he was doing, so when he got to me, I put my hand up. I was not going to let him skip over me. I wanted to let both the professor and the class know that I was an intelligent human being who could function and who could think. I wanted to make that point very clear.

I thought Providence College had a very good impact on me. First of all it was run by Dominican Fathers and discipline was important, and I believe in that. Most of them went out of their way to help me. The thing I liked about Providence, too, was that it was small, and they got to know me as a person. I think you lose that in huge universities. Because of that and, because of the highly disciplined academic program they had, I felt it was very good for me. I enjoyed my four years there immensely. That doesn't mean I didn't have negative encounters. I remember dating an Italian girl.

Her father was very upset and spoke to one of the priests at the school, who in turn tried to talk me into not seeing her. This floored me, because this was a man of God. I'm mature enough to realize now that he was just a human being and susceptible to weakness like anyone else, but back then I resented it. So my college years had its ups and downs, but there was one thing I always made sure of: I was going to get my education and I was going to graduate on time, because I that was very important to me.

My perspective changed between my freshman and senior years. When I was a freshman I was, of course, very open-minded, and I still am. But I think I looked at what people told me as if it were the gospel. I was very patriotic. If we had been at war, I would have volunteered for service. But by the time I was a senior, I began to realize that everything that glittered wasn't gold. I had to make my own way in this world, and my success wasn't going to rely strictly on what I knew, but who I knew. Just because a book says something, doesn't necessarily make it so. You have to use your own common sense and knowledge and apply yourself.

PROFESSIONAL YEARS

What a lot of people don't know about me is that I never planned on a professional career in sports. That was something that just happened because I worked hard and was able to navigate various situations. I was really lucky. I only played a half year of high school ball, so I was very fortunate to get a scholarship, and it was important to me to make that scholarship pay. I majored in economics and during my senior year I received a couple of propositions. There was a firm in New York that wanted to me as an economist. Also, I received an assistantship to Boston College to work on my masters, which I would then have used to come back to Providence and teach. Those were the choices I faced. I thought I'd have my degree and a good job.

Then in 1960, I was the number one draft pick of the St. Louis Hawks, and they wanted me to come out around April. Even then, I did not go out and see them. A friend of mine was getting married and wanted me to be his best man, and that to me was more important, because I didn't really have any aspirations to be a professional athlete. But the Hawks kept calling and trying to talk to me. There used to be a league called the Industrial League, the old AAU league, and they had teams like the New York Tuck Tapers. They sent a guy up to entice me into working for them and also playing on their team, because they knew I was from New York. When their representative came up to Providence to talk to me I didn't want to go to dinner with him alone, so I asked one of the players on the team, a good friend of mine, to go with me. Well, my friend wanted to go to the Boston game. He was a diehard Celtics fan and they were playing for the championship. The representative got tickets for the game, and we went. I had never seen a professional basketball game live before. Interestingly, the Celtics were playing the St. Louis Hawks. I watched the game, and there was such an excitement in the arena. The fans were going nuts!

As I watched the game, I came to the conclusion that I was as good as their guards. It wasn't cockiness. I knew I could handle the ball better than they could. After seeing that, I started thinking, "Maybe I ought to try this for a year and see," although I still thought becoming an economist would give me a better life. We knew professional players were paid well, but at that time they wouldn't discuss my pay until I came out to St. Louis to speak with them. My first year's contract was for $8,000. Back then accountants were getting $6,600, economists $6,000. I said "Okay, I'll try it, and make a couple grand more." When we went to the playoffs we were given a little extra, although it wasn't a whole lot of money, even then. For the finals that year we received $2,327 and the winners got $3,300.

I wasn't very kindly disposed to the Hawks because in 1958, my junior year of college, we played St. Louis University in St. Louis. At that time you couldn't eat at the restaurants downtown; they were all segregated. Initially I hadn't been particularly intrigued by their offer or the city because I knew how they felt about black people down there, but after seeing that game I decided that I would go try it. I joined the Hawks in September of 1960, and when I got there I found that the racism I had previously experienced still existed. Of the rookies on the team, there were about seven of us who were black and about five whites. I remember they had us staying at the Sheraton-Jefferson Hotel downtown. One evening we decided to go to a restaurant. It was right across from the hotel and they wouldn't serve the black players, but most of the white rookie players went in and ate. We left and went back to the hotel, because they would feed us there. I started to wonder, "Boy, will I have to deal with this all year?" Because of that kind of discrimination, I marched once in a demonstration. I know the St. Louis Hawks had to think I was a little crazy, because you didn't see many athletes doing that then.

After I moved there I got to know St. Louis a bit. At that time St. Louis had a big black population and I began to make friends, but there were still a few racial incidents. I remember the first year some of the players on the team always looked at us like we had horns on our head or something. But I didn't pay them any mind. Once I proved to them I was a good athlete they accepted me right away, because they could see that I was going to help them win. By the end of the season I could go into any restaurant that I wanted, because St. Louis opened up to me.

When the season ended, the number one thing I was thinking about was leaving and getting back east to New York. I was seeing more of the world because we traveled a lot, and I was beginning to be exposed to a lot of prejudice I had never seen before. We played seventeen exhibition games that year. We played in Albuquerque, New Mexico; Edinburg, Texas; and Denver, Colorado. I began to see more racism, and while to me it was a sad state of affairs, I still had high hopes that the situation was going to change because I felt that white people were going to get more and more exposure to black people. At that time I also saw that people my age were not putting up with it. They were starting to demonstrate against segregation in the schools; they were just not going to tolerate it.

After my rookie season I went back to Brooklyn. In those days the season ended around the end of April. I had been in ROTC in college and I thought I had to go into the service right after the season ended, but I received an extension. I was supposed to report in February, but I did not go until sometime in May. The reason I went into the advanced ROTC in college is because they paid you. Also the draft was still in effect, and I wanted to go in as an officer. I figured I'd spent four years in college, why should I go in as an enlisted man? In May of 1961, I reported to Fort Lee, Petersburg, Virginia.

The Hawks knew that I was going in, but they figured it was only going to be for six months. They thought I'd get out around the beginning of the season, but at the end of my six months we had the Berlin Crisis and, because I was an officer, I was extended for a year. I was going to be in for a year and a half now, which shook up the Hawks. They tried to see if there was some way to get me out on a hardship release, but they couldn't do it.

After the Hawks realized I would have to stay the full year and a half, they wanted me to play on weekends if I could get a pass. I was on troop duty and the general wasn't too happy with that idea. I had decided I wasn't going to play while in the service, because I had seen guys who had done it and they didn't perform very well once they came back to professional ball. If I played for the post team, however, I could get a three-day pass whenever we didn't have a game. So I decided to do it, and some weekends I played for the Hawks. It ended up only being twenty games, because that was all we could fit in. They paid me reasonably well for those games.

I think that if you talk to anybody from the service who knew me, they would tell you I was a good soldier. That's the only way I would operate. No matter where I am, I'm going to do the best job that I can do. That's why I liked having troop duty. I was responsible for getting these guys in shape.

I was an executive officer to the company commander and, when he was shipped over to Berlin, I became company commander of a student battalion, although I was just a second lieutenant. They assigned me a couple of other young "seconds" because I had more time in grade, and I was due for "first." I also had a mass of sergeants under me, people who had been in the service for many years. Your troops had to be ready for inspection at any time. I had to give a couple of guys, who had gone AWOL under the former company commander, general courts-martial because once he left I had to take over. Of course I read everything on it to see what would be the maximum and minimum sentences I could give, and tried to ascertain what the circumstances were. It was a great experience for me. I know one guy resented me. He didn't like the idea of having to report to me, but I couldn't have cared less. We were in the military and he had to respect my rank. I was going to treat him like everyone else, and I wasn't about to walk around with kid gloves.

The army was an interesting experience. When I played for the post team we would travel by bus. We went to Camp Lejeune, North Carolina; Fort Gordon, Fort Benning, all those places. One time we stopped along the road in Georgia and again, the white restaurant owners didn't want to serve black people. The white guys on the team were eating and getting their stuff, and the black guys had to go around to the back. My pride just got the best of me. I refused to eat, and when we got to the base to play that night I wouldn't play. I didn't like the way we were treated and I didn't like the way my teammates went ahead and ate. I think we had about six or seven black guys on the team. Our coach was a civilian, a GS-18,[3] I think, and he was all shook up and upset. When we got back to our base, news of my refusal traveled around. The guy who was the head of special services was a major, and he was annoyed that I did not play. But when I talked to the general and I explained my actions, he agreed with me. Then no one bothered me. The general was a sharp soldier as well as a guy who loved athletics. He thought what I had done was important for the morale of the troops.

I had another experience, too. I traveled with the post football team once. They were going down to Fort Benning, Georgia, and they needed another officer to accompany them so they asked me. I wanted to go because I was very interested in football. We stopped at one place for gas and one of the black football players went into the restroom. Immediately, one of the white guys sitting out front went in there with a shotgun and told him to get out of there. He said, "Boy, you know you're not supposed to use this bathroom." The team coaches, all the white officers on the team, lieutenants and the rest, everyone was scared to do anything. When I saw this guy with a gun on him, I ran over and I grabbed the barrel and held it up in the air and took the shotgun off the guy. I hadn't been in a situation like that before, so I just reacted. It wasn't like I knew what I was doing. I was really angry about it. After that the coaches and the captains came over, took the gun, and tried to calm everything down. Then they got us on the bus and we got out of there. The players were very upset, because the coaches were just saying, "You know we can't control situations like this." The people who owned the gas station didn't give any apologies; none at all.

That incident left a very bad impression of the South on me. It really did. I didn't want any part of the South, and I'm serious. I felt all southern people were like that. Of course years later I found out that that was not the case, but at the time I was very resentful toward anyone with a southern accent. But time passes and you get to meet and know people. I've since met some wonderful people from all parts of the country. It is customary to speak badly about the South, but Massachusetts is just as racist as any southern state. Just look at what Bill Russell had to go through in Boston. It's unbelievable.

I was happy when my military service was finished. I wanted to pursue a career in professional basketball because I thought I'd had a good first year, considering I didn't become a starter until the middle of the season. I broke their guards' records, which I didn't think was a big thing, but now I was anxious to see if I really belonged. I was excited about it, so when my time was up I looked forward to getting back to St. Louis. I thought I could be one of the better guards in the league, and I wanted to be in that class with players like Oscar Robertson. I had gotten to know him, we were rookies together. He was in Cincinnati and I was in St. Louis, and we played against each other a lot. I had tremendous respect for him. I also knew Jerry West, another good guard. We had played in the college All-Star game and we shared the MVP award. I was anxious because I wanted to see if I could achieve something in the professional ranks, among players like these.

The Hawks had stayed in contact with me, but when I got out of the service, it was a different team. They had had some dissention problems, and by the time I got out the coach had been fired. During my first year the coach was Paul Seymour. He played for the old Syracuse Nationals years before. When I came in to play those twenty games while I was in the military, the coach there was named Fuzzy Levane. When I got out of the service, the coach was a guy named Harry Gallatin who had played for the Knicks. The only guys that I had played with left on the team were Bob Pettit and Cliff Hagen. Everyone else was gone. St. Louis was a lot more open then than ever before, and we had a pretty decent team. The team had changed so much that we had about five or six black players. When I was a rookie they didn't have any more than two or three blacks on any of the teams, and some teams didn't have any black players at all. Everything had changed a little.

But even though there were more black players on the team, there were not a great many black people coming to the games. I don't know if they couldn't afford it, or they just weren't used to going, but the seats were always taken up by white people. Attendance began to slip because Bob Pettit was at the twilight of his career and they were going to have to promote black players as stars. I don't know if people in the franchise were used to that; they didn't do a whole lot of promoting. But the money was starting to escalate for salaries. I'm sure the owner at the time could see this coming, so eventually he sold the franchise to two guys from Atlanta, Tom Cousins and Sam Banks. At that time I was in the last year of my contract. Since we couldn't get together on a new one, I was traded to Seattle.

I came to Seattle in November of 1968. I was very impressed with the city. I saw things I had never seen before. I saw white guys with black women, and I had never seen that, I'd always seen it the opposite way. The people were very warm and friendly. Not that they hadn't had problems in the past, I'm sure they did, but I met a lot of nice people. I couldn't believe how friendly they were. The black people did not immediately welcome me, and that threw me a little, but in time people get to know you and it changes. Seattle was a blessing in disguise. In my years in St. Louis, there weren't a lot of people who were willing to advise you on investments, as they did for a lot of white players. When I went to Seattle, all of a sudden there were so many more opportunities with which to get involved.

There was a guy, for example, who owned a percentage of the team, and he would invite me to lunch with him from time to time. He introduced me around. No one from the Hawks ever did anything like that. I took advantage of the financial opportunities presented to me. I made a few investments, and we were fortunate enough to make some money and get out. I think this guy tried to help me because he wanted me to feel good, to feel comfortable. He certainly didn't need anything from me, because he was a very wealthy man. When he introduced me around I got a very warm reception, people were very friendly. Of course my reputation as a player preceded me, so when I spoke at dinners, the reception was even greater because now people saw that I had something to say and that I could contribute something.

I was introduced to a black doctor who started the Odessa Brown Children's Clinic, a medical and dental facility in a low-income area. It was small at the time, and they wanted to build a new place. They were getting ready to break ground, and they asked me to do a public service announcement spot on the clinic and narrate a piece on Odessa Brown. I checked up on it and found that they were providing medical and dental care for low-income families, who only paid what they could afford. Once I saw what it was about I wanted to be involved, because as a youngster my family used to have to go up to St. Mary's clinic where they treated everyone like cattle, just a number. No dignity at all. I became involved with that charity and with others as well. Years later, after we won the 1979 NBA championship in Seattle, I was "roasted," and we raised $26,000 for the Odessa Brown Clinic and $26,000 for Children's Orthopedic Hospital. I also hosted a golf tournament at Jefferson golf course in Seattle for ten years, and half of the money raised went to the Special Olympics and the other half went to the Odessa Brown Children's Clinic. I played in a tournament at the Broadmoor golf course, which was segregated, to raise money for the Fred Hutchinson Cancer Society. Dick Vertlieb, the general manager for the Sonics, was also playing. He's Jewish, and he told me that we were making history, because they had never let minorities play their course before.

In my first season in Seattle, the coach was a guy named Al Bianchi. At the end of August, after the season was over, the owner fired Al. I was vice president of the NBA Players Association, and at the time Al was fired I was in a meeting. One of the guys I was negotiating against was the owner of the Sonics, Sam Schulman. At that time I didn't know he had fired Al. When I got back to Seattle, Dick Vertlieb offered me a player-coach position. I said, "No, you got to be crazy. I don't want to do that." He kept saying, "You can do it, I know you can do it." He argued that if he had to go out and hire a new guy, everything would be messed up because the new coach wouldn't know the players. He said, "I know you're a coach on the floor anyway. I know you can do it." I thought about it for awhile, and I thought this would be a good way to get some experience. I decided to do it.

To go back to the meeting I was in, as I mentioned before, at this time I was vice president of the NBA Players Association. When I first came into the NBA they did not have a pension plan for players, and very few teams had medical insurance. During my first year they circulated a petition to support a pension plan, but strangely, not all the teams wanted to sign. The Detroit Pistons wouldn't sign because their owner threatened to get rid of anyone who did. He intimidated them. When I got out of the service, Bob Pettit began grooming me to be the player rep, because he wanted me to replace him. He didn't like the pressure that went with the position. The year I got out of the service, Bob and I both made the All-Star team, and we traveled to Boston together for the All-Star game. When we got into the lobby of the hotel, we ran into Bill Russell, Tommy Heinsohn, and another guy who was with them, Larry Fleisher, who later became a top agent for players. At that time he was the legal counselor for the Players Association. They stopped us and said we had to talk to the new commissioner because the owners had refused to give us a new pension plan. The NBA had been off TV for a year, and the first game they were going to televise again was the All-Star game. Fleisher insisted that we go in and talk to the commissioner. If the owners still refused, we would tell them we weren't going to play.

The commissioner at that time was Walter Kennedy. When we met with him, he couldn't believe that we would threaten to strike a game. Such a thing was unheard of. He went down the line to each guy: Tommy, Russell, and to me. He said to me, "You mean to tell me you're going to strike this game." I said, "Yeah, I'm with the group." That evening we all went into a locker room and explained to everybody what we were doing and why we were doing it. Russell commanded a lot of respect because of his impact on the game, and the players certainly viewed Pettit and

Heinsohn as superstars. I just happened to be there, I guess. Well, the game was supposed to start at 8:00, and at 8:15 we were still in the locker room. ABC went to the commissioner and said if they didn't have a team on the floor in five minutes they were going to go with another program. In the meantime there were threats coming in from some of the owners. I remember Bob Short, who owned the Lakers, sent a message in to Elgin Baylor and Jerry West that they better get out there. But we had great unity. Everyone decided this was what we were going to do. Eventually the commissioner came in and signed a letter that said by June 1963 we would have a pension plan.

They gave us an acceptable plan. Every year after that the Players Association would have a meeting and most of the players would attend. Larry Fleisher helped set all this up. He talked to the airlines and the hotels and arranged it so we would get a package deal. At that time "Heinz" was in his last year and he was out, so at the meeting we elected new officers. Fleisher suggested that when we elect player reps from each team, it should be a star player because that way the owners couldn't intimidate us. We elected the new player reps, and then we elected the officers. We made Oscar Robertson president, I was vice president for the Western Conference, and John Havlicek was vice president for the Eastern Conference. We had all the areas covered. I guess the other players remembered I was at the meeting we had with Walter Kennedy, so I happened to wind up on a lot of committees that negotiated against the owner's committees. Whether it was pension or meal money or what have you, I would be on one of those committees. It was sort of semi-formal. We just had a group of guys that would handle a lot of negotiations. Oscar was there, I was there, John Havlicek, and we had one or two other reps, but always either Oscar or I was going to be there.

My participation didn't really create any problems for me in terms of being viewed as a troublemaker. In fact, the meetings went really well. The owners had a chance to see that what we were asking for wasn't totally unreasonable. And Sam Schulman was very reasonable. This might have been because in his younger years he was a maverick himself. When the general manager told him he wanted me to be the coach he thought it was fine, which was surprising because player-coaches were not common. The first was actually Bill Russell with the Celtics. Al Attles and I came into the league the same year, but he became a player-coach just after I did. He was at Golden State.

In 1969, I became player-coach, and the negotiations went okay. I was still a little bit naïve in that respect, but they offered me more than what I was making as a player. In that sense it looked really good. It was just a one-year contract, because I wanted to see if I liked it. I didn't want to be pinned in for three years and X amount of dollars. The first year was moderately successful, and they wanted me to continue. We negotiated for a two-year contract and I made them increase my salary considerably. I didn't get a chance to talk to Bill Russell, but I did speak to a couple other people who were coaches to see what they were making. There was no hassle. I was probably their best player so it would have been hard to hassle me.

Some might wonder why I wanted to coach and play, to do both. At first it was a novelty to me. I figured, "Why not try it and see?" In my last year as a player-coach in Seattle we won forty-seven games. We had some injuries, but there were some second-guessing going on with the guy who was our general manager at the time. Dick Vertlieb was gone at this point. The new guy convinced the owner I should do one or the other. I could see as the game became more and more sophisticated it would be tough to do both. When they approached me to talk about it, I told them, "You don't pay me enough for this aggravation as a coach. I'd just as soon be a player." I felt I still had some years left, so I decided I would just play, and they hired a new coach, Tom Nissalke.

The general manager convinced the new coach that I was a step slow and that they should probably get rid of me. They thought I could be a problem for him because the players might look to me for leadership instead of him. I met with the new coach and he seemed to be satisfied with me, but when he got back from meeting with the general manager things weren't so fine. The next thing I knew, they had traded me to Cleveland.

I talked with the new coach and with the general manager because I had heard rumors that I was going to be traded. They said, "No, no." I said, "Listen, I understand, but if you're going to trade me I would like to go to a team that I feel has a chance to go to the playoffs, a contender." And they said, "We respect that and all the things you've done for the Sonics, so we will try to do that." Well, they didn't do that at all. They traded me to Cleveland, which was an expansion team, a team I couldn't help much. I was very upset by this, and I sometimes wonder if they would have handled it better if I had been a white player. That did cross my mind.

I learned of the trade in August or September, when my father-in-law called me from New York and said that he had heard on the radio that I had been traded to Cleveland. I said, "That can't be. I didn't hear anything about it." Of course my father-in-law was right; it was released back East. I had gone out to play golf that morning with the team dentist. While I was putting around, getting ready to tee off, my wife called and said the Sonics had called her and said we were traded to Cleveland. I was really upset because one, they should have called me, and two, they said I would be traded to a contender. I was very angry about the way they handled the whole thing. We don't handle trades like that anymore. We try to talk to the people first. But they didn't call me in or anything, they told her over the phone.

When you go to a new team they buy the contract, and they have the option to pay more but not less. I didn't really want to go to Cleveland at the time, and I refused to go. I said, "To heck with it." I had another job offer. Then the coach came to Seattle to see me, and the owner got involved. They felt that if I didn't come to Cleveland, no one would else would either. It was not a city that had a great reputation back then. In the meantime they're talking to the guy who represents me, Larry Fleisher. Finally I decided I would go, but Larry wanted me to wait because they had made some overtures to him, and he thought they would increase my contract. When I finally agreed, they did increase my contract and I ended up making twice what I was making in Seattle. I played there for two years, and then I was offered coaching jobs in Seattle and Portland.

Portland wanted me because my record was good. My last year in Seattle we won forty-seven games. That was the fifth or sixth best record in the whole league. Also the guy who owned the Portland Trail Blazers, Herman Saskowsky, was a neighbor of mine in Bellevue. He knew I always wanted to get back to the West Coast. We were at a function in Seattle when he came over and started talking to me, saying, "You know, you want to get back to the Northwest. I want a coach in Portland, and we would like you to take the job." I kept putting him off and putting him off, but he kept asking. Finally I said, "You know it's something I would be very interested in. Talk to the guy who represents me." I had him talk to Larry Fleisher. This was in the summer of 1974. I'd had two good years with the Cavaliers, I'd made the All-Star game playing there, but I knew that I would probably only play two or three more years. Here was someone offering me a four-year contract. The offer was better than what most coaches were making. Back then the highest paid coach was getting between $75,000 and $100,000 per year, but in my last year in Cleveland I was making $125,000. I decided I would take the job.

Once we made the deal to coach in Portland, they decided that they wanted me to play for a year. I said, "Well, if they want me to play, they will have to pay me $150,000." They agreed. I signed a four-year contract with them, three years as a coach and one year as a player-coach. After my first year in Portland, Herman Saskowsky left. He bought into the Seattle Seahawks and became the managing partner of the team so he had to liquidate his interest in the Trail Blazers and we got a new owner, Larry Weinberg.

When Larry became the owner there was a lot of shuffling going on in the front office. He really didn't know me well, and I didn't know him, and I took some heat from the press because I played a lot of young players. They just assumed I didn't know what I was doing. Bill Walton was in his first year and he was going crazy with his stuff, and I knew this team was close to becoming a good one. I wanted to make a trade for a player, but they wouldn't trade the player I wanted. After the end of my second year there, Weinberg wanted to make a change. He didn't feel the team had made enough progress. My response to him was, "We have eight new faces." I felt we had made a lot of progress. I told him if we trade the player I want to trade, we could get a good deal for this guy. If Bill stayed healthy, we had a chance to win a championship that year. But it was his decision and his team, and if he wanted to make a change there was nothing I could do about it.

I left and moved back to Seattle and, from 1976–77, I worked for CBS as an analyst. That year, the Knicks coach came in and told me that Portland had traded the same player I wanted to get rid of, and gotten Maurice Lucas. Bill stayed healthy and Portland won the championship. I felt good because what I predicted came true, and also there were bonuses in the contract that they had to pay me when they won. As a TV analyst, I would fly to wherever the game was being televised, get in the daily report, and the game would come on Sunday afternoon. There's lots of money in that now, but I had this taste for coaching and I knew I could be successful because I had predicted correctly what would happen with the Trail Blazers. I wanted my opportunity to prove I was right.

After that year with CBS, Sonics owner Sam Schulman hired me as the director of personnel, because they had already hired someone as a coach. Bill Russell had coached there after me, and they fired him. Then they hired a guy named Bob Hopkins. When I first returned to Seattle, the team was in disarray. They were trying to rebuild their image. When I took over, we evaluated the personnel. I talked to Hopkins and tried to make some suggestions to him, to let him know that I would be behind him and I would help him acquire talent. When I worked for CBS we covered all the games, and I saw all the talent in the league. I knew who was available, who I thought were good players. The year I came back to Seattle, Hopkins had done some scouting and he liked two players, Jack Sikma and Ernie Grunfeld. They were both good players, so I researched them. When I came back I said, "You're right. Both of them are good and I think based on what you're saying, the player we need is Jack Sikma." He agreed with that. Then he changed his mind and he wanted us to take Ernie Grunfeld. I tried to get another draft pick that year so we could draft Grunfeld but we didn't. I said, "Look you were right the first time, Sikma's the guy we need. That's the guy we should stay with." I assisted with that, and we drafted Jack Sikma. Then I was able to acquire Gus Williams from Golden State. The Sonics had a center named Tom Burleson who we traded to Denver with Bobby Wilkerson for Marvin Webster, Paul Silas, and another player. I was able to help them acquire a lot of players. I picked up John Johnson that year for them. We had all this talent, but Hopkins just got off to a bad start and he blamed everything on the players when things didn't go right. You lose players that way. The first time the owner wanted to get rid of him I said, "No, give him some more time. He's young, be patient." But they kept losing and finally the owner decided to make a change.

I felt some anguish watching the brother stumble. I gave him the best players, advice whenever he wanted it, but I couldn't insist that he do certain things. I wanted him to have his freedom. But every day he'd come in and he'd say this guy isn't doing the job and someone else isn't doing the job. You can't knock your players like that. If you do then they'll tune you out, and then ownership starts looking at you. He lasted only a couple of months, after five wins and seventeen losses. That's why they said they wanted me to take over, because I knew the players. I did what they wanted, but even then I said, "I'll do it for the rest of the year, and then if I don't like it I want to be able to go back to being director of personnel." They said, "Fine." We turned it around and we went to the finals in 1978. We didn't win it, but we went to the finals.

After that success I wanted to see how far I could take this team; I wanted to see if we could win a championship. I really felt we had good, young talent. Sikma was now a second year player. We had Dennis Johnson, Gus Williams, Fred Brown, Lonnie Shelton, Paul Silas, a kid named Dick Snyder, a couple other kids, Wally Walker, and Joe Hassett. With these players we won the championship in 1978–79. The championship season was a great experience. I thought we had a good team and we would be good for a few years. Now the thing you have to be smart about is bringing in new players to continue winning. We needed scouts but they never hired anyone to replace me as director of player personnel, and that had the predictable results.

I wanted to stay in coaching. If you're going to continue to build a team you need good scouting out there, and you need someone in the front office who knows basketball, especially if I'm going to be out coaching. We didn't have that. Our general manager was a super guy, but he didn't know basketball. So we lost some players over time. Paul Silas was toward the end of his career and Dick Snyder retired after the championship year. There were trades and things like that as well. But I enjoyed coaching and I stayed with the team a few more years.

Eventually Sam Schulman sold the team to Barry Ackerley. Before Sam left he wanted me to be his general manager, but I still enjoyed coaching and I didn't want to move into the front office, so they hired a guy I recommended, my assistant Les Habegger. Then the new ownership took over, and the new general manager and the new ownership started getting rid of players to get the salaries down, and the team declined. They fired the general manager, and by then I needed a break from coaching so I took the position. I was general manager for a year, from 1984–85, and I made sure we did some good things. I got us Xavier McDaniel and Dale Ellis. Jack Sikma wanted to be traded and, of course, they wanted to get rid of that salary, so I traded Jack, but I made sure we got two first round picks along with Alton Lister. In the meantime, while all the trades and acquisitions were going on, I got a call from Wayne Embry, who was a general manager in Cleveland, to see if I would be interested in a coaching job there. I told him he had to get permission to talk to me. He called the general manager, and the new president of the Sonics, and got permission to talk to me. Since I wanted to get back to coaching I eventually took the job in Cleveland. I had played in Cleveland before, but I had never played in the new building. I had played downtown in the old arena. The other reason I was very interested is that I saw the draft and the young players that they had obtained, and I thought it would be kind of fun to coach this young talent. It was a franchise that was starting over, and they were going to build from the bottom up. So I went to Cleveland.

I have been very lucky to have people like my mother and Father Mannion in my life because they did everything they could to make sure I'd have a real future. They made sure opportunities were not only made available to me, but also that I took advantage of them. That's what we need to teach minority children, to make the most of what they have. And on the other side, we need to make sure they have something toward which they can aspire. I think the reason that there are so few black people in sports broadcasting is because they do not have the opportunity. How many black play-by-play guys do you see covering the NBA or baseball or football? They just don't get the opportunities. I think it's good that some of us were able to leave a good impression so that they won't be afraid to contact black sportscasters. I think ten years ago there was real pressure felt by people in the places of power in the industry to do something. I don't think they feel that way anymore. The "Reagan Era" relaxed it all.

Now our approach can't be the same. We can't go in there and cry that the white man's got us again, or we can't do this or we can't do that. What we have to do is go back to the old philosophy that we need to be twice as good as everyone else. And those of us in good positions must help others get those opportunities. I know that when the season is over I could just go home and relax, but I do the games on TV. African American youth need positive role models, so I think we should keep doing these things, even though they may be an inconvenience for us. People don't realize that we need to keep doing the show. That gives opportunities to other black youth who might want that opportunity or need to have that aspiration. They might see us and say, "I'm going to do that someday."

NOTES

1   The others were Bill Russell with the Boston Celtics, and Al Attles with the Golden State Warriors.
2   For more on Lenny Wilkens, see his autobiography, *Unguarded.*
3   GS stands for government service. The 18 refers to a grade within that ranking system.

KEN HUDSON

NBA REFEREE

September 11, 2007
Atlanta, Georgia

In 1968, Ken Hudson became the first African American to serve as a full-time referee for the National Basketball Association (NBA). For twenty-two years, Hudson was a marketing executive for the Coca-Cola Company, and during his time there he managed all media-related activities and community-based events for New England Coke. In 1972, while vice president of community affairs for the Boston Celtics Limited Partnership, he founded the Boston Shoot-Out, a program designed to showcase the city's high school basketball talent. Hudson has continued his dedicated support of community organizations, and holds positions on the board of directors for the Boys and Girls Clubs of Boston, Southwest YMCA, and the Jackie Joyner-Kersee Community Foundation. His awards and recognitions include the Atlanta Technical College Presidential Award (2002), the Trailblazer Award from the African American Ethnic Sports Hall of Fame (2003), and an induction into the New England Basketball Hall of Fame (2003). He currently serves as an advisor to the NBA evaluating referees' standards during games.[1]

CHILDHOOD

I was born in Pittsburgh, Pennsylvania, on September 24, 1939. I went to elementary school and high school there. My parents, John and Jane Hudson, were a very interesting couple. My father was a good athlete in his youth. My mother was the youngest of fifteen children. She dropped out of high school in the eleventh grade. My father continued on and received a partial football scholarship to Ohio State University. But it was during the Depression and, because it was just him and my grandmother, he only stayed a semester before coming back home to work in the steel mills. I think that my interest in sports while growing up was encouraged by him because he was my role model. Everyone in the city knew him, and he continued his activity in sports by pitching softball while I was growing up. He was a pretty good left-handed pitcher. I was very proud to watch him perform and I guess it was only natural to become involved in athletics myself.

I was fortunate that even though I did not have a heck of a lot growing up, I had a lot of love. As a family, we were very supportive of one another. I was an only child. My parents are now both deceased, but we used to have some interesting conversations about progressing in life. They encouraged me and were very supportive of anything I tried to do. There was one stipulation: that I did not embarrass them in any manner, which I had no problem with, so it was alright. I had a lot of friends growing up, some of whom didn't exactly stay on the straight and narrow path, but we all have had those types of friends.

I think one of the good things that happened to me was that I attended an integrated school. It worked out very well because I developed some very positive relationships with people who didn't look like me, and through my athletic abilities and endeavors those relationships became even stronger. I was fortunate as far as education was concerned because the elementary school I went to was a very positive school. First through eighth grade was elementary, and then high school was nine through twelve. In my elementary school class alone there were seven or eight students of color out of twenty-two or twenty-three students. All of us had to hold our own because back then they didn't have remedial education, or what have you. Either you did the job or you failed, and when you failed you were kept back. Because of my competitiveness and the desire to please myself and make my parents proud about what I was doing, I was not going to be kept back. The big thing was to see your name on the honor board when we did well in our classes. It was a challenge.

I did all the normal sports, things like baseball, football, and basketball. Baseball was probably my best sport, although I probably would have been pretty good at football. I just didn't feel like getting hit all the time. I concentrated on baseball and high school basketball. Those were my strong points. The other thing about sports activities was that my parents had a rule that as long as I acted with good sense and did what I was supposed to do in school, I could participate in sports. That was motivation enough to do well in school.

I was a good student. I probably could have been better, but as I told my mother one time, "If I'd done any better, I'd have been a genius and you wouldn't have been able to have anything to yell at me about, so I figured I'd just be a decent student." She just rolled her eyes and looked at me like, "Yeah, right."

I'll never forget the story my parents told me about how they bought their first house. I grew up in the projects of Pittsburgh's Hill District, and one day they decided that they were going to buy a house. They had no idea where they were going. They drove out to an area of Pittsburgh, with a lot of woods and trees, that no black families had ever moved to and they bought a house. That was in 1942–43, and the war was going on. They moved out there when I was about two or three years old. It was interesting because you might have expected some hostility from the neighbors, but it was just the opposite. My father was working in the mill on the swing shifts at the time from seven to three or eleven to seven; it would rotate. One day Mr. Steel, our next door neighbor, came outside and said to my dad, "Mr. Hudson, if anybody comes around here unwelcome or I don't know," while pulling out his shotgun, "Everything will be fine, so don't worry about a thing." It was interesting, because all of the neighbors were white.

In elementary school I played Little League baseball. My father was the coach of one team, I played on another, and we competed against each other. Growing up with Italian, Irish, and Jewish children, I can honestly say that the racial experiences I encountered were not the "flamboyant" type. When I was about twelve or thirteen years old, Reverend Patrick, who was a very outstanding leader in the community of Pittsburgh, came to my parents' house and said, "We want to integrate the swimming pool in our neighborhood, and we'd like for Ken to go swimming." I swim, but I don't care for it one way or the other. If I have to I will, but I would rather sit around and watch other people. My mother said, "Fine." Reverend Patrick went back and told the people in the community that tomorrow we're going to integrate the swimming pool with Ken Hudson, Ronny Henderson, and George Blackwell, two friends I grew up with. The people in the community said, "Oh we don't have any problem with that." And Reverend Patrick said, "What do you mean you don't have any problem with that?" They said, "Well they live here. They play with our kids every day. They play baseball and football together. Why wouldn't they go swimming with their friends?" The pastor was stunned.

Back in elementary school there was segregation, but in my class we were never seated based on race. We were seated either alphabetically or by height, and I sat next to the same Italian young lady for five years in elementary school and that's just the way it was. Because of how I grew up, I benefited from other cultures. I tell people all the time that I learned how to play bocce right after I learned how to play Little League baseball. The father of one of my good friend was a member of the Italian Club, so after we finished playing baseball and he'd say, "What are you getting ready to do?" I said, "I'm going home." He said, "Let's go play some bocce." We'd go into the Italian Club and no one said anything, because I was with one of the guy's sons. We just had a good time.

I started high school when I was thirteen and went straight through. Westinghouse High School was a legendary high school noted for academics, athletics, and talented people. I'm a member of the Westinghouse High School Hall of Fame. Looking at the list of students who attended that high school is incredible. They have all the photographs on the walls, it is amazing. Our class football team was the best in the city. Our basketball, baseball, and track and field programs were always integrated. We took full advantage of that when we played against other teams.

In high school there were no racial problems in my class. In fact, my class was death on substitute teachers on that topic. When a substitute came into the room, someone would get up and say, "Excuse me, I have a problem." The teacher would say, "What's the problem?" The person replied, "I really don't like being in this class. There are too many black kids in here." Then the substitute teacher would say, "Huh?" And someone black would get up and say, "Yeah, I'm tired, I can't put up with this." Now we're all in the same class, and you could tell that the teacher was thinking, "Oh my God, what is going on?" Soon she'd walk out and we'd start laughing because we all knew what was going to happen. We knew the teacher would go down to the teachers' room and say, "Those kids up in so-and-so, they're crazy." Finally the principal would come up and say, "Cut this mess out." He knew what we were up to. We were having a good time. I look back on those years as probably some of the most influential in my life. High school had such a profound effect on how I was able to deal with people as I moved around for the rest of my life.

Back then, a lot of people only went to college for a couple of years, just to say they had been. I figured I'd go for a couple years to have the experience, but I received a baseball scholarship to Central State[2] and after the first year I said, "I kinda like this." It was a four-year deal, and there were all these sisters there. I said, "This is the place for me," especially since my classmates were going. I refused to have my classmates outdo me.

COLLEGE

I decided after I finished high school to go to Central State. I had an opportunity to go to Pitt (University of Pittsburgh) or Penn State, but I wanted the black college experience. I could have gone to Morehouse or Florida A&M, but I had never been to the South and I wasn't comfortable going there. Central State University provided a good experience for me because it allowed me to see black people in high positions of leadership. In Pittsburgh we had a black city council person and an assistant superintendant of police, so there were some examples but not as many as I would have liked. At Central State, I saw that the president of the college, deans, and heads of departments were black people. That was a motivating factor. In fact, our commencement speaker was Dr. Martin Luther King Jr., because he and Dr. Wesley, the school president, were the best of friends. It was a great, great time in my life.

My competitiveness in academics was based on my athletic experience. In athletics, I was always a thinking person. I once had a job working as a vendor at Ford Field where the Pirates played. I watched what the big leaguers did, and I learned from them. As a result, I was able to take back what I learned while watching them and implement it when I played. Those were things that stayed with me as I moved along in life, because I believe that if you participate in any type of athletics, it has a profound effect on how you live your life. Through sports you understand the art of competing, of recognizing that you're not going to win all the time, but as long as you put forth your best effort, you can compete. There will always come a point where you encounter some people that are just a little more talented than you, but you can't use that as an excuse. You need to put forth your best and see what happens. I remember my college commencement when Dr. King spoke, he said, "If you're nothing but a bush on the side of the road, be the best bush that ever lived. And whatever it is you decide to do, work as hard as you can to be the best you can be at it." That has always been the foundation on which I operate.

In college I was elected captain of the baseball team my junior and senior years. I had always played second base, but in my first year I played third base. The year before I started at Central State, the team had been undefeated so the only position open was third base. I hadn't played third base since Little League, but I decided to play it. I thought I was going to be killed out there, but I survived and ended up playing second base in my senior year. In my sophomore year, we won the NAIA (National Association of Intercollegiate Athletics) District Championship, the first championship the school had won. We couldn't go any further because the school didn't have the money for it.

The athlete's life then was different from what it is now. We had a coach who was one of those old time guys. He made us shave our mustaches, and when we traveled we had to wear a sports coat. We would arrive in the morning, play a game, and leave right after. If we asked, "Can't we stay over?" he'd say, "You better get on that bus and get back to school. You got class in the morning." We'd get back to school at 4:00 a.m., get two hours of sleep, take a shower, and get to class.

PROFESSIONAL LIFE

After graduation I intended to be a teacher and I went back to Pittsburgh to teach. I soon found that teaching was not the way I was going to earn a living in this world. It was just too confining and didn't pay enough. I had a vision that my living habits would outdo my salary.

After teaching I took a job with the Joseph Horne Company, a large upscale department store in the Pittsburgh area. I was their first black manager trainee. I interviewed with George Palmer, vice president of personnel at Joseph Horne, and the interview went very well. "Call me in two weeks," he said. When I did, he said, "We haven't made a decision yet. Call me back next week." Next week I called again. He said, "We'll get back to you." After about three or four calls, one morning the phone rang, and they hired me. They paid me about $130 a week, as a manager trainee. They hired me in November and my first assignment was as a trainee in the toy and sports departments. It wasn't so bad leading up to Christmas, but the day after Christmas customers brought in all their returns and I thought, "What did I get into?" I worked there for about a year and a half, and then I said, "I've had it."

When I applied for jobs, I didn't have any reservations about being a black guy from a black college. I just assumed they would hire me. I had a family friend who is now deceased, Elizabeth Giddens, who was one of the first people of color to be a secretary to a major executive of a major department store in Pittsburgh. She was my confidence builder. She put together résumés for me, making sure that they were very well done, and always gave me the encouragement to be anything I wanted to be. The thing about it is, when companies sent me letters saying, "Well, right now we don't have a position," I just said, "Okay." I would say I was disappointed, but I didn't allow that to affect me. I didn't allow it to stop me from doing what I wanted to do.

When I was young I had a vision of doing two things. First of all, I wanted to be the best person I could be. Second, I wanted to have a job in professional sports. Like all kids playing baseball, I had a dream of going to the major leagues, but when I got to Central State I ran into a young man by the name of Jimmy Wynn, who played for the Houston Astros. As good as I thought I was, I knew when I watched him play that "I better get my degree." But I ended up in professional sports anyway, in the NBA. But that was after my time at Gulf Oil.

I started at Gulf Oil by a series of eliminations. One day I looked in the Yellow Pages and made a list of twenty companies that I thought would want to hire me. I knew that I was a very talented person, but no one else knew it, therefore it was my job to convince them. I interviewed with Atlantic Richfield Oil Company, TWA, and the Cascade Company. Back then, the people who interviewed me were a little nervous because I wasn't the shy introverted person they expected. Gulf Oil was different. They interviewed me, liked my style, and offered me a job.

Gulf Oil sent me to Boston, but first they had me train in Philadelphia. This was in 1964. They realized right away that I was not mechanically inclined. We had classes five days a week. Two days of the work week we'd have class and then work in the service station. One day we watched an operator with some of the tools. He said to me, "Here's what we're going to do. You stay out of the garage. You wait on the customers. When they drive up for gas, you go put gas in the car and wipe the windshield, and we'll take care of the rest." Now in the classroom I was decent, but I told people, "I'm here to sell gasoline and motor oil. I'm not here to work with tools."

The week before we finished the trainers said, "Okay, we're going to give out assignments." This was for the eastern region. I knew I wasn't going to go back to Pittsburgh because there were two people of color from Pittsburgh there, and if they sent both of us, they'd ruin the company! I knew the other black guy was going back to Pittsburgh because his father owned a gas station there. They said, "Ken Hudson, you're assigned to Boston." I said to myself, "Boston? Boston? How'd you get there?"

When I got to Boston, I thought, "Aw, what am I doing over here?" I think I knew two people in Boston. I knew a young man I had gone to college with, Stacy Johnson, and I had met Sam Jones, of the Boston Celtics, the year before in Pittsburgh because the Celtics had played a game there. Back then teams would sometimes play games in non-NBA cities, and through some mutual friends I ended up having lunch with Sam Jones. The great Bill Russell owned a restaurant in Boston at that time. I went there soon after arriving in Boston, and Sam was there, too. He said, "I know you." I said, "Yeah, we met in Pittsburgh." I became friends with him and his wife. He introduced me to Bill Russell and some other people, and since I was working for Gulf Oil, I made sure those guys got Gulf credit cards!

I did sales and marketing for Gulf Oil. I worked out of an office, but I had a company car and I had a territory. I had about fifteen service stations and a supermarket chain that I called upon to sell Gulf products, through promotions. These were company-owned stations that were leased out and you had to convince people to buy Gulf products. I had a tough territory in Boston. It covered the black, Irish, and Italian communities, but I had a good time with it because Gulf was very supportive, and I got along well with all kinds of people. But you were also dealing with some people who owned stations who were not exactly brilliant, and their stations failed. You never want to have a station close in your territory, because it looks bad. I once put a guy in a station in South Boston who used to suffer fits every now and then. You had to learn to deal with things like that. Then you had to deal with guys who put two dollars in the cash register and one dollar in their pocket. There were also guys who would come up short for the gasoline they bought. You go in and say, "Okay, this is what you owe," and the reply is, "Well I don't have that today." Then you have to go lock the pumps, so they couldn't sell any gas. I stayed with Gulf for four years. It was a good experience, and I got to know some nice people.

I went to Boston in 1964 with Gulf Oil, but after about four years I said, "I think it's time to do something different." They wanted me to stay in the area, do some other things, but I was ready to move on. Soon after, looking in the paper and there was an ad for Eastman Kodak. They we hiring, so I applied and they offered to send me through their training program in Atlanta. Being a sociable person, I walked around, met a lot of different people because I was staying across the street from the Hyatt Hotel that they had just built at the time.

As it happened, I was talking to a gentleman one day, and he said to me, "You ought to come to the reception tonight." "Reception?" I asked. He said, "Yeah, Coca-Cola's having one over at the Hyatt Regency." In the meantime the people from Eastman Kodak had hinted that their company was not my cup of tea, and I should consider other options. I went to the reception and someone said, "You're in Boston, huh? We're trying to hire minority folks in different cities." The company had never hired many minorities in the North, so when this person said, "They're going to hire someone in Boston, you may want to talk to the people there when you get back," I said, "How about that." A few days later I went to Rochester, went through my termination with Kodak, and went on to Boston. I said to myself, "Boy, this is going to be interesting." When I got back to Boston I didn't have a car, because before I'd had the company car. For about three weeks I was on public transportation. I did not have a job either! This was in 1968.

I rented a car and arranged to have a meeting with the Coca-Cola people. After two or three of these meetings, they said to me, "We'd love to offer you this position but we must let you know that we interviewed some other people, and there's a gentleman in Philadelphia we're waiting to hear back from." He was a black guy. "If he decides he's not interested in moving, we might offer you the position." Little did I know that the person they offered the job to was the brother of a classmate of mine at Central State. A week and a half later the people from Coke called and asked, "Can you come in and meet with us? We'd like to talk to you about the position." I went to the meeting and they said, "Well, the young man from Philadelphia decided he does not want to move to Boston, and we'd like to offer you the position. Think about it and let us know if you're interested." I could have told them right then, "Yes, I'll take it," but I said "I'll give it some thought." The next day I went back and said, "I talked it over with a few friends and I would be more than happy to accept the position." The interviewer said, "Great!" then he sat down and said, "Here's what we want you to do. We'll provide you with a company car and an expense

ou to help us develop the Coca-Cola image, and help
iness." To put it mildly, it was an unbelievable develop-
ie a truly satisfying relationship.

make such an impact on the city of Boston. I received
iad relationships with everyone around, in government
: I didn't allow it to make me think I was better than
anybody else, and I always tried to include other people in anything I was
doing. I'd hire kids for the summer and offer opportunities for jobs in the
company. I'd get some of "us" involved. But don't get me wrong, I still
maintained great relationships with people who didn't look like me. And I
was always very supportive of any activity that would positively relate to my
company, sports teams and the like.

I was with Coca-Cola in Boston from 1968 through 1988, and then
through 1990 in Atlanta. I moved to Atlanta because Coca-Cola decided
they needed me there. Most people never thought I would ever leave Boston. I never thought I would, either. Having the association with Coca-
Cola and with the NBA, my efforts to do things with the other people in
the Boston area, gave me an entrée into the community.

I went back to Boston in 1990 because I was homesick. Boston had
become my home. All my friends that I had grown up with, who had
helped me develop as a person and allowed me to grow, were in Boston.
I took a job as vice president of the Boston Celtics, but after I got back to
Boston I found it wasn't the same. It wasn't the same level of enthusiasm
that I had felt when I was there before. My friends and people that I had
known had gone on with their lives, and since I wasn't around I was not
part of their lives anymore. I accepted that and moved back to Atlanta. Plus
I was tired of the cold weather.

I got the job with the Boston Celtics because while I worked for Coca-
Cola, I was also a referee in the National Basketball Association. I was the
first black person to referee an NBA game on television. I started refereeing
in 1966, while still in college. I went to Central State on a scholarship, but I
had a job during the off seasons. The first job I had when I got to college was
working as a landscaper on the grounds crew and I knew I wasn't cut out for
that because my mother would have to beat me up to cut the grass at home.
If I didn't cut grass at home, I certainly wasn't going to cut it on the Central
State campus. They gave me another job working in the laundry, but too
many of my friends got their laundry done for free, so they said, "We gotta
get you outta here." They finally assigned me a job with the basketball team.

One day I was sitting in the stands watching practice and the basketball coach said, "Since you're here, are you planning on doing any work?" I said, "Yes, whatever you want me to do." So I became the manager. Sometime later he said, "Well since you're here, why not referee practice?" I said, "Okay," and that's how it started. Soon after that I started refereeing intramural games at school and semi-pro games around Ohio. When I moved back to Pittsburgh I didn't get into it, but when I moved to Boston I really got into it, refereeing for summer leagues and high school. Then I met Bill Russell.

One day, Bill and I were standing outside his restaurant in Boston, and I told him, I'd been refereeing for summer leagues and the Boys and Girls Clubs. Just to backtrack a bit, when I was in Boston I walked into the Boys and Girls Club one day and said, "I just moved to town, what can I do to help? What can I do with the young people to help out?" They were stunned because most people don't just walk in off the street and say, "What can I do?" I got involved and I became the part-time physical education person in the evening.

Bill Russell and I were standing there talking. We had developed a very good friendship. In fact, he once invited me to his house for Sunday dinner, and I forgot to show up. His wife fell out laughing. She said to me, "I can't believe it." I said, "What?" She laughed, "He sat around here all day waiting for you. He doesn't sit around all day waiting for me!" I sent him a telegram apologizing.

We're talking outside his restaurant and I said, "You know something? I think I'd like to referee in the NBA." He looks at me and says, "What?" I said, "Yeah." This was about 1966. He said, "Okay, so big deal." A couple weeks later during the summer, we were standing outside again and he said, "What are you doing?" I said, "Nothing." "Come on with me," he said. We got into his car and we zoomed down the highway to Marshville, Massachusetts, where Red Auerbach had a basketball school. We showed up, and a camp's going on, and Russell says, "Red, I want you to meet my friend Ken Hudson." Red's personality was, "Why do I want to meet him?" Red was like that. Bill said, "He wants to referee in the NBA," and Red being Red, said, "Now I really don't want to meet him." Red Auerbach always had this gruff personality on the outside, but inside, he one of the nicest people you could ever meet. I miss him dearly because he really took me under his wing, and he would always show up for every event, or activity, or anything for which I ever received an award. He became upset with me when I left Boston because he thought I should never have left. "Why," he asked, "do you wanna go down to Atlanta? Stay here."

I kept refereeing summer league, semi-pro, and then one day the NBA called me and said, "We want you to go down to McGuire Air Force Base." The New York Knicks were practicing there. They had me go down and referee their practices, because I had refereed the Boston Celtics' practices in the spring. I really got into it. The Knicks observed me, and I guess they must have said something to the NBA administration, but for a while I heard nothing. I kept refereeing for the summer league, even though I had this new job with Coke beginning in June of 1968.

In September '68, while I was listening to the radio, I heard, "Bostonian chosen to referee in NBA." The NBA hadn't said anything to me. I was lying in bed, listening, and my phone started ringing, people calling with congratulations. "Congratulations for what?" I asked. "You were chosen to ref for the NBA." I was stunned. That first year I was the only black person refereeing in NBA. The first game I ever refereed was a preseason game in Toledo, Ohio, in September, because back then that's when they played preseason games. But it was interesting, because I went from watching "the Big O" on television to telling the Big O, "I don't wanna hear your mess."[3] That's when it all started. I was the first person of color to referee an NBA game on national television. They did a story on me in the *New York Times*, that's where I got the title for my book, *A Tree Stump in the Valley of Redwoods.*

No one I knew, outside of Boston, knew I was going to be a referee. None of my friends around the country, not even my parents, because I'd forgotten to tell them. When I showed up on national television, they nearly died. They were big sports fans, and they were watching the Pittsburgh game on a Sunday afternoon when the TV sportscaster called my name as one of the referees. My mother thought, "There has to be another Ken Hudson in the world." They're watching the game, they look up, and my mother says, "Oh, my God." My father's reading the paper, and my mother said, "John!"

"I'm reading the paper, will you quit bothering me?" She insisted, so he put the paper down. By this time I was off-camera, and my father said, "What are you talking about?"

"You gotta watch." Then the camera zeroes in on me.

"What's he doing out there?"

"I don't know! He didn't tell you?"

"No!"

Every Sunday I would call home regardless of where I was, just to check on them. After the game I called and my father answered the phone. He said, "What were you doing there?"

"I was refereeing."

"Here, talk to your mother." My mother got on the phone.

"Who told you to get out there?"

"Nobody told me, that's my job."

"You better be careful."

"What do you mean, be careful?"

"You gonna get hurt out there. Keep me posted."

My mother might have worried, but my parents were proud of me and very supportive of my new position with the NBA.

You didn't go to referee school back then, you just refereed high school and learned. I did only one game at referee school. To this day, Russell and I laugh about it. I probably became a NBA referee quicker than anyone in the history of the game. What helped me was the experience I had refereeing the Celtics practices. It wasn't so much getting to know the guys; it was that I learned the game. I learned how to referee in the NBA. The thing that surprised a lot of people in the NBA was that I was pretty good at what I was doing and they never expected that, because of my size. Then there were a couple guys on the court who said, "He can referee pretty good. We didn't realize." I found out later that some people in the NBA never expected I would last more than one year.

I refereed and worked for Coke at the same time. When the Coke people heard about this, they said it was great. It was good for their public relations. When I sat down with them, they said, "You can referee, but if you're not going to another city, try to get back to the office the next morning, as early as you can. Whatever you do, make sure it's legal, and make sure we know what you are doing." These people were helping me. I was surprised, because they could just as easily have said no. Soon after this, Coca-Cola raised my salary!

I was a referee from 1968 to 1972. After the four years, Coke decided that this double duty was too much. "Sorry," they said, "but either you work for us or you work for the NBA." I got the message. At the time the NBA wasn't paying that well, not as well as Coke, so the NBA and I parted on good terms. As fate would have it, I'm now working for the NBA again, this time observing referees. I've been doing that now since 2002.

When I left Coke in 1990, I went back to Boston as vice president of the Celtics. The owner at the time thought highly of me, and the organization had always tried to figure out a way to bring me back to Boston. I later found out that when I left Coke, people there said, "Well if he wanted to go back to Boston, all he had to do was tell us. We'd have sent him back." But I stayed there for a year, then came back to Atlanta in 1992 and have been here ever since. I was vice president of the Celtics for just a year. Somehow Boston didn't have the same appeal the second time around.

In my life I didn't have any trouble because I was black. When I refereed, people would say, "Don't get stepped on out there," because of my size, but nothing racial. I had only two interesting racial incidents. One was in Atlanta. I had finished refereeing a game and I was walking up Peachtree Street when a guy walked up to me and said, "You Ken Hudson? The referee?" I thought, "Oh God, what's gonna happen now?" He said, "No, no, I just wanted to say I was at the game and I thought you did a nice job. You did a good job refereeing." I said, "Thank you," and he went about his business. The other time was in Phoenix, Arizona. There was this black guy out there who was a little bit crazy and he would wait after the game to harass the referees. I had been working with Daryl Garrison and he and the referees all knew about this guy. Once when we were leaving the arena and getting into the car, we saw him and I said, "Daryl, I'll take care of this." I said to the guy, "Hey brother, cool it will you?" He said, "If you don't get out the way I'm a shoot you, too." We drove away quickly, and Daryl turned to me and said, "I thought you were gonna handle it?" I said, "I am, that's why we're getting the hell outta here!"

In refereeing, in the heat of the game you pretty much block everything out. You hope that the arena's packed because then you really don't hear anything. I can honestly count the times that I've actually heard racial hostility directed towards me. When I was a patrol boy in elementary school, a white kid behind me said, "Hey nigger!" But the interesting part is that the white boy that I was on patrol with was the one who ran after him. Once coming back from Tennessee State University our bus broke down in Goodlettsville, Tennessee, and the team went into this restaurant to get something to eat. After we ordered and we were sitting down to eat, the manager said, "You can't eat in here." I said, "Oh? We can't?" So we got up and left.

Compared to when I started, some of us people of color have moved forward, a lot of us have remained the same. Some of us have gone backwards. I think race relations are at an interesting, if not critical, period in our lives because the attitude of certain government officials has caused race relations to deteriorate. There's not a whole lot of communication between the races. I think in our own race, we have had some setbacks because of lack of communication, lack of reaching out to one another. I think it's so hard out there, that we often forget we're only here for a short time.

We can do a better job by putting in more effort and make ourselves more available to those who are less fortunate. We should recognize that there but for the grace of God go I. Regardless of who I am or where I come from, I cannot be totally happy and successful if my brothers and sisters aren't experiencing some joy. I get more excited giving stuff away to other people and seeing the smiles on their faces than I do when receiving things.

Looking back on my life, I think my parents were proud of me before they moved on. My participation in sports definitely helped me. The lessons of life I learned about winning and losing gracefully came from the great people who helped me, like Elizabeth Giddens, Bill Russell, Red Auerbach, Sam Jones, the people at Coca-Cola, among others. All these people helped me achieve a good life. I am grateful.

NOTES

1   For more on Ken Hudson see his autobiography, *A Tree Stump in the Valley of Redwoods*.
2   Central State University, a historically black university in Wilberforce, Ohio, was founded in 1965. It originated from Wilberforce University, which was founded in 1856 and named in honor of the abolitionist William Wilberforce.
3   "The Big O" is the nickname of Oscar Robertson, who at that time was considered to be one of the two greatest players in professional basketball. The other was Bill Russell.

ARTHUR ASHE JR.

TENNIS

December 3, 1990
New York City, New York

ARTHUR ASHE JR. IS THE FIRST AND ONLY AFRICAN AMERICAN male tennis player to win the U.S. Open (1968) and the Wimbledon Championship (1975). Raised in Richmond, Virginia, he played on the neighborhood courts next to his home under the guidance of his mentor, Dr. Robert W. Johnson. As a teenager, his outstanding performance on the court brought him to the attention of tennis legend J. D. Morgan, who offered him a full athletic scholarship to the University of California at Los Angeles based on nothing more than his tournament record. Though he faced discrimination, Ashe's athletic talents prevailed and he soon emerged as a true pioneer in American sports, remaining a top contender in international tennis competition throughout the 1960s and 1970s. A politically active figure who strove indefatigably to raise the social consciousness of both Africans and African Americans, Ashe's work culminated in a three-volume history of black athletes in America entitled *A Hard Road to Glory: A History of the African-American Athlete,* which was published in 1988. Ashe contracted HIV from a blood transfusion in 1983 and died of AIDS-related pneumonia on February 6, 1993. The Arthur Ashe Stadium in Flushing Meadows–Corona Park opened in his honor in 1997, and is the headquarters of the National Tennis Center.[1]

CHILDHOOD

I was born July 10, 1943, in St. Philip Hospital, a hospital for blacks in

Richmond, Virginia. My mother's name was Mattie, and she worked for one of the two major department stores in Richmond, Miller and Rhoads. She died when I was six. My father was Arthur Ashe Sr. and he worked as a laborer on the Richmond, Fredericksburg, and Potomac Railroad, which is now defunct. When I was three or four years old, my father became the caretaker, and special police officer, for the largest public playground for blacks in Richmond. A house came with the job, and it was right on the playground, on Sledd Street. Within a third of a mile radius from our house, standing out in a 180-degree direction due west, was an Olympic size pool, four tennis courts, a utility field with a large basketball court, and railroad tracks that ran right through the middle of the playground. Just across the railroad tracks there was a parking lot, three baseball diamonds, and two football fields. It was also right across the street from Virginia Union University, a historically black college. That's where I lived until I was seventeen. Then I moved to St. Louis.

Growing up I worked with my father sometimes. We had a landscaping business on the side, and one Saturday morning I was raking leaves at a woman's house in Richmond. I was sitting, taking a break, and she came out with a bundles of magazines, with yellow borders around them, all tied up. I had never seen them before in my life. They were just sitting there, and she asked me to please throw them out. I saw the cover and I asked, "Do you mind if I look at them?" She said, "Oh sure, go ahead." I think I must've sat there for two or three hours looking at those magazines. That was my first exposure to *National Geographic*. In school, I loved the books we had about faraway places. I was always intrigued by geography and history, so those magazines really tweaked my interest. I'll never forget that day. When I went on to play tennis in college and professionally, I never got homesick. I absolutely loved the idea of traveling across the country or going someplace new.

While growing up I always went to church, and I attended two churches rather frequently. One was the First Presbyterian on Monroe and Catherine, which has been torn down. Its membership has switched over to All Souls Presbyterian in the north side of Richmond. The other was Westwood Baptist Church, where my maternal family attended, and that was a very powerful little church. I would say it was easily one of the most influential churches in Richmond. A lot of very famous people have pastored there, including Samuel D. Proctor. Membership probably isn't more than a few hundred people. This enclave of Richmond was originally cornered off, almost, as a place where black domestics could live as they served the wealthy whites in the western side of Richmond. It is a self-enclosed area and miles from any other blacks. It's probably about three-quarters of a square mile in area, total. When I was growing up you couldn't find a black person who lived three miles from it. My maternal grandmother lived there. This church was the absolute center, the bedrock of that little community and that church did very well, I think because they felt like an island in a sea of racism.

The churches I went to never took an interest in my career, but they certainly did have an effect on my educational and moral outlook. Later, when I went to UCLA (University of California at Los Angeles), I stopped going to church. For one thing, while growing up I always had to go and I didn't like it. Although I listened and absorbed all the lessons and so forth, I never thought they were saying anything I didn't already know. If you want to distill religious lessons, what more do you need than the Golden Rule or the Ten Commandments? I'm not going to be bad to anybody; I'm not going to steal, kill, or covet my neighbor's wife. I didn't think life was that complicated.

We had a few churches where most of the people of the black ruling class attended, and it was very important to belong to one of them. A college professor would not belong to a storefront church, he just wouldn't. That was just the way it was. The black community was stratified to a great degree by skin color and most of the people in storefront churches are very dark complected. I'm not saying that it is much less so in the churches that the ruling class attended; it would be quite mixed. But if you were to walk into your smaller churches, I would say the ones that had maybe fifty members or less, almost all of the members were darker skinned.

You can see that among southern blacks that the figure of the preacher is very strong. We had an expression called the "Sacred Six." Those were the six occupations in the segregated South that gave you a lot of social status: undertaker, teacher, preacher, doctor, lawyer, and dentist. These occupations gave you a fair degree of economic independence because you didn't depend so much on whites to make your living. They also required a good amount of education, except for the preachers, because one difference between Baptists and the other Protestant denominations is the motivation behind one's authority to preach. With us, if someone got the call, they didn't have to go to seminary, because God had put his hand right on this person, and they were going to preach the gospel and end up being a lot more spellbinding than someone who graduated from Union Theological Seminary. Of the "Sacred Six" that was the only profession in which you could gain quite a bit of social status even if you never went to college, because it didn't matter.

I moved to St. Louis in September 1960, on the recommendation of Dr. Robert W. Johnson, who was my long-time tennis coach when I was younger. Dr. Johnson felt that I was doing very well nationally and was keeping up with my peers, but that this was a rather important juncture in my life. If my tennis was going to keep pace with the people in my peer group and age category, I would have to play all winter long, which I couldn't do in Richmond. My father trusted Dr. Johnson because I started with him when I was ten and I had done exceptionally well under his guidance.

Arrangements were made for me to live with a friend of Dr. Johnson's, a man named Mr. Richard Hudlin, who was just as much of a tennis nut as Dr. Johnson. Mr. Hudlin was a high school teacher and had captained the University of Chicago's tennis team back in the 1920s. Mrs. Hudlin was a registered private nurse. He willingly agreed to have me stay with him in St. Louis during my senior year at no expense. He didn't charge me one dime for room and board or anything! He didn't know me, but I had a reputation as a polite, well-mannered, good player, and I already had a U.S. National Tennis ranking, which was something very, very few black youngsters had.

I went to Sumner High School in St. Louis, a rather famous high school. I thought it would be integrated, but there was de facto segregation. Emotionally it was a very momentous time for me. I went to Sumner as a senior with a very high academic record. I'd had straight As all the way through the Virginia Public School system. Because I didn't know a soul in the school, I could be whatever I wanted to be rather than continuing in the mold people thought I fit for seventeen years in Virginia. I matured a lot.

While I was at Maggie Walker High School in Richmond, we had the idea that even though we produced brilliant black citizens, somehow things were better in integrated schools. In St. Louis I discovered that was absolutely not true. Had I gone to Sumner for three years instead of just that one, I might've been the valedictorian of my graduating class. That was one of the most disillusioning realizations of my entire life.

My tennis game improved after I moved. At that time St. Louis happened to be a major center of tennis influence in the country. There were a lot of good players. In fact, two of them were my contemporaries, Cliff Bucholz and Jimmy Parker. Both Cliff and Jimmy ranked in the top ten in the country along with me, and we were all from St. Louis. Jimmy was local, he lived in Creve Coeur. He and I played doubles together, and in the Juniors we won quite a few doubles tournaments. In addition, Chuck McKinley and Cliff's older brother Earl came to St. Louis from time to time. We all played on the wood floor at the Armory on Kingshighway during the winter.

Every day after school I went to the Armory to train and play. It was a public facility, so if you belonged to the local tennis community and wanted to play there, you could do so. If you weren't as good as I was you probably wouldn't have been able to play with Cliff Bucholz or Jimmy Parker, but you could play. Elsewhere it was different; there were some places I could not play, such as a club in Forest Park. Mr. Hudlin couldn't play there either, but he didn't make it into a problem. He just wasn't going to fight that battle in 1961. Blacks also faced discrimination in accommodations. The Chase Park Plaza Hotel, which was one of the last to desegregate for the Major League Baseball players, wouldn't let blacks stay there.

I made a major breakthrough in the fall of 1960 when I won my first USLTA (United States Lawn Tennis Association)[2] national event. I won the National Junior Indoor title at the Armory. Soon after this the UCLA tennis coach, J. D. Morgan, offered me a tennis scholarship, sight unseen. Here was J. D. Morgan[3], one of the greatest tennis powers on the earth, who never met or spoke to me, saying "I'm going to offer him a full scholarship." He took a big risk. I also received offers from University of Michigan, Michigan State, Arizona, and three or four black colleges. Had I chosen to go to a black college, I would've gone to Hampton, because the son of Hampton's tennis coach was a good friend of mine. I had stayed in their house quite a few times. But I decided to accept J. D. Morgan's offer.

COLLEGE

I started at UCLA in 1961. I think southern blacks thought of California as the land of milk and honey. We thought there was always sunshine, people weren't prejudiced, and you could play sports outdoors. There were palm trees and there were beaches. Virginia Beach is one of the biggest beaches in the world, but when I was a kid I couldn't go there because it was segregated.

I remember getting off the plane in Los Angeles. The airport we landed in wasn't today's LAX, it was a pink stucco building nothing like the modern structure you see now. Someone picked me up and took me straight to J. D. Morgan's office in the administration building at UCLA. J. D. Morgan always looked after me. I'm sure he saw me as an average black kid from Virginia, three thousand miles away, but he had promised my father that he would take care of me, and he did. I received a warm welcome and efforts were made to make me feel at home. One of my teammates, David Reed, was assigned as my roommate. He was very gracious. He asked me, "What do you want to see first?" I said, "I want to see Hollywood Boulevard and Sunset Strip, made famous by that TV show." He and another guy named Ronnie took me up to Hollywood Boulevard to see Sunset Strip. The whole atmosphere was quite different from St. Louis, and certainly very different from Richmond.

Every freshman at UCLA had to test for Subject A, a remedial composition course, before you even started school. You wrote an essay, and on the basis of this essay it was decided whether or not you had to take the class. Every freshman had to take the test, not just minority students. I had always received very good marks in English composition in high school. I also gave lots of speeches in churches, in school, and I was on the Easter program at church year after year. I even had a letter I wrote printed in the *Richmond Times Dispatch*. I thought that the test would be no problem, but I flunked! I couldn't believe it. This was something I thought I knew how to do. So I had to take Subject A the first year. I passed it easily and then graduated to English 1A, but that test result was a rude awakening. I remember learning some things in Subject A that were helpful, but I certainly didn't think I needed an entire semester to learn them.

When I first arrived at UCLA, I had a nagging worry that academically the school might be a little dodgy for me. Society tries to make you think that black institutions are of less value and, I thought that because I'd gone to all-black schools, my education was not to be compared to that of someone coming from white or integrated schools. Even though I had been on the honor roll and had straight As, I went to college thinking I was not as good. I quickly found out that I was just fine and that the black schools I attended had prepared me well. Academically, that first year I sailed. I had no problems with the schoolwork.

One thing I constantly hammer away at now is the fact that a minority student's ability to communicate correctly is always being called into question. Even if you are very good at reading, expository writing, and analytical thinking, you're always going to be impugned. No question about it. Consequently, I always advise minority students to take some type of English course every semester of their college career because learning to express yourself correctly has applications to other courses as well. It is a determining factor in how fast you might be promoted in your job and improve in life. Obviously I can speak black English if I want, all African Americans can do that. But you've got to be able to navigate the King's English, otherwise you're not going to get very far.

Academically I did very well in college and, of course, my tennis game improved as well. In the fall we would play tennis when we felt like it. As a matter of fact, there were no organized practices. My athletic scholarship provided me with no extras at all. I received whatever the NCAA (National Collegiate Athletic Association) allowed: free room and board, tuition, books, and laundry. That's it. My father sent me some money sometimes and I had a off-the-record job at a local sporting goods store in Westwood, California, for some pocket money. Every Saturday morning I would clean the store. I would go down there and clean for an hour and a half, and they'd give me five bucks, which I would say is about the same as twelve dollars now.

There were some tournaments in which, traditionally, A-League tennis teams of Southern California were invited to Palm Springs. There was one in Phoenix called the Thunderbirds. Fall of 1961 was my initiation into the world of tennis played at the senior level. It's a world of country clubs and fancy organizations, but I never had any problems with the people I met. For one thing, I was a good player. I went to UCLA, and was very polite and well-mannered. By that time I had quite a bit of self-confidence, and I wasn't afraid to go up to someone and introduce myself or engage in conversation over just about anything. It wasn't like I went to a tennis club in Palm Springs and sat in the back and waited for someone to say hello. Even if I were the only black person in the room at the Phoenix Country Club during breakfast, I would not be a bit shy. It also helped that I was part of a group of guys who I had known for at least six years. The guys were on the tennis teams from USC (University of Southern California), UCLA, Santa Barbara, Cal-Berkeley, and Stanford; we had all grown up together and played in all the big junior tournaments.

I was comfortable in this setting, but there's no question that I went through a period I would say of about two or three years—my senior year in high school and maybe my first two years at UCLA—when I was definitely co-opted to a marked degree by white American culture. Looking back on it now, I'm certainly not ashamed, because I think I can understand how it happened. There were no other blacks but me. For half the summer, we continued to play in the American Tennis Association (ATA), which were black tournaments, and a lot of my friends were obviously still black, but you never got any publicity for ATA titles. You did in the Afro or the black press, but not in the white papers. And UCLA was rather isolated from black Los Angeles. After all, the university's northern boundary was right across the street from Sunset Boulevard, literally. You could walk over to Bel-Air from the Athletic Department. You had Beverly Hills to the east, and Westwood and Santa Monica were to the west. Watts was a long way away, a good twenty-five minute drive. I was enveloped by white society and I learned to navigate it.

While I was at ease in my new environment, and although I had received a scholarship from the great J. D. Morgan, I still experienced racism. For instance, in 1961 I won the Middle Atlantic Junior Championship in Wheeling, West Virginia. I was the only African American in the under-eighteen age section of the tournament. A group of players had ransacked a cabin and the boys tried to pin the blame on me, I'm assuming because I'm black. But even in West Virginia in 1961, I was completely exonerated and they found the boys who did it. I don't know if it's my Christian or southern black upbringing, but I believed "The truth will set you free." I really wasn't that worried. The people that meant the most to me believed me. I didn't lose much sleep over it, although the experience certainly taught me some life lessons.

Another incident involved the Balboa Bay Club. They had a tournament in Orange County that was traditionally held in the fall and they invited teams from the elite colleges. In 1961, although my teammates were going, I was pointedly not invited. J. D. Morgan called me into his office and we had a long conversation about it. At that time I was a freshman and freshmen didn't play varsity tennis, but he said, "I'm aware of the situation at Balboa Bay Club. How would you like to handle this? I want to feel you're comfortable with it one way or another. I can ask the other team members not to go; I can come down hard; I can make sure I get the word out that if you cannot play next year then the team will not go. Or we can leave it and hope that one day things will get better." I said, "I like the last option a lot better." I had just turned eighteen and certainly wasn't a crusader, not in the least. I said, "Look, let the other guys go. We can see what happens next year, and if you want to talk to them then, fine."

But there was also an encouraging incident that happened just four months earlier, after I won my second USTA (United States Tennis Association) Interscholastic National Championship in Charlottesville, Virginia. It was the only integrated tournament I ever played in my home state as a junior. A lot of my cohorts from the summer junior wars were there. We were all staying at the same place, and we decided we wanted to go to the movies. I thought, "Hey, this is Charlottesville, Virginia, I'm not going to be able to go," but I didn't say anything because I wanted to belong to this group. I was very apprehensive about it, but we all went, and of course my friends thought nothing of it. We went up to this movie theater, and this lady was looking through the Plexiglas window and was about to sell tickets to everybody when she said, "You know he can't come in." I wouldn't say it was malicious, she simply said, "I can't let him in." Just like that, they said, "If he can't go in then none of us are going in." It was done in a way where they didn't have to hold a group meeting about it or anything, it was just, boom!

That experience certainly made me think these guys were good fellows, and several of them were southerners. I remember one in particular, Butch Newman. He's from Beaumont, Texas. He backed right off. There was another one from Louisiana. Back then, I didn't think the times were going to change very soon. Though I don't think the other kids thought about it one way or the other, I guess what was in the back of my mind were the sit-ins that had started just two years earlier. I knew of the Woolworth lunch counter and Greensboro, but I certainly hadn't read about any sit-ins in Charlottesville, Virginia.

After my freshman year, in the summer of 1962, I was a member of the USTA Junior Davis Cup team. I was playing in some ATA tournaments, and then in the last part of the summer I played in some USTA tournaments. All of these were senior events because I was over eighteen. This is when I really began to be immersed in competition on a continuous basis. We would play in these very fancy clubs in the summer, Marion Country Club, Marion Cricket Club in Philadelphia, West Side Tennis Club, and Longwood Cricket Club in Boston. Once a year, the "cricket" clubs still played cricket just to maintain the validity of the name.

At that time you could earn a little money on the side and it was legal. You weren't contravening any NCAA rules. In fact, I was starting to do quite well. You were paid expense money, but it was really the experience that was invaluable. The multicultural, multiethnic mix of people was certainly very interesting. I was starting to meet people from all over the world, because a lot of foreigners played in those tournaments. As a matter of fact, as a result of the draws and the seedings, you had a domestic seed and a foreign seed in the tournaments. Usually they would seed the top eight American players and then they would have the top eight foreign players. Those sixteen would be placed in a subjective manner, most of the time depending on how the committee felt it should go. In those days the International Tennis Federation, which is the governing body of the sport around the world, ruled the players with an iron fist. Players had very little say. You had your travel paid and you had your own room, but a lot of the time we stayed in people's homes. The club would provide lunch and dinner and you would have breakfast in your hostess's home and so forth. You had pretty girls driving you around, and you had privileges. You could go to clothing stores and get a discount and movies would let you in free. I'm still friends with a lot of the people I met then. I know if I ever need anything, they would come through for me if they can.

I would say, comparatively speaking, by the beginning of my sophomore year I had become quite integrated. I certainly never had a problem with being able to negotiate the social graces. I knew which fork to use and how to sit and so forth, because one of the other odd jobs I had when I was younger was working with my father and some other blacks who owned catering businesses. I would have to put on a white coat and I would serve at parties. I had to set the table, so I knew exactly which fork went where and what it was for. The other thing about growing up in the South is that manners are extremely important, extremely important. You said, "Ma'am," and "Sir" to adults no matter what, which was even further reinforced in Virginia. In fact there was a pervasive gentility in Virginia society, black or white, that you didn't find in other states. It was no less racist than the extreme, but Virginia would not have tolerated a George Wallace or a Bull Connor. It was sophisticated in the sense of being exposed to other cultures and to almost every socio-economic stratum the United States had to offer. My exposure to all of that helped me to navigate the social aspects of my sport. I think it was part of what saved me from some of the problems other African American athletes faced.

While I was at UCLA, a large percentage of the male black students were athletes, and I was very aware of the unwritten, sometimes subtle attempts, usually by assistant coaches, to get black athletes to act a certain way. You were sometimes advised to watch it if you did this or if you did that, with the knowledge that if you make too much trouble, they'd yank your scholarship, although it was never said explicitly. I didn't feel it personally, but there were other black athletes who definitely felt, "Oh geez, I've got to watch my mouth around here," especially if they weren't a member of the basketball, football, or track teams, because the bulk of the black athletes were in those three sports. At the time, we didn't have any black swimmers or black golfers, and I was the only black tennis player. We had some African students who were on the soccer team, but they may as well have been from Mars.

I was not in those three sports either, but there's no question that I was considered different because I was in a somewhat privileged position. Not only was I in an elite sport, but my coach was the most powerful person in the athletic department. By the time I finished school, J. D. Morgan was the athletic director. During his tenure in the athletic department, UCLA had an almost unbeatable record in intercollegiate athletics. He was the most powerful athletic director to come out of one school. He found the resources and had the political muscle to broaden UCLA's athletic department; he hired the coaches and he negotiated the TV contracts. He had tremendous vision and he had been a UCLA student himself. The athletic establishment wouldn't think of committing any ill toward the tennis players, because they were J. D.'s boys. You didn't mess with them. I was especially protected because he'd told my father that he would look after me, and he kept his word.

Even though I wasn't in the same position as some of the other black athletes, I was still conscious of changes in America's political and social atmosphere. I'll never forget the day JFK was assassinated. I was walking down the main walkway that led from the dorm past the parking lot to the main campus up on the hill, on my way to a business class, and there were coeds walking very quickly out of the student union, Royce Hall, and the library, crying. I never saw so many people crying. I thought, "What is going on?" Then I found out JFK had been shot. By the time I got to class everyone knew. Classes were cancelled and people congregated in front of the library. Without having to be told, that's just where you went. You gravitated to the library and Royce Hall, the oldest buildings on campus. As a black person I felt Kennedy was going to help, I really did. Dr. King was just getting started in earnest. You could sense a rising tide of militancy, of impatience, and a lot of it started on college campuses in the South. A lot of the sit-in students were athletes. Some of our hopes died when Kennedy was shot.

There were two events that internationalized the Civil Rights Movement. One was the 1960 Olympics in Rome where Muhammad Ali proved he could back up his boasting. The other was that we all started reading a bit more closely about colonialism. In the early 1960s, Charles de Gaulle[4] and Harold Macmillan[5] decided, "Look, we better free up these colonies now." When I was at UCLA, the Afro-American Studies department was always very large. The African students almost always dressed in African garb and we didn't really associate with them too much, but when these countries—Nigeria, Kenya, Tanzania—started gaining their independence we would talk about it in the cafeteria. Yet the Africans mostly kept to themselves. There really wasn't as much intermingling as I thought there should have been.

The summer after my sophomore year I went to Wimbledon. It was the first time I went overseas. Let me tell you how I physically got there. One of my teammates, Charlie Pasarell, was a very good friend. We were playing an exhibition for the head teacher at a place called the California Club, on Motor Avenue just south of Pico Boulevard in L.A. It was a nice, beautiful day. We played the exhibition and afterward a lady came up to me as I was about to head out the door. Her name was Julie Ogner and her husband owned the Beverly Hills Volkswagen dealership. She was a member of the club. She said, "Oh, we certainly enjoyed your exhibition today. I really love the way you play. What are your plans?" I said, "Well, I've got final exams coming up in a couple of weeks, and if I can get enough money together I'll try to go to Wimbledon, because my ranking would certainly allow me to get in." I had been looking into it, but I was thinking there was no way I was going to be able to afford it unless some money dropped from heaven. She said, "Well, how much will it cost?" I happened to know exactly. I said, "About $800." The Junior Davis Cup would pay for my ticket from L.A. to the East Coast for the summer tournaments and back, so all I needed was a ticket from New York to London and back on Pan Am. She asked, "Is that all?" I said, "Yeah, it's a lot of money." She said, "Wait here a minute." She turned to her right, went down a long hallway, toward the card room. I could see guys at the end of the hallway, sitting at tables, smoking, and playing gin rummy.

I later found out what she probably said was, "Look, there's a nice, well-mannered Negro boy out here who needs some money to go to Wimbledon. I want each of you to give me a hundred dollars." I could imagine that when people like that are playing it's not so much about the money, it's the fact that you've beaten your buddy. I'm sure without even looking up each of them went, "Here. Leave me alone." She came back with eight crisp one hundred dollar bills. I was floored! Later I concluded that those card games were serious. They probably went to the bank and said, "Give me some crisp bills." After I got the money I went back to the dorm. I remember telling Pasarell that I could go to Wimbledon. In those days you had to ask permission to go from the man in the USTA who was in charge of overseas play. Permission also entitled you to a certain amount of spending money once you were over there. It was a hundred pounds.

I think there are two morals to that story. One, it was a reaffirmation, however you want to characterize it, of what I had learned all my life in the church: you do God's will and it will come back to you. When I was growing up my grandmother always used to say, "If you always do the right thing, you'll be looked after. You do for people and it will come back to you sevenfold." The other thing is that an overwhelming majority of the white people who went out of their way to help me, going back to the time I was ten, were Jewish. The Judeo-Christian philosophy is very close to what black people are taught in the church.

When I first went to college, my focus was really single-minded. At that time there was no such thing as professional tennis as we know it today. I was going to use the sport to get a college degree. I was going to graduate in four or four and a half years, and then I was going to go off and play in places all over the world that I knew the senior players on the tennis tours went: Istanbul, Australia, Asia, Europe, and South America. I was going to do that maybe for three or four years, then come back and go to graduate school and probably study law. I don't think I would have gone into business, because in those days very few blacks set their designs on those kinds of careers, although I did get a degree in business administration. I graduated from UCLA in 1966, and became a tennis professional in 1969.

PROFESSIONAL LIFE

I was apprehensive at the beginning of 1968 for one main reason: the black track athletes' announcement that they were not going to run in the upcoming Mexico City Olympics. For a trial project to see what the unity was amongst them, the New York Athletic Club held games in Madison Square Garden. That competition was boycotted by almost all of the major black Olympians. O. J. Simpson said, "I wouldn't run in that meet if my mother promoted it." Bob Beamon[6] did happen to run in it, but in his book he said he did it more because the promoters gave him a round-trip ticket from Texas to New York, and he wanted to see his family. He just used it for that.

Harry Edwards started the Olympic Project for Human Rights as a kind of test case, and it went off pretty well.[7] But then the year just got worst. First Dr. King was assassinated, then three and half months later Bobby Kennedy was assassinated, and there were more riots in the summer. For me personally, the danger was the South Africa issue. I was on the Davis Cup team at the time and South Africa and the United States were scheduled to meet in the third round. No way could I stand the heat if I played against them. Unfortunately for them, and fortunately for me, South Africa lost to Germany, in a match played in France under armed guard and with no spectators.

Nineteen sixty-nine was the first year I formally applied for a visa to play in South Africa. They turned me down. In 1968 I had applied to go play, but in '69 I actually went to the South African Consulate here in New York and filled out the application. It came back a few days later, rejected. They gave no explanation. But the rationale given to me was that I had made a statement about apartheid, so the South African government wouldn't let me in.

It was fascinating where the Davis Cup took me—Spain, Brazil, Ecuador, Mexico, Australia, and India—but I was the only black on our team. They have never had any other blacks on the team. They have never had any black males to rank high enough to even make the short list. From 1963 to today there haven't been any. No one has even come close.

By 1970, I was doing very well financially. I got my first endorsement from the Doral Resort and Country Club. This is my twentieth year being with them. Other endorsements soon followed, such as Head USA, which produced a racquet with my name on it.

In 1975, I became the first male African American Wimbledon singles champion. There is a personal vindication in winning tennis's most acclaimed event. I immediately called my family. I remember coming back on the Pan Am flight from London to Washington. My family physician, Dr. Jackson, met me at Dulles airport. That was a very memorable July 5. I always had trouble being the first this and the first that, because ideally you would like to get to a position where it didn't matter anymore. After Wimbledon I had a severe heel problem, but I lived with it for three years, from 1975 to 1978. In 1977, I won the doubles with Tony Roche. After that I came home and did two things. On February 10, I had an operation on my heel, and on February 20, Jeanne and I got married. I then took all of 1977 off, just letting my heel heal. In 1986, my wife and I had a daughter, Camera.

In 1988 I published a book on the black athlete.[8] There's a lot of discussion going on right now on whether or not African Americans are superior athletes. My heart tells me yes, black athletes have an edge, but my head tells me no. In working on the book, the evidence I ran across was so startling that it leads you to believe that, "Hey, a lot of the successes we had were so rare and so unique, and had nothing to do with trying harder." If you are truly talented you can win without trying hard. There are lots of examples of that. Let's take Howard Porter Drew. He was the co-holder of the world 100-yard-dash record in 1911, and Howard never trained. As a matter of fact, he came upon the race by accident. Take Dr. Meriwether. He just said, "Hey, I can do that." He walked up to the line with his suspenders and hospital gown and boom he was gone; he never trained. How many other people just walk up to the line and say, "Hey let me try this," and win? There are just so many instances where we have done well without training, without superior facilities, and without coaching. But my head says, "Wait a minute." The first argument against that idea is very simple. It's your anthropological one: is there such a thing as a black race? No. Therefore, it's a moot point.

Right now I feel pressed for time. I think anybody who has heart problems like I do, feels pressed for time. I wake up every day and I know, statistically at least, this could be my last day. My first goal now is rather basic and that is to make sure my family is provided for. That's number one, my wife and my daughter. Secondly, I would like to see the situation with minority athletes improve. I would like to see the graduation record improve. I would like to see a much more balanced perspective taken by public school student athletes. I would like to see minority athletes in general assume a more leading and proactive role in trying to alleviate some of the problems we're having in the black community. I would like to see the general condition of minority Americans improve. In my own upbringing in Virginia, the rule of the house was strictly, "Nobody is going to do you any favors. You're going to have to make your own way through life." Since the advent of free agency, when salaries started to skyrocket, I am absolutely convinced that too many black athletes started to come up thinking, "The world owes me a living," and "People will do things for me for the rest of my life and I don't have to reciprocate. I can be a little disdainful if I want, and they are still going to come through." A lot of our kids are victims of this entitlement mindset. It's nonsense, and that mentality needs to change.

The first thing I would ask the black athlete to do is to be a better example of what we would want to hold up as paradigms for our nation's youth, black or white. Secondly, I would urge that they would stay connected, in more than just a tangential way, with the minority community. Many of them, like me for instance, have white agents or white lawyers. In many cases these agents act as a buffer, keeping them from contributing in a positive way to the minority community. I would ask that they specifically get involved in some projects, especially with minority youth who are woefully short of live role models.

At the other end, there aren't too many minority ex-athletes who are doing that well. There are a few boxers who are doing well, but there are a lot of minority ex-athletes who are, if not destitute, living ordinary lives. And I don't mean those who retired before big time money came into sports. Many of these younger guys aren't experienced in having that much money. In too many cases they have not been able to control their spending habits and try to live in a manner they expected to live in the rest of their lives, and realize too late that they can't. That's another tragedy that most people don't recognize.

I see a very strong connection between sports and social change. The connection between sports and political change is much, much less strong. The black athlete has had an indelible and profound influence on the social changes that have taken place in America. Profound! As evidence, I'll give you a recent example. Last month's *Life* magazine listed the one hundred most important Americans of this century. Four of them were athletes, and two of the four were black: Jackie Robinson, Babe Ruth, Muhammad Ali, and Billie Jean King. To that list I could have added Jack Johnson, Joe Louis, Jesse Owens, and Kurt Flood.

A lot of our national sports heroes have been apolitical. Babe Ruth couldn't have cared less, and they didn't want him to. Arnold Palmer is apolitical. Joe DiMaggio is apolitical. You don't have any enemies because you sit on a fence. As long as you don't have any enemies you're alright. Michael Jordan is not political because Coca-Cola and Wheaties would tell him, "Alright Michael, you can get involved, but don't say anything that will prevent sales." It is almost an axiom that the real All-American sports hero has to be apolitical, and that's not what our youth need.

Let's just see all the black athletes that went to the Rose Bowl in the last twenty years. What were they able to do from the fact that they went to the Rose Bowl, winning or losing? Let me tell you something, the answer's probably going to be, "nothing." Take all the teams from the 1970s, both winning and losing, that played in the Rose Bowl and ask the question, "Where are they now?" I would be very interested to take these benchmark events, like the Rose Bowl, and say, "What did you get out of it? How did it change you?" If you reach that pinnacle in the Pac-10 and the Big 10 and you're with a team that is good, you have come through one helluva screening process. You've come through the playgrounds, the clubs, the high schools, college, your conference, and especially if you're first string, man, you're a pretty good player! Did you take advantage of it?

NOTES

1 For more on Arthur Ashe Jr., see his autobiography, *Days of Grace*.
2 The United States Lawn Tennis Association was renamed the United States Tennis Association in 1975.
3 J. D. Morgan won eight national championships in fourteen seasons as tennis coach at UCLA. Appointed athletic director in 1963, he revolutionized the athletic department and led UCLA teams to thirty championships in seventeen years. Morgan is credited as one of the most successful athletic directors in the university's history.
4 Charles de Gaulle was president of France from 1944 to 1969.
5 Harold Macmillan was prime minister of Great Britain from 1957 to 1963.
6 Bob Beamon established a world record in the long jump of 8.90 meters at the 1968 Olympics in Mexico City. In the thirty-three years prior, the world record had progressed by twenty-two centimeters, but Beamon's new record advanced it by fifty-five.
7 Harry Edwards was a professor of Sociology at San Jose State University in 1968. With the support of other black leaders, Edwards organized the Olympic Project for Human Rights to protest American racism through a boycott of the Olympics by black athletes.
8 Ashe, *A Hard Road to Glory*.

WYOMIA TYUS

TRACK AND FIELD

September 22–23, 1994
Los Angeles, California

WYOMIA TYUS WON THE 100 METERS AT THE 1964 OLYMPICS AND successfully defended her title at the 1968 Olympics, establishing her as the first person in Olympic history to win consecutive gold medals in that event. A member of Coach Edward Temple's celebrated women's track team, she ran as a Tennessee State University "Tigerbelle" from 1963 to 1968, breaking a number of world records during her tenure. At the famous 1968 Mexico City Olympic Games, she established an Olympic and world record of 11.0 seconds in the 100 meters, and earned another gold medal in the 400-meter relay. In addition to those accomplishments, Tyus received a gold medal at the 1967 Pan American Games for the 200 meters, and once held a total of eight national Amateur Athletic Union titles. In 1974 Tyus, Billie Jean King, and other prominent female athletes collaboratively established the Women's Sports Foundation,[1] which is dedicated to enhancing opportunities for women in sports. Tyus was inducted into the U.S.A. Track and Field Hall of Fame in 1980 and the U.S. Olympic Hall of Fame in 1985.

CHILDHOOD

I was born in Griffin, Georgia, which is about forty miles south of Atlanta, on August 29, 1945. There were four children in my family. I was the youngest and the only girl. My mother's name is Marie Tyus and my father is Will Tyus. I grew up on a dairy farm in the country, in a predominantly white community.

I got into sports because of my older brothers. I participated with them in all kinds of sports. My father was never the kind of person to say, "You're a girl; you can't do certain things." He was more, "It doesn't matter what you are. If you are capable of doing something, do it." My mom was always the person to say, "Well, you're a girl. You shouldn't be playing so much with the boys." But I really didn't have anyone else to play with. We were the only black family in our community, and the white girls were not allowed to play with us "coloreds," but it was okay for black girls to play with white boys. So my childhood experiences were always with boys, because I played with my brothers and the white boys in the neighborhood.

I was aware of segregation even before I went to school because we lived very close to the white elementary school. My brothers could not go there, and neither could I. We had to take the bus to our black school. The closest black family was probably a mile or more away, so we never had an opportunity to actually play sports or do anything with our black "neighbors." We played mostly with white neighbors, because they lived right across the road from us.

The person my father worked for owned the dairy farm; the other neighbors just lived around the area. Our house was on the dairy farm property, which was hundreds of acres, and the owner lived in a mansion on a hill above us. My father refused to let us work on the farm because he felt we should never be where he was. He wanted his children to have a life that was a lot better than what he had. I think he worked himself to death.

Sometime after my sixth birthday I realized, "Hey, I am a black person living in this world, and there are certain things expected of black people." My father was always saying to us as children, "You can do whatever you want, but it's not going to be easy. You can't give up. If you really want something you always have to strive to do it." When I look back on it, I realize my family was poor, but I never thought of us that way. We had a garden so we had food all the time and we had clothing (although it may not have been the best).

In elementary school I was a typical kid, just going to school and enjoying it. I did not think much about white kids going to that school, and me going to go to this school. But we were always told, "You do not let white people call you 'nigger.'" You should never be called that, and you must defend against that. That's how we were brought up. You do not let these things happen because if you let them do it once, then they are going to do it again and again. Everyone in the neighborhood knew that, black and white.

I can remember times when new families moved in, people we considered poor white trash, and they came in trying to call us names. They were soon told, "Hey, you cannot do that, and if you are going to do that, this is what is going to happen to you." It was not just the black families saying that, it was also the other white children in the neighborhood who said to them, "You don't do that around here, these are our friends." And that was in Georgia! When I moved to California, I realized people in Georgia were different. People would say, "Oh, why don't you come to visit," but when you went over they'd say, "Who are you?" In Georgia, when they extended a hand, you knew that it was a good hand, and you knew it was in good faith.

I didn't start running competitively in elementary school. All they had for girls was sack racing on May Day. I started athletics in the seventh grade when I got to junior high school. I think I was twelve. In Griffin, we had a lot of black elementary schools, but only one high school. Many of the people didn't go any further than elementary school. They had basketball and they had track for girls, that's all they had in junior high and high school. I thought I was a better basketball player than I was a track person. When I first started out in basketball I played guard because I was not a great shooter. I was fast, I could get the ball, I could pass, I could make a play, but I couldn't shoot. I never scored points or anything, but I thought I was a good player. I could rebound and I could do all the other things that it took to be a basketball player.

I started running because the guy I liked in junior high ran track. My father was still living then, and I was never really allowed out of his sight to go many places. I was involved in track and basketball, but that was about all I could do. I couldn't do anything else. I played more basketball than I did track. I never really ran that much. I played whatever was going on with the boys. Playing football was easy. I was either going to be on my brothers team or someone else's team, even though some of the other kids didn't want me because I was a girl. My brother would say, "Oh, we'll just take her," but they would always put me where I would go out for the pass, catch it, and out sprint everybody. I would even out sprint my brother. I never looked at it as, "I'm a girl, I'm not supposed to out run boys," because I knew I had to be better than the boys in order to play. But I never got in a race with my brothers in front of people. It was just respect. My father brought us up never to compete against each other. You never fought in public with each other that was the rule. You could settle whatever you needed to settle at home and no one had to know about it.

In junior high school they had meets and I started to compete with others from the surrounding neighborhoods. You would run against the people in town or people that were there at the track. I guess they looked at me in junior high and thought that I had a natural ability because I was winning. I never trained. My training was playing ball with my brothers, but I could beat all the girls anyway. It was not a big thing. We would have track meets with the surrounding towns from ten or fifteen miles away. I would go out there and I would run and I would beat them. We didn't have a coach, it was usually a teacher who took responsibility and said, "Okay, we will go there and we will do that." When I went into high school we had regular physical education classes. We played softball and basketball, among other sports.

In high school I tried out for the track and basketball teams. Those were the two sports for women. I was basically a benchwarmer in basketball, because everyone else could play a lot better than I could. By ninth grade I had moved up, because now they saw that I could play. The track team was more organized and we had more meets. We would go different places, not more than twenty miles outside the state. The same woman coached both basketball and track, because she was in charge of physical education and had all those jobs. In our P. E. classes we learned how to play volleyball and softball. I had no idea in high school what sports would eventually mean to me. I didn't care, it didn't bother me. It was more a love for all sports. I didn't even think I was good. I had always beaten the boys in track, and I knew I could beat the girls. I never doubted that if I wanted to be the best runner on the girl's team, I could do it.

When I was fifteen, Coach Temple saw me compete at a track meet. Coach Temple was like a football scout, he traveled through Georgia and the South, attending different state meets and local track meets for girls. He was the pioneer of women's track. He had a program with Mae Faggs years before at Tennessee State University. He saw me run at a track meet in Fort Valley, Georgia. After the meet he came up to me and asked if I would be interested in coming to train in his summer program. I said, "Oh yeah, sounds good." Of course, I thought my father was not going to let me go, but at fifteen, I'd have gone anywhere to get out of Georgia for the summer.

After the 1960 Olympic Games, Coach Temple wrote to my family. His letter stated that he had been the coach of the 1960 Olympic team and that he had trained Wilma Rudolph, who had won three gold medals.

That was the first time I had ever really heard of the Olympics, and I didn't even know who Wilma Rudolph was. I didn't keep up with any women's sports and had no reference as far at that was concerned. Coach Temple said that if I attended Tennessee State University, and if I kept my grades up and continued to do well in track, I could have an opportunity to go to the Olympic Games, too. He came and visited in the hot, hot summer, and he was in his tie and suit. He was like a father-figure to me. I remember him coming to my mom's house and talking to her, telling her about his rules. He said, "If they don't follow my rules, then I send them home." He assured her that the girls lived in an all-girls dorm, they trained at this and this time of day, and nothing could happen to them. My mom was a very trusting person, and she said, "Okay."

As I said before, the word "Olympics" didn't mean a thing to me. I learned what it was about when I went to Tennessee State that summer, and everyone was talking about Wilma Rudolph. My parents drove me in a car from Griffin to the train station in Atlanta, and Coach Temple met me at the station. Coach Temple usually had ten to fifteen girls in his summer program, and he also had the college runners there. That summer in Tennessee was horrible, because I'd never trained before. We were training at five in the morning, nine in the morning, and one in the afternoon. We had to be on the track at five, and you could never be late. All you did was brush your teeth, put your clothes on, and when you got there the coach was waiting. I think the reason he made us junior high school girls train at five, nine, and one was so we would not want to go out. He had to keep his promise to our parents, and we were young enough not to question it. When the track season started back in high school, I began to think of myself as a runner. My high school coach could see the change in me; they could see I was winning going away. I went back to Tennessee State for three summers, until I graduated from high school.

In my senior year of high school, they wrote in the yearbook that I would go to the Olympics. I was always decent in my schoolwork and in my senior year I really applied myself. I had come to understand that you had to have good grades to get into college, and you had to have a C+ or better. I knew I could do it, but it was just that if I had to work six hours to get a B and I could work two hours to get the C, I'd work the two hours. It was like that even for track, but I was forced to do that. In subjects I liked, such as history and biology, I would make As. Otherwise I didn't do much, but I was able to bring home the necessary grades.

In the summer of 1963, before I went to college, I went to Europe with the AAU team. We went to Russia, Germany, and Poland. I didn't win anything. I was beaten by one of the Russian girls and by Edith McGuire, who was my best friend. Edith's dad died when she was young too, when she was fifteen. Edith was from Atlanta and we had known each other since we were fifteen or sixteen years old. The coach didn't say anything about my losses, he seemed to think it was just good experience for me. And I was not beaten too badly; I was right in the mix of things. The first 50 meters I was there. After that I didn't have it. I can remember not having it. So when I got back I had to practice running more hills.

In high school, I never thought I could go to college because my parents couldn't afford to send me. We were too poor. I just thought of having a good time and enjoying school. After training with Coach Temple, though, Tennessee State offered me a scholarship.

COLLEGE

I went to Tennessee State University in 1963. I was the first in my family to go to college, but we didn't sit down and have a mother and daughter talk. My mother's attitude was more, "This is what you need to do, you are eighteen, and you can leave." I was brought up to understand that at eighteen you are an adult, and you have to get out and start working. I had always thought I would get a full-time job after high school, because we never considered college to be in our realm. But when I was presented with the opportunity, I wanted to go.

In my first year at Tennessee State, 1963–64, school started around the second week of September. Track practice started the first of October, and we began by running cross-country for a month. We had certain standards to meet in each race, from the 50 to the 400 meters. Unlike the summer program, in college we didn't practice at five in the morning. We only practiced once a day, from 3:00–5:30 p.m. at the latest, because athletes had 6:00 p.m. classes. In the winter we had the indoor season. We couldn't run outdoors until March, when the snow was gone.

In college I was trying to figure out who I was. I had gone to Europe and done poorly, and now that I was in college, I had to study and train. I was wondering if I'd be able to do all that. I would think, "I just don't know what I've gotten myself into." I didn't have great study habits, and my classes were terrible. In my first year I had an English class at six o'clock at night, the worst thing in the world for a freshman. We certainly weren't given any special treatment because we were athletes. The football and basketball teams got all the attention, and we got whatever help was left.

I didn't "go" to that English class. I didn't skip, because Coach Temple made us go, but it was as though I was never there. I was never late, I was always a punctual person because of Coach Temple, but I was still in high school mode and I never participated. I would just go there and listen, and if she called on me I would say something. Most of the time I thought, "God, six o'clock, I cannot wait until eight." As a runner, I had to travel, and we had to get permission to leave from our instructors. Once when I went to do this, the instructor said, "You know, you cannot continue to run track and think you are going to pass my class." I told her, "Well, I cannot be in your class, because if I don't run track, I won't be here. Now if we can't work anything out, you might as well fail me now." Of course, you know what she did? Right! I had to go to summer school and make up the class.

Coach Temple never let freshmen go to summer school, but he did allow me to go, since I was going to be out the next year because of the 1964 Olympics. If you make the team, you are going to be out that quarter, so those freshmen who he thought had the potential of making the Olympic team had a chance to go to summer school that year. But all I was concerned with was doing well in summer school and getting through college. I just thought, "I've got to get through this year. Olympics? I'll deal with that when it gets here." My main concern was making the grade in college, because if I couldn't do it, I would be going home, and I wouldn't be going to the Olympics anyway.

By Christmas of the first year, things were looking bad. I don't know what it was, but in my first quarter I just didn't do well academically. Right off the bat, I flunked English. You had to have a certain grade point to stay in college, and in my first quarter I had a 1.8. Coach Temple said, "If you don't make it up the next quarter, you are going to be kicked out." I thought, "Oh gosh, I can't leave school, what is my mom going to say?" After that, I made a complete turnaround. I made Bs and Cs, but more Bs than Cs, because I had to bring that grade-point average up. Spring quarter went better because I knew what I had to do. I knew my task. In order to stay there, I had to continue to get good grades and continue to do well on the track.

Before the Olympics, Coach Temple never changed his training schedule. It was always the same. He trained us all year to lead up to the big meets. Just because it was the Olympic Games, that didn't make it any bigger than running in the AAU championship. He would always say, "If you do all the things necessary to compete, then you don't have anything else to worry about. When you go to the meet your job is done. It's a practice then, because you have done all the hard work before you get there." I shouldn't say he never believed in changing anything. For example, I was never a great starter. He tried to change my starts when I was there in the summers, but I never could change. I had a bunch start. It got worse, so he decided to leave it alone.

We went to the Olympic trials at Randall's Island in New York in 1964, when I was eighteen. It was not really a meet; we were trying to make the Olympic team. Edith won the 100 meters. Marilyn White, who ran for Fred Jones on the Los Angeles Mercurettes, was second. I barely made third. When it was all over, the Olympic team was Edith McGuire, Marilyn White, Debbie Thompson, and me. Once you qualified and made the team, you didn't go back home. You stayed together as a team. Coach Temple was the coach of the women's Olympic team in 1960 and 1964. We stayed together in New York for a week.

In Tokyo, I had to do more practice than normal because we could never get the relay team together. I was running the second leg and was having a lot of trouble with every person Coach Temple tried as first leg. I ran a lot. After finishing my 100-meter workout, I had to work on relay. And now I'm not just working on relay between the first and second leg, I also had to work on relay between second and third, because I had to pass off to that third person. Coach Temple wanted me to run second leg, because Marilyn White is short in stature and he felt she would be good for the third leg, to run the curve. He thought I'd be better because I ran a great 100 meters and the person who runs the second leg had to run the longest anyway. I was working overtime and I was getting very tired. There were three or four people vying for running the first leg, since three spots were already filled. Edith was anchor, Marilyn was third leg, and I was second leg. The people vying for first leg were Willye White, a 100-meter runner and long jumper; Debbie Thompson, who took fourth in the 100; and Rosie Barnes, who was a hurdler, but also ran the 100. Willye eventually won the starting leg.

I had been running well leading up to the finals of the 100 meters in Tokyo and in different trials. I ran relaxed, I ran comfortable, and it was because of Coach Temple. He said, "When you go to the Olympics, it's a practice, that's all it is. Just think of it as a practice." That's how I was running. I was not looking to win; I was just out there to do my best. And that's how I felt, like it was so easy to win. I kept saying to myself, "This feels so good, just running." I was in four heats before the finals and I won them all.

Edith was not in any heats with me, but she qualified. Coach Temple always said, "Just qualify." He never said she had to win it, although he also said, "Now that doesn't mean you coast, because you don't want it close." Then I got to the finals of the 100 meters and Coach Temple came up and talked to me. He always called everybody by their last names, and he said, "Tyus, you look really good in all your races. You really look like you have a good chance of winning one of these medals, so don't worry about it. Remember, just stay relaxed. Run your best. No matter what it is, we're going to be proud. People try all their lives just to get where you are today." I said, "Okay, fine." And I'm thinking, "Gosh, I've been running really well, I could win." That's how I was feeling inside.

Edith and I said to one another, "Hey, good luck. See you at the end." Because our philosophy was always, "We are the best of friends, but when they say 'Take your mark,' I don't know you." It was my regular start, it wasn't a great start, but I wasn't left in the blocks. Marilyn was in lane eight, I think, I was in seven, and Edith was in six. We were all there together. When the gun went off Marilyn White was gone, like she did earlier in the Olympic trials, when I couldn't catch her. Now she got out again, but I was thinking, "I can catch her; I know I can catch her." I was relaxed.

I kept thinking, "I can catch her." She was out there and I could see my stride and Edith was still back behind me, though not that far back. And then when I got to about the 80-meter mark, I said to myself, "I wonder where Edith is?" Because at 80 meters, that's where she would usually catch me. I kept saying, "Gosh, where is Edith?" I didn't look around, because we had always been coached not to do that, but I kept thinking, "Edith should be here." But she was not there, not until right at the 100 meters. I ran 11.4, she ran 11.5, so she was right there, and when we got to the tape, I leaned, and I still didn't know who won. Edith was grabbing me, yelling, "Tyus! Tyus! Tyus! You won!" I said, "I what?" I felt good. For me, all I kept thinking was, "Gosh, I beat Edith. She was right there behind me, but I beat her." She was so good, and we'd always had that competition between us, so my first thought was, "God, I won, I beat Edith." Only later did it dawn on me, "I won the gold medal."

I got telegrams and things from men in the army over in Vietnam saying how great my victory was. It made me feel good and wonderful. I was still only nineteen and I was busy just trying to have a life. Even when I was on the victory stand, I was so happy but I thought, "Now I have to go back to school and try all this over again? Oh, no!" Before we'd gone to the Olympics, I thought, "I will win in '68, not in '64. I'm just on the team here; I'm not expected to win." But I won! Then I thought, "What am I going to do with my life? How can I top this?" I said, "Well, I've just got to do it, and that's it." I went back to school and acted like nothing had happened, which was good, because after a few banquets, no one remembered.

In the 400-meter relay, there was Willye White. She ran the first leg and passed off to me, and I passed off to Marilyn White, and she passed off to Edith. Willye started out and didn't lose or pick up any ground on the first leg. She passed off to me and I passed off to Marilyn and we were out in front, but when we went into the curve of the relay, one of the girls from Poland ran a great third leg. The Pole was 5' 11"; Marilyn was maybe 5' 1". Willye and I were yelling, "We got the gold! We got the gold!" But then I stopped and I started to look. For every ten steps Marilyn made, this girl made one, and she made up the lost ground. When Marilyn got to Edith, Edith took off, head back, but with no baton. By the time Edith got the baton she was in fifth place, but she went from fifth to second. If she had another 10 yards she would have won, because she had pull on that girl. We got second in the relay. And that was it for the 1964 Olympics.

After the Olympics, we women weren't invited anywhere. We flew back to Nashville, and Tennessee State University gave us a welcome. They met us at the airport, and we had a parade down the streets, honking horns, driving down Campus Drive into Tennessee State. We stayed there for a week and went to banquets. We took the train to Atlanta and they had a parade for Edith and me, and both of our mothers were in it as well. All this was done for us, and you're talking about two black women in 1964. It was really nice, they did a good job. When I went home to Griffin two days later, they also had a big parade for me. They gave me a Wyomia Tyus Day and well wishes.

I didn't go back to school until winter quarter. I stayed in Griffin until then. I was nineteen, what else was I going to do? I was not allowed to do too many things, because I was still a child, as my mom told me. I was not able to travel, I still had no money. It's amazing that now my kids ask, "You mean we're not going anywhere for the summer?" I never went anywhere for the summer! Where would I go, where would I stay, and who was going to pay for it? But I was not unhappy, I was with my family. Those were the people who made me who I was. I went back to Tennessee State to register for classes, stayed on campus for two weeks, and went back home to Griffin.

My second year at Tennessee State was a good year in a lot of ways. I was a lot older, not so much in age, but in experience and wisdom. I think I was a little more outgoing than I had been, and that helped me a lot in my classes. I had initially chosen elementary education, but then I changed my major to physical education. I really wanted to be a physical therapist, but I was never encouraged to do so and no one helped me to do that. Physical education was the closest I could get at that time.

In 1965, I traveled a lot because I'd won a gold medal and was invited to a lot of the indoor track meets. I went to all the major ones; it must have been six indoor meets. I went to the Milrose Games and the Mason-Dixon Games. In California there were a lot of well-known teams, with girls who were really running great times, and they all wanted to beat me. But they didn't. That whole year I went undefeated, I think. Then when we went outdoors I was still running well. We (Tennessee State) went to the Penn,[2] but I didn't run the 100 meters; they only invited us as a relay team. They didn't have the 100 meters for women, they just had the relay. We weren't even invited to the Drakes.[3]

Nineteen sixty-six was a good year, too. Not so much in the sense that I was breaking records, but in the sense that I was growing as a person and becoming more aware of who I was and where I wanted to go. Training was the same as always. Coach Temple was working on me, trying to change my start, but I was too stubborn. He was trying to move me up to the 200 meters. When he'd put me in it, I would try to lose, because I knew if I won he was going to make me run both the 100 and the 200, which I didn't want to do. I would win off and on, just so I wouldn't look bad. He'd say, "You are too good of a 100-meter runner to be looking that bad, you could run the 200. We're going to work harder." I used to tell him, "You're going to burn me out for the 100."

Nineteen sixty-seven was a bad year for me. I was losing and had no interest in going to the Olympics anymore. It was not really something I wanted to fight for. When I look back on it, I think I was just tired. But

Coach Temple had no sympathy for tired. I was also just fed up with what had happened during the indoor season. We went to a track meet in California and I was bitten on the leg by a spider. I didn't know it was a spider at first, and weeks went by and I still had this blister. I thought, "Oh, I must have just burned myself or something," because we had radiators in the dorms. But then it got bigger, and I went to the trainer and he said, "Let's put you in the whirlpool." It got worse and Coach Temple had to take me to the doctor, who told me, "It's a leg ulcer. You can't practice; you have to stay off that leg." I was laid for up two months or so. Wherever I went I had to keep the leg elevated. I couldn't practice, I couldn't do anything, but in order to stay in school I had to go to practice. I started training and we went to meets. Every now and then I would win one. After a month of practice, I went camping and someone threw a piece of paper on the fire and it landed on my other leg and burnt part of it, and I couldn't train again because it was all blistered. I was so frustrated, and I thought, "All I want to do is get out of college." I was starting to feel that I didn't really need to go to the Olympic Games. I had already won a gold medal. Everyone had said, "Go to the Olympics; win a gold medal." I thought to myself, "I did that. And I'm done with that."

In 1967, they had the trials for the Pan American Games in Frederick, Maryland, and I was still running badly. I think I took fourth in the 100 meters. Coach Temple was furious at me. "What's wrong with you? You've been training, you looked decent in training. You're out there looking like slow motion." I said, "Well, I don't know." I was supposed to run the 100 and the 200. Coach Temple said, "Well, we might as well just pull on out of here. You're embarrassing yourself and me, too. You don't need to run the 200." I said, "Well, Coach Temple, if that's what you think." And he said, "Well, you don't even like the 200 meters. It doesn't make sense for you to go out there and continue to embarrass yourself." I said, "Can you just give me a day to think about it?" The 200 meters was in another day or so. The next day I said, "Okay, Coach Temple, I have decided that I will run the 200 meters. It's me who's going to be embarrassed if I don't win. It has nothing to do with you. I'm getting old enough to make some decisions in my life." I had never said anything like that to him before. He said, "I don't even understand. Why are we doing this? You just need to go on back to Tennessee State, and we'll just work all summer." I said, "Okay, if that's how you really feel, Mr. Temple, but I do think you should give me a chance, and that's all I have to say."

I ran the 200 meters and won. I didn't want to go to the Pan Am Games; I just wanted to prove to Coach Temple that I could do it. Of course, before I'd won the 200 meters, the rumors were, "Oh Tyus is washed up, she's lousy," and the coach of the Pan American team didn't want me on the relay team. I said, "Fine." I went to the Pan American Games, running nothing but the 200 meters. Then they wanted to have a run-off, so if I won they could have me run the 100 meters. I said, "I thought you said I wasn't good enough for the 100." Then they wanted me to run the relay. I said, "No, I can't run the relay. I only qualified for the 200 meters; it wouldn't be fair to those other women." The Pan American Games were in Canada. I ran the 200 and won it, and didn't have anything else to do except stand, yell, scream and talk, and have fun. I had a great time. When I went back Coach Temple said, "I knew you could do it, I told you that you could do it. You gonna run that 200?" I said, "No, don't want to." After the Pan American Games I decided, "I'm going to go to the Olympics. I am going to win the 100, and I am going to be through. I will graduate from college, I will have a new life, and I will be done with this."

I started training for the Olympics. I just went back into the regular routine, trying to make sure I could end everything on a high note. Before we had even gone to the Olympics the black athlete boycott movement had already started, but it was on the West coast, really in San Jose. That's where it started with Tommie Smith, John Carlos, Lee Evans, and Harry Edwards. They argued that black athletes should definitely not go to the Games because of the unfair treatment of all black people in America. But as far as the women were concerned, we were never really approached to be a part of that movement. It was more like, "We're doing it, so you should follow." The women at Tennessee State got information from reporters who would call Coach Temple and ask him, "What are your girls going to do about this?" Our standard line was, "Well, we haven't made the team yet, so we can't say whether we're going or not." We went into Mexico City with that still over our heads.

My first thought was, "Gosh, these people have trained all their lives to do this, and now they're going to give it up for a protest that's not even guaranteed to work." I felt at the time that the movement was only in California, and I felt we needed more people to be supportive of it for it to really work. I also thought it was the best thing that could happen, because it definitely exposed the world to what was happening to black people in America, how unfairly we were being treated.

Even before I went to the protest meeting in Mexico City, we had basically decided that everyone should protest in whatever way they felt was right. No one came up to me and said, "Hey, we're going to do this or that." The whole group never agreed to not participate in the Olympics. From what I can remember, it was left up to you as the athlete to make your own protest, to make your own statement. I felt that whatever I did, or whatever I could do, it wouldn't make a big difference; the only thing I could do was speak out anytime I was interviewed, and the only way I would be interviewed a lot was to win.

I ran the 200, and I placed fifth or sixth. I won the 100 meters, and then had to get ready for the 400-meter relay. Barbara Farrell ran the first leg. She passed off to Margaret Bailes who had made the team. Margaret Bailes must have been about seventeen or eighteen years old. She'd been running quite well before the Games. She was a big girl in stature. The third leg was run by Mildred Netter from Alcorn A&M. I ran the anchor leg. I felt that we had the best four girls ever because I knew Barbara had a great start and she could run a great curve. The only thing we were really worried about was Margaret Bailes, because she was so young. She had really never been in a competition like that before, and she was always nervous. I remember in workouts she would take off, and Barbara hadn't even hit the mark. We kept saying, "Just wait, just wait, if you wait, it'll be okay." And she did it, she stayed in the box. Margaret really didn't make or lose any yardage, and she passed off to Mildred, who ran a fantastic third leg. Then she passed off to me. I guess I must have had one or two yards lead or more. I could coast in. We had a good pass, and it was just smooth sailing all the way. I came away with two gold medals. Now I had three Olympic gold medals and one silver.

After the famous protest on the victory stand by John Carlos and Tommie Smith, they were put out of the Olympic Village. I thought that action was wrong, and I always said that. It was understood that people would do whatever they wanted as far as the protest was concerned. I think what John and Tommie did was one of the best things that could have happened. Once they did that on the victory stand, there was nothing anyone else could say or do, because you could not restate it any other way.

I graduated in August of 1968. I received a degree in recreation from Tennessee State University and moved to California, because the guy I was dating, Art Simburg, worked for the Puma shoe company, and he was from Berkeley. I had always wanted to move to California. On my first trip out there when I was sixteen, I decided that's where I wanted to live. What I remember about it when I first visited was how huge it was, how clean it was, how different the people were, and how free I felt.

PROFESSIONAL LIFE

I left Georgia on December 30, 1968. My mother didn't want me to go, but she knew I was not going to stay. No one was offering me a job in Georgia anyway. I would have stayed if I had gotten a good job offer. I moved out to California and was going to start work in San Francisco, but my boyfriend had an opportunity to move to Southern California for a job, and he said, "Oh well, I'll make enough money so you don't have to work right away." I thought, "Okay. That sounds good."

I moved to Los Angeles to find a job and a place for us to live. I had teammates from Tennessee State that lived out here, so I stayed with them for a while. I stayed with Marcella Daniel from Panama. She was my room-mate in college, and she was already established in L.A., teaching school at a junior high. The assistant principal there was a guy who also went to Tennessee State, years before I did. He gave me a job as a long-term sub. Then my boyfriend moved down here, and we got married in April 1969. We decided we should get married because my mom was always saying, "Now you're not living with that man are you? You should not live with him. You can't do those kinds of things, you have to be married."

I was hired briefly at UCLA in the Black Studies Center to work in its library for about seven months. I got bored with that and started teaching in 1971. I became pregnant that year, so I stopped teaching to raise my daughter, who was born in January 1972. My husband made enough money for me not to work, and I don't think I had a real job until she started going to school at six or seven. In the meantime I did a lot of personal appearances, as well as track clinics in the summer. My husband traveled a lot for work, and we went to the Munich Olympics as spectators in 1972.

My husband and I separated in late 1974, after about seven years together. After my marriage ended, I continued to do the personal appearances and things like that, more so now because I was on my own. By 1974, they had also started doing Women Superstars, like the Men Superstars, and I became involved in that. In the Superstars you were paid for however many points you got. I participated in tennis, bowling, bicycling, and the obstacle course. They were held once a year and I participated for three years.

Around the same time I became involved in Women Superstars, some other female athletes and I created the Women's Sports Foundation. It did well because of Billie Jean King's support, and the pool of people she knew. It started out very small, but now everyone knows about it. It was very instrumental in getting Title IX passed. Donna de Varona was president for a long time and did a great job.

I met my current husband, Duane Tillman, at a girlfriend's wedding. I married him in 1978, and we've been very happy. I have a son who is fifteen; he was born in 1978. I've done so many jobs over the years, but I always felt that I should be home with my children. The first eight years of my marriage to Duane, I really didn't have a full-time job.

In 1982, I had a sixty-city pro-track tour. They had started in '76 or '77, before my son was born, and it was an attempt to start professional track. When it first started they only had men, and I asked, "Well, what are you doing for women?" Eventually they brought Barbara Farrell, Lacy O'Neal, Mable Ferguson, and me on the tour. They gave us a token race, the 60-yard dash, and we were the four that competed in it. We would go to different cities and it was kind of like a circus, just put on a show. Even though my last Olympics was in 1968, I was still in good shape in 1982. They paid $600 a race, and they paid expenses, but the men got more. We mostly ran indoors, and there were a couple of weeks we ran outdoors in El Paso, Texas, and a few other places. We even went to Japan. In the 60-yard dash, I was running 6.7 and 6.8 seconds. When this thing ended I was not sorry. I felt my day was finally gone.

When I talk about sports, I concern myself with what you learn from being involved in sports. You learn to get along with other people; you learn to take your knocks. When I say that, I mean you learn to accept winning and losing gracefully. That is how I grew up and that is what sports did for me. I learned to have a lot more pride, and to look more deeply within myself to see what I could do. It taught me to set goals and make sure that I stayed with them, and be happy with what I did accomplish. Sport was a way for me to get an education. Not just a college education, but an education about people, because I had to learn to live with a lot of different people. I went to different countries and learned to either eat the food or starve. I had to try to communicate with a lot of people whose language I did not speak. I learned to make decisions quickly, and then act. Being in sports gave me confidence in accomplishing goals. Going to the Olympics and winning gold medals helped me put things in perspective.

Since 1960 black women have won more than 60 percent of all medals in track and field. Yet black women are only about 6 percent of the U.S. population. It is astonishing to me. Being at Tennessee State put me in a situation where all these black women were not just running track, they were also getting a college education and talking about what they were going to do when they left school. Coach Temple always encouraged us to do better. He was always saying to us that no matter how many gold medals we won, we might never get the recognition we deserve, and we always have to put forward our best.

When you talk about black women dominating in track and field, Coach Temple is responsible for so much of that. He was a man that took a genuine interest in not just one girl, but in all of his girls. He made sure that we all went to college and got an education, and he made sure that we all graduated. If you look at statistics all the Tigerbelles stayed there and graduated.

Arthur Ashe said, "Somehow, we as black people are more motivated whenever we are given the opportunity to do well." When we are given the opportunity, we go after it and do it. We have always been taught to do the best job we can do. That's all we are doing. It bothers me that people always try to dismiss our accomplishments by saying it's because we're inherently superior athletes. We made it to the top through hard work. It's obvious that we are a people who simply believe in doing our best, against all odds.

I enjoyed my whole track career, and I have enjoyed the life that I have lived, with all my ups and downs. I didn't enjoy the downs, but I learned to put them in perspective. For example, when I was still in college, the State Department sent me and some other athletes to Africa. We went to East Africa, Ethiopia, and Kenya. The trip was really eye-opening for me. I am happy for that, and for all the other opportunities track gave me.

NOTES

1 For more on the Women's Sports Foundation, visit the official Web site at http://www.womenssportsfoundation.org.
2 The Penn Relays are held yearly and sponsored by the University of Pennsylvania for select colleges and high school teams.
3 The Drake Relays, similar to the Penn Relays, are held on the same weekend and sponsored by Drake University.

ALAN PAGE, J.D.

FOOTBALL

July 21–23, 1994
St. Paul, Minnesota

ALAN PAGE DISTINGUISHED HIMSELF AS A NINE-TIME ALL-PRO defensive tackle in the 1970s and as a Minnesota Supreme Court Justice since 1992. An All-American football player at Notre Dame, he joined the Minnesota Vikings in 1967 and became an integral part of the Vikings' fearsome defensive line, popularly referred to as the "Purple People Eaters." Page is the first defensive lineman to earn the NFL's Most Valuable Player Award (1971). He ended his career with the Chicago Bears (1978–1981). He was inducted into the Professional Football Hall of Fame in 1988 and the College Football Hall of Fame in 1993. During the off seasons, Page attended the University of Minnesota Law School, earning his law degree in 1978. He practiced law after retiring from football until he was elected to the Minnesota Supreme Court, where he is currently serving his third term. In 1988, Page established the Page Education Foundation, an organization dedicated to increasing the participation of Minnesota youth of color in post-secondary education. The foundation offers mentoring and financial assistance for college in exchange for volunteer service. As of 2007, 6,871 Page Foundation grants have been awarded to 3,320 students.[1]

CHILDHOOD

I was born in Canton, Ohio, on August 7, 1945. My mother is Georgiana and my father's name is Howard Page. I have two sisters and a brother. I'm the youngest of four. The oldest is Marvel, the next is Twila, and then

Howard Jr. My brother is about eighteen months older than I am. I went to Market Elementary School through the fifth grade and then we moved to East Canton. I ended up at the East Canton Junior High School, where I attended sixth through eighth grade, and then on to Central Catholic High School. I think it was my parents' belief that we were going to get a better education there. My two sisters went to Central Catholic High School, and my brother and I followed in their footsteps. My parents felt very strongly that education was important, and that we should have the best education possible. They saw that as the only way that we were going to have a better life than they had. They made it clear by both word and deed that they were willing to spend the additional money for education.

We weren't wealthy. I guess "poor" is relative. We didn't live in poverty but at the same time if I had to describe it on a scale of one to ten, one being the poorest, we were probably a four. My father had a jukebox business, which was iffy. He owned a couple of bars, serially, not at the same time. My mother worked as an attendant at a country club.

I don't think I displayed any sporting abilities in elementary school. I was more of a scholar than an athlete. In elementary school I was a pretty decent student. Unfortunately, it was a little too easy. I could do well with little or no effort, and that came back to haunt me later because at some point, the schoolwork became difficult. If you haven't developed the work habits or the study skills necessary, it comes back to bite you. I wasn't particularly large in elementary school. When I went to junior high I was a little bit larger, but I still wasn't the biggest kid in the class. By the time I entered the ninth grade, though, I was probably bigger than most of the kids. I really didn't develop an interest in athletics, other than playing on the playground and the parks and the streets, until the ninth grade. Sports were just one of those things that happened for me. I had a cousin who in the mid-1950s had gotten a football scholarship, but he was the only athlete in the family. My older brother began playing football in high school and, needless to say, football is important in Canton, Ohio. He started playing and because he seemed to enjoy it, I gave it a try the next year. My father didn't put any pressure on me to go into football, and my mother died in 1959 so she never saw me play. She died during my freshman year of high school, the summer that I went out for football. When I began playing I had dreams of glory, thinking I was going to be good. I think it's a personal sense that we all have that we are going to do great things, and be good at whatever we do.

I entered high school in 1959. I maintained a good grade point average, but that was because it wasn't too difficult. I don't remember the exact number of blacks in the entire school, but it was fewer than eight out of eight hundred. Not many at all. But I was there to go to school, so, to me that wasn't an issue. I didn't feel out of place. Again, I think I had a sense of where I was and where I belonged. I'll be honest. I would have been surprised had I felt out of place. When I first made the team I was playing both offensive tackle and defensive end. I can remember being horribly disappointed that I didn't make the varsity team my freshman year. My first year in high school, I didn't have a clue. I hadn't played the game before and I didn't know what it was about so my failure to make the team shouldn't have come as a surprise to me. I don't recall anybody else commenting on it one way or the other. I don't think that it was that big a deal.

As I grew older I began to think about my future. That was about the time I began to see some of the ugliness in the world. I don't know if I had any extended or deep thoughts on the matter, but I'd had a sense from early on, probably nine or ten years old, that I wanted to be a lawyer. Don't ask me why, other than the fact that most people in Canton worked in steel mills, and I knew I didn't want to do that. I had a healthy distrust of the steel mills. Working in the steel mill was dirty and dangerous work, and didn't make sense to me. I have an uncle who spent thirty-six to thirty-seven years in the steel mills. As it turns out, he is now eighty-nine years old and in extremely good health. It's absolutely amazing. Maybe he knew something I didn't, but I didn't want anything to do with it. To me, being a lawyer made more sense than hanging around the drop forge all day long.

I tried basketball in the eighth grade but I was just all thumbs. Dribbling the basketball and chewing gum at the same time was not my strong suit. In the ninth grade they made football players go out for track. It was an awful experience because it's so hard, so much more work than football. I wasn't fast enough to be a runner. I had the strength but I just couldn't get the technique. During that first year of track, they had us running 200s and 400s, and I got to the point where I was about to throw up. I had promised myself that if I ever threw up while running track I would never, ever do it again! One cold spring afternoon, the track meet was one person short and they needed someone to run the 400 meters. I had never run that before. I remember taking off and trying to stick with the leaders and getting further behind. Starting into that second turn, it's like somebody put the piano on your back, and you can't quit. Everyone is watching. That was the worst! Nobody told me it was normal to throw up the first two weeks of training. It just felt awful. It's one of those things that you don't have any control over. I'm a bit of a control freak, and I like to be in charge of what I'm doing. Having my insides come out is not my idea of a good time.

When I was a sophomore I played more and more on the football team as the year went on. They said, "You're a tackle." I think I played eleven games that first year, five or six of which were home games. My high school team was not top in the state, but we had a good team. We were at the top of the second tier but that was nowhere compared to Massillon, which was the best team in the whole northeastern corner of Ohio. Still, my team was 10–1, and we maintained that record the next year as well. In my senior year everybody left the team and it was 4–4–2. In my sophomore year there was some local coverage, but there wasn't much talk about offensive tackles and defensive ends. I started to establish myself, and by the end of the year people recognized I had some potential. During my junior year I played defense nearly all the time, and some offense.

It was always an assumption that when I graduated from high school I would go on to college, and I had not forgotten the idea of being a lawyer. Don't ask me how I was going to do it, that part of the assumption hadn't been sorted out. As it turned out, there were athletic scholarships available. But there is one thing I should have seen in my senior year. Had I been paying attention, I would have realized that all of the academic ease I'd enjoyed up to that point would begin to turn on me. The As and Bs that used to come easily were gone. I was in for a rude awakening and, when I got to college, it could well have buried me.

COLLEGE

I went to the University of Notre Dame. I chose to go there because I thought I would get the best education, in the sense that I could handle the coursework. My other two choices were military academies, and I was smart enough to recognize that math and engineering were not my strong suits. Ohio State also tried to recruit me, but I absolutely did not want to go there. Woody Hayes, an outstanding and very exacting coach, was there. I also visited Michigan State, Michigan, Purdue, University of Toledo, and a few others. There were ten or eleven schools interested in me, but I was most interested in Michigan State, Notre Dame, and Purdue. I can remember Michigan, and the trip that I took there and the hoopla and all that. I became sick while I was there, and whatever interest I may have had in Michigan ended about that time.

In the balance of things, it seemed like Notre Dame had the best academic reputation, and its alumni network was far more active. They sold the idea of, "When you graduate from this school, you've got it! You'll have it made!" To me, the message was clear: "If you want to play football you had better to go to school." I was there to play football and to go to school, and one pretty much depended upon the other. They treated me very well at Notre Dame. Back then it was an all-male school, all white, and isolated both physically and philosophically.

The first year was difficult. You weren't allowed to play in games as a freshman, and the coach who had recruited me was gone. It was a lonely year. There were about thirty black people in the entire school, but I got along just fine. I was part of the campus life. The team didn't treat me any differently because I was a black athlete. It was wonderful. No one took any special interest in me. Maybe if I had been focused on the issues instead of on athletics, it would have been different. It was isolation I guess. It was a Catholic school, all male, where football is very important. I could watch things from afar, and it was amazing to see what was going on in places like Berkeley.

My sophomore year I made it. We had a new coach, Ara Parseghian. It was his first year and I became a starter after the first game. We had a successful year, going 9–1. When I was there we didn't go to bowls, thank goodness. Football was just fun and I loved it. There were a lot of people there who wished we could go to bowl games and I didn't understand it. The first year I played I think they thought I was okay. The second or third game of the season, I think we played Purdue, and I played reasonably well. Somebody blocked a punt that I picked up and returned for fifty-seven yards. I'm one of those runners that could run as fast as I had to. Put me in a 100-yard dash or a 40-yard dash and the times are mediocre, but it's different when you've got the ball and somebody's trying to catch you, or vice versa. Then there's something on the line!

I think it was apparent that I was a fairly good football player, or at least it was to me. But at the same time I always had the sense that football was secondary. It wasn't the only thing going on. My future didn't lie on the athletic field. To be honest, it didn't become clear to me that there was any future for me on the football field until I was in my third or fourth year with the Vikings. When I started playing professional football I figured if I played five years it was going to be too long.

In the classroom I was still thinking of becoming a lawyer, but my performance was going in the other direction. The bad part was that I didn't know how to turn it around, so I let it slide. Those were not good years. I didn't really tell my father, I just said, "I'm at Notre Dame, I'm a football player, and I'm passing!" By all appearances, it didn't look so bad. I was a football player, doing well on the football field at Notre Dame, a good school, so I wasn't expected to get As all the time. Never mind that I had the ability to produce As if I had my act together.

Junior year of football was rough. In the middle of my sophomore year I dislocated my shoulder. Over time the shoulder began to pop out spontaneously. It got to the point when it could happen while I was walking down the street, or I'd wake up in the middle of the night with it popped out. I didn't have control over it. When football started the next year, it became an obstacle because there were times I'd be out on the field and the arm would just go. It wasn't good physically or psychologically. I reported it to the coach, but I looked alright so they thought I wasn't playing up to my ability. I was benched because I would say it was out, but it didn't look like it. They just thought I was goofing off. Usually it didn't hurt all that much, it was just awkward because I would lose control of my arm. The injury was not that uncommon, it happened to a lot of people.

One day at practice my shoulder popped out and wouldn't go back. It had gotten so loose that it just wobbled out. We had to stop practice and the trainer came over and tried to get it back in. It wouldn't budge, so they eventually sent me to a hospital. They gave me a shot of morphine and tried to get it back into the socket for about half an hour to forty-five minutes. After that, they began to believe me. They ended up giving me a shoulder strap, which limited my range, so it couldn't pop out. Once I got used to it, my performance went back up to my previous level. I played with that shoulder harness until the end of the season, and then I had it surgically corrected. I think I had surgery just before Christmas and it was immobilized for a month. It was pretty awful. I couldn't get it wet, I couldn't do anything, and it was tied to my body. Then I started the rehabilitation process, which went reasonably well and, by the time spring football came around, I was ready.

I worked construction jobs, which I had gotten through the alumni, for two summers. The summer before my senior year, I worked for a large construction company back in Canton, Ohio. I dug ditches, pushed brooms, worked with a jack hammer on a wall, just manual labor. It became very clear that I didn't want to have to do these kinds of jobs for the rest of my life. One day I had to do traffic control and that was even worse than the physical labor. It was torture.

My senior year went very well. By the end of the year it was clear that I was going to have the opportunity to play professional football. This was back in the days when the NFL and the AFL were competing, when both leagues were sending out babysitters. If the NFL got there first, the AFL didn't bother, but before the season was over the NFL and the AFL received permission from Congress to merge and my babysitter disappeared.

I received calls from a few teams including the Cleveland Browns. They indicated that if I was still available in the first round, they were going to take me. I didn't necessarily believe that, nor was I certain that I would be available. I would not have been surprised if I had not been drafted. I guess I had very low expectations. I don't trust the newspapers; I have a healthy distrust of the press.

On the day of the draft I had classes. It was a normal day. I remember thinking, "If I should get drafted in one of the high rounds, I should hear from somebody relatively early in the day." Lunch came and went and I hadn't heard from anybody. At about four or five in the afternoon, I got a phone call from a Minneapolis reporter. He said something along the lines of, "You've been drafted by the Vikings, what do you think?" I'd had no preconceptions about where I was going, but there were two teams I didn't want to end up with. One was Minnesota, because they were in the division that played with the other team that I didn't want to end up with, the Chicago Bears. Neither were very good football teams because they spent more time fighting than playing. I didn't want to be in a place like that. It turns out that's exactly the places where I did play. Later in the day, I got a call from the Minnesota Vikings. They told me I was the team's third first-round pick, which made me think, "First-round pick? Okay. The third one? But they wanted me bad, hmm?" I was thinking about the money and, obviously in the back of my mind, I knew the higher I was drafted the more I'd be paid. I guess I also knew that the two leagues had merged, so whatever players had been paid before, it wasn't going to be the same now. But the fact that I was going to be a professional football player didn't change the realities of everyday life.

I didn't know how my future was going to unfold at that point. If I hadn't been going to play football, it would have been a question of going on to law school. They don't give football scholarships for law school, so I needed to figure out how to pay for it. There was a lot of uncertainty about that. First, however, I graduated from Notre Dame and played in the college All-Star game. I'd gotten married in December and my wife was in school in D.C., so I went there for the summer, and became enamored with milkshakes. I could now afford all the chocolate milkshakes I wanted. I put on a few pounds. I probably did deserve it, but I regretted it. I think the highlight of the summer was playing in the All-Star game. The next day I was in Mankato, Minnesota, playing in the intrasquad game. Given that I hadn't seen a playbook before I got to Mankato, and that I had played in the All-Star game the night before, I was pretty beaten up.

PROFESSIONAL LIFE

I got to Mankato, Minnesota, at four o'clock in the afternoon and they shoved a playbook in my face, like I've got some clue as to what all of this means. Then someone said, "By the way, here's this card to sign." It was a licensing agreement that gave the NFL all rights to my name, likeness, etc. I asked, "Do I have a choice?" And they said, "No, you don't." I signed it and away I went. There was a whole series of these kinds of things. Anyway, we didn't have any problems in Minnesota because we had "Minnesota nice!" It went well the first year, other than the fact that I was a little rotund. The coach at Minnesota was Bud Grant and it was his first year.

It was a different game. In college I was a defensive player and offensive players would try to beat me up, overpower me, outmuscle me, and do bad sorts of things. Professionally all they wanted to do was get in your way and I learned that really quickly. I found that out in the All-Star game. I would be rushing the passer and the defensive player would be in my way, and they'd let me beat on them. They didn't care because while you were beating on them, the game was still going on. That was a real eye-opener for me. When I came to training camp I was fortunate enough to have Jim Marshall, Carl Eller, Gary Larsen, and Paul Dickson there. They were the four defensive linemen. They were very helpful in teaching me the mechanics of the game, and also its philosophy, particularly Jim. I think he got there when the team started in 1961. Carl, Gary, and Paul had been there for three or four years. The interesting thing was, although I had been drafted to take one of their jobs, they were all extremely helpful.

Eventually I took Gary Larson's position, and he ended up taking Paul's. At the beginning of training camp I was a defensive end, but it wasn't clicking. That's what I played in college but there was a difference in the way it was done. During the week of the third game of the season, they started practicing me at tackle. I had never played defensive tackle before. They just decided they wanted to take a look at me there, and midway through the third game, they actually put me in the game. I must have done something right, because I was there the rest of my career.

When I came in the league I didn't feel out of place. I felt at home. Things kept getting better and the team kept improving. The next year we were 8–6 and made it into the playoffs. We were beat in the first round, but that was quite an accomplishment because until that point, the team had never shown any promise whatsoever. I think that was about the time the name the "Purple People Eaters"[2] began to develop, because our four defensive linemen were selected for the Pro-Bowl. That's when it began and it took on a mystique because we were good. To a large degree the success of that team was built upon the performance of the defense. We started to come together even more and build on the confidence we'd developed. In 1969, we still had Joe Kapp, but we got a new quarterback in 1970. For the most part, we won in spite of what our offense did (the offensive people would probably disagree). During games it would drive us crazy because the offense's philosophy seemed to be, "Three or less plays and out," which should be the defense's philosophy. There were times when it seemed like the defense scored more often than the offense. Worst of all was getting an interception or recovering a fumble. We had to concentrate not only on getting the fumble or interception, but also on scoring because that was the only way that we would score any points.

I think I always saw the world differently. In my second year, I enrolled in law school at William Mitchell College of Law. It didn't last long because I was still too focused on football. I remember standing on the sidelines during the national anthem and looking around the stadium at all these people and all this hoopla. I was thinking about what was going on in Mississippi or about what was going on in Southeast Asia, and trying to figure out what the hell was wrong with this picture. I thought, "What am I doing? Much less, what am I doing here?" I would question all that, and then the anthem would end and the whistle would blow, and I had to go. It almost became a weekly thing and I thought, "This is crazy, this is absolutely insane." It was one of those things that goes on and on that troubles you, and at some point, you have to act. Clearly I wasn't acting, and that was troubling and wearing. At the same time, all these good things were happening for me in football. I had a hard time figuring out how to resolve that conflict. I never did completely sort it out.

In 1970, in the midst of all these good things going on, my marriage to my first wife began to fall apart. In early 1971, I met my current wife. That year was another good season for the team, another good season for me personally, and I was named the league's Most Valuable Player. I said to myself, "Okay the team has done well, I've done at least as well as people expected, so where do I go from here?" By 1974, it was clear that I was not going to play too much longer. It was time to act on my next step, which was law school.

Finally, in 1975 I started law school. I absolutely loved it, it was a fantastic experience. I am not going to say that it was easy. It was different for me for a couple of reasons. One, I had been playing football for so long and I really was at a point where I not only wanted to do something different, but I needed to do something different, and obviously to do that you have to prepare yourself. Two, by then I had had some experience with lawyers and had a sense of what the profession was all about. I developed a better sense of what one might do with the law. I was bored with football, but in law school I was challenged and forced to think in a different way. I had the opportunity to undo those years at Notre Dame when I was caught in a spiral, and to at least begin to correct those mistakes. I found the whole experience just fascinating and extremely liberating.

I had no trouble getting into law school, I'm sure in large measure it was a function of my fame, but even though my LSAT scores may not have been at the top of the heap, they weren't at the bottom either. I went to the University of Minnesota, but I had the good fortune to start off down at the University of Texas, which had a program for entering students which began in June. I took two courses start to finish in thirteen weeks. I walked in not even knowing how to buy books and ended up taking the contracts and torts exam. Along the way it was a big challenge. I felt like I was in over my head and thought that none of it made any sense. I didn't have a clue. That was six weeks into law school. Seven weeks later, everything came together! That is a feeling that you can't buy!

There are some professors that you enjoy. At Minnesota there was one professor, Don Marshall, who taught torts and evidence, who stood out for me. Another interesting one was a professor named Tom Waterbury.

He taught tax, a course that most people would find just dreadful, but I thoroughly enjoyed it. Tax is important, but not a class many would necessarily go out of their way to take. I finished law school in three years. I did the full three years, but I also took summer school classes and then had a lighter load each fall. It turned out that the year I enrolled in law school, I was also in line for a new contract. Up front I said, "I am going to law school and it's going to require I go to summer school, which means I will miss training camp," and they said, "No." We dealt with it up front, so it was not a problem.

We had gotten a new defensive coordinator and a new defensive line coach in 1978. The new coach had a different philosophy that didn't fit my makeup or my skills. I went to training camp and it was awful. First of all, coming in from law school and being suddenly thrust back in that environment, I thought, "These people are crazy! This is awful! This is dumb!" Not only that, they are going to make it difficult as well. This was clear when I walked into that first team meeting and everyone else had been in training camp for awhile. When I walked out of the meeting I said to Jim Marshall, "I will never make another quarterback sack as long as I'm here." It was just clear as day this wouldn't work for me.

I don't think Marshall responded to me. He is no dummy. He knew and understood. He's a bit of a free spirit, but very thoughtful. I survived training camp and the season started and it was just as I anticipated. Whether I predicted it or was just fulfilling my own prophecy, we'll never know, but it was clear that this wasn't going to end well, and that it was going to be ugly. Two weeks into the season, I received my Bar Exam results, and I had failed. About ten days after that, I was fired by the Vikings. I was at home, unemployed and, at least for a few days, unemployable. I said to myself, "What is going on here?"

I'd been running for about three years and the excuse I was given for being fired was that running had led to the natural erosion of my skills. It had a nice touch to it, and if you look at numerical categories like sacks, assists, all the things you quantify, the things that offensive linemen play by, they were down substantially from the year before. The year before they had been the highest they had ever been. But although there were no quarterback sacks, I was leading the team's defensive linemen in all categories. Fortunately, the day after I was fired, I got a call from the general manager of the Chicago Bears, Jim Finks, who was the former general manager of the Vikings. The coach that had left Minnesota had gone to

Chicago to become the head coach and defensive coordinator. He said to me, "We think you can still play. We'd like you to come to Chicago, and if you come here you will play as who you are and perform up to your potential. We'd love to have you, not only for this year but into the future."

I wasn't so sure that I wanted to go to Chicago, but at the same time since I hadn't passed the Bar, I couldn't begin working as a lawyer. I went to Chicago, sacked my first quarterback of the year in the fourth game of the season. I ended up tying for the team lead in sacks with three fewer games than everyone else. I also led the defensive line in all the other categories. After my first year there, the Bears wanted to extend my contract. I took the Bar Exam again and fortunately passed it, but I can remember really questioning whether I was going to play anymore. I had intended to play out the year's contract and that would be it, but the Bears wanted me to stay longer.

That was very good, except that I wanted to get on with the future, even with the cut in pay that would come with beginning a law career. I felt it was time to move on, but the Bears really wanted me to stay. We began a bidding discussion. They asked, "What would it take for you to stay?" I figured, "What the heck, let's be outrageous." I gave them a figure and said, "For that I'll come back for a couple of years." Lo and behold, they said yes! I was not anticipating that. But because I had been fired before, I asked for some security in addition to the dollars. They replied, "We can't do that. We don't guarantee contracts; we don't even guarantee Walter Payton's contract."[3] I was thinking, "If they say they won't do it, that's okay, because I will go practice law." They said, "Well, we really want you to play."

"That's fine, but I need some assurances."

"How about we give you more money?"

"More is good, but I need some security."

"No, but we'll give you more money."

They really wanted me to play. They refused to give me security, but thought everything would be cured with more money. But as the amount of money increases, you get closer and closer to that guarantee. By the time it was over, I had all the security I needed and wanted, and about half again as much money. It was a really strange situation.

We never talked about it, as such, but it was clear that Finks has a philosophy that if you had a contract, you weren't going to get any more than that. You agreed to it. That was the way most people functioned. But the flip side of it was, when you don't have a contract, and they want you to have one, they are going to do what it takes to get it. It certainly worked for me. I have to be honest; my time in Chicago was really a wonderful experience. It was a fantastic time, both for me and for my family. It was really healthy to get out of Minnesota. I was in Chicago for three and a half seasons. Finks and head coach Buddy Ryan were my sponsors. Buddy liked good football players. I decided to retire from the Bears when I agreed to those last two years. It was time to go, not skill-wise, but mentally I was ready to retire.

I felt confident that I could make it in the legal profession. I had passed the Bar and from my perspective that was all I needed. My family shared my point of view absolutely. My two youngest children were four and six at that time so they really didn't understand what was going on, and the two eldest were sixth and eighth graders. I think they liked the football life and I think they had a fairly normal life, whatever that is. We've been lucky, my wife and I, in that we have grown at about the same pace, and in the same direction, so she was ready to move on, too. It wasn't at all threatening for her, because she had her own life.

I came back to St. Paul because of my family. My wife is from here, and my children were all born here. This is home. We bought the townhouse in Chicago and lived there during the season, then came back here during the off season and I practiced law. I had the good fortune of knowing people in my firm. The firm represented the players' association, so I had worked with them before. My interest was labor employment and I had connected with a very good lawyer from the firm whom I had worked with at the association, so it was a natural fit in that sense. But there was also some expectation that I would bring in clients. That has never been my interest in law. Ultimately that's why I left that firm, because they were looking for business and I was looking to practice law. There is a big difference. I started there in 1979, and I was there through the end of 1984. I worked the three off seasons and all of 1982–84.

I almost went to work at the Illinois Attorney General's Office. I would not have had to take the Bar again because you have reciprocity after five years. But the family took a vote and it was five to one against my going there. The opportunity then arose to work in the Attorney General's Office here in Minnesota and I took that job even though it was not as good as the Illinois position. I could practice law without having to worry about bringing in business or keeping clients. That's what I wanted to do. I was at the Minnesota Attorney General's Office from 1985 through 1992. It gave me the chance to practice law and develop as a lawyer. If a case came in and was assigned to me, I would take it wherever it led. In the Attorney General's Office, because of lack of resources, the attorneys did just about everything, which meant if witnesses need to be interviewed, you were there. If depositions need to be taken, you were there. If it went to trial, you took it. If it was appealed, you handled the appeal. If it went to the U.S. Supreme Court, you did to. It gave me the full breadth of experience especially in areas that are not static, such as issues of sexual harassment and discrimination, in all of its facets. And as a defense attorney, you could get a different perspective. Having been on both sides, I have seen that you can have as much or more influence in limiting discrimination and harassment, and other kinds of issues, than you can when representing the plaintiff, and more so than you can in private practice. As an attorney for a state agency, you can give them your best independent advice, without having to worry about the extraneous stuff. You don't have an axe to grind.

But that position would not have satisfied me for a long time and I was able to leave prudently. The timing was right. In Minnesota there is a court of appeals, which is below the Minnesota Supreme Court. I was initially trying for an appointment to a district court as a trial judge. My skills and my interests are more suited to the appellate courts and the way to get there was to work my way up. I tried to play the game the way every-one else played it, but I couldn't get appointed. I think it was because I'd been known to march to the beat of a different drummer and therefore considered an outsider and because I was black. It was clear I wasn't going to be appointed, so I started looking at the choices.

I decided to try for an elected position. How does one go about doing that? You go over to a wall, look in a book, and it tells you the criteria, the procedure, and all the ground rules. I thought, "That's what the rules say. I can play by the rules." Needless to say, everyone plays by the rules differ-ently, and the rules can be used to keep the insiders in and the outsiders out. The challenge is to understand what the rules are and to use them to your advantage. It's a little like playing football. If I had any success as a football player it was because I took advantage of the rules that allowed me to do something more than protect my area. I knew that if I was going to have any success in getting elected to this court, I, and the people who helped me, needed to know and understand the rules better than every-body else. The press made a connection between me and a political party, but there was no connection. It was just me, my wife, and a group of very close friends. We worked very hard. You have to get on the ballot first, and in Minnesota it's easy to get on the ballot for virtually every office. You go to the secretary of state's office and write a check for three hundred dollars. If you've got three hundred dollars and a law degree, you can get on the ballot.

I was going to run for the court in 1990. I showed up with my three hundred dollars and signed the filing papers for the seat I was going to challenge, but before the ink was dry the judge resigned. That created a vacancy. Whenever that happens the seat is filled by appointment, and the appointee remains until the next general election. That's the state's general election, which was about two years away. We looked at suing the state, but decided that it was a long shot. It would have taken forever and, in the final analysis, we might not have been successful. By filing those election papers, we had taken on a system in which no one new had been elected to the court in thirty years. That burned a number of bridges.

The governor at that time was a Democrat, a DFL (Democratic Farm Labor) type. It was as a DFL that I had been trying to be appointed to the District Court. When the seat I was after was taken off the ballot, I went back to work at the Attorney General's Office. At least I had a job, and there would be another seat available in 1992. As best I could tell, they couldn't use any technicalities to stop it from going on the ballot, except a provision in the Minnesota State Constitution that provides for the retirement of judges. The Constitution states that the legislature can provide for the retirement of judges, one of the provisions being that a judge may have his or her term extended for up to three years in order to attain full retirement years. I didn't think that would be a problem because the seat coming up was occupied by somebody that had been there for around seventeen years, so I planned to file. The Friday before I filed, there was a newspaper article about the governor extending the term of the individual whose seat I was going to file for, so he could get full retirement benefits. I said, "Wait a minute, there's something wrong with this picture." I investigated a little, talked with people, and was told the governor was arguably correct, given some of the case law that had been written by judges protecting their own turf.

I had a choice here. I could have gone back to the Attorney General's Office, but I thought, "One time is fine, but the second time, I don't think so." Couple that with the fact I didn't see the state's supreme court ever having a person of color on it. Court of appeals? Never! My advisors said,

"You're talking about taking on an incumbent governor, an incumbent supreme court judge, and really the entire judicial system." But we went to court because the onus was on them to justify two actions: one, the state's denial of the opportunity to get on the ballot; and two, the fact that they were not going to have an election. The court had to explain why they were contemplating an unconstitutional action. We filed a petition for issues dealing with elections. The attorney representing me was a member of my campaign, a very good attorney and friend whom I had met years ago. He did a phenomenal job. The other side's argument hinged on full benefits; the justice already had benefits, but each additional year of service would increase them. We were playing the game in their ballpark, with their ball and their officials, but we won.

Once I got on the ballot, the media began to question me, and they asked me the same two questions over and over. One, "What's your interest?" and two, "What makes you think you're qualified to do this?" I thought, "You're asking me what makes me think I'm qualified and these fools can't even read the Constitution?" The very first salvo, after the court ruled there was going to be an election was, "He's only a football player." That came from one opponent, a district court judge. Kevin Johnson, the other opponent, said, "He's not qualified as a football player." I had to answer the same question until the general election: "Why do you think you're qualified?" They weren't asking anybody else if they were qualified, they were only asking me. I knew what was going on, but I couldn't do or say anything because I would be perceived as whining or sensitive. I just had to keep answering that question again and again. They didn't want to accept my answer because once they did the story would be over. There would be nothing else to write about. It was pretty bad. It was always some variation of "He's not qualified; he's just a football player," and "He's not qualified; he's just a black jock."

On a personal level, that was very hard to fight. At times I thought, "I don't need this. I'm here because I think I have something to contribute, and I've got to go through this?" I was in the middle of a campaign and I became extremely single-issue oriented, which is no way to live. All this was going on, and it got to me. But if you are what you think you are, you keep plugging away and smiling, and eventually the election comes and you hope a million plus people think, "He's alright." We had no pollsters. The only indicators were from going around the state and talking to people. The primary gave us a good indication of the way the electorate was feeling. I won the primary with 47 percent of the vote. That was good, because the other two candidates shared the remainder. But then all of a sudden I realized that over half the voters did not vote for me. I could have started thinking, "We might as well go home now," but when you are in the middle of an election you don't do that. In the general election, Kevin Johnson just got uglier and uglier. On election night I was sitting there and waiting for the returns, which come in slowly. But I won and it was absolutely lovely.

If you take a good look at my track record, you will see that I obviously don't stay anywhere too long. I will stay on the court as long as people continue to elect me, and as long as I think I'm doing a good job. When it comes to the point where I don't feel I'm making a contribution to the community or I lose interest, it will be time to move on. I think at some point I'd like to teach. I know that teaching doesn't pay as much as practicing law, but pay isn't what it's all about. Actually I have a vision of teaching third or fourth graders, or law school. Law school would be natural because of my background, but I've spent time in classrooms with young children, and I think that would be absolutely fascinating. If you don't catch them then, it is impossible to catch them later.

I think a number of things have brought me here. One, having some internal mechanism that said, "You can make a difference; you can make this a better place;" and two, another internal mechanism that created an incredible fear of failure; and a third mechanism that pushed me out there and said, "You may be afraid of failure, but you're out here now." I have thought about the genetic argument as it pertains to black athletes and sheer athletic ability. I haven't come up with an answer. We do excel far beyond what our numbers would indicate, but I don't think it's genetic. It may or may not be innate intelligence as much as drive. Maybe that's where it comes from. When you look at the great athletes, no matter who they are, they have something that drives them that other people don't have, something in their emotional makeup, something that they can't get rid of if their lives depended on it. I've always had the view, at least in team sports, that athletes are made up of three categories. There are those who are great and are great all the time in anything they do. They are driven to be great, psychologically and emotionally. Then there is the group in the middle, who may have the same skills but perform only some of the time, and don't know why they can't be anything different. Then there's the third group that performs when they want to. I don't know why that is, but virtually every team that I've been on, I see those layers where the first group and the last group are small, with most of the people right there in the middle. But it's also characteristic of law offices. It requires a certain amount of discipline to be successful on the athletic field. Any success requires the same discipline, which is not always utilized even though a person has the ability. There are a lot of undisciplined people out there.

I think there is some truth to the assertion that black athletes have lost a sense of community, but I don't know that those black athletes are acting any differently than anyone else. If you have a sense of ethnicity, a sense of race, and you have a desire to help others, then obviously you should try, but I don't know if that is inherent in any of us. The reason that things have changed from thirty to forty years ago is that we as a nation have lived in this "me-my-mine" generation. There's a sense of, "It's all about me. As long as I get mine, to hell with anybody else," and that is a failing for all of us.

Where I came from, I grew up in a hotbed of football. I didn't have anybody I aspired to be like. What had more of an influence on me was my desire to not be like certain people. In college I suddenly became the hero, and I didn't handle it well. As I progressed, I fought it, and then realized that I could fight it if I wanted, but I wasn't going to win. I could either sit back and let whatever happens happen, or I could take advantage of it, and use it in a positive way. Looking at it with that perspective, you have to realize that most of these guys dealing with this hero worship are very young. Life does have its idiosyncrasies, but the reality is that athletes are role models. They will continue to be role models as long as society designates them as such.

As a society we have gone overboard. If you are paid a lot of money, you are an instant celebrity. Just because someone has athletic skills, which someone else will pay for, doesn't mean that they have a strong moral fiber. We idolize people simply because they're athletes, and we turn them into heroes simply because they are there. We don't stop and think. We don't sort out the good from the bad. It's a sad commentary. The whole tragedy of O. J. Simpson shows just how bad the problem can be. Never mind that we have got two people dead. We've got our soap opera.

NOTES

1   For more on the Page Education Foundation, visit the official Web site at http://www.page-ed.org.

2   The name "The Purple People Eaters" came from the 1958 song of the same name.

3   Walter Payton (1954–1999) was an outstanding running back for the Chicago Bears. During his years in the NFL (1975–1987), Payton won several awards and set a number of records. He was inducted into the Professional Football Hall of Fame in 1993.

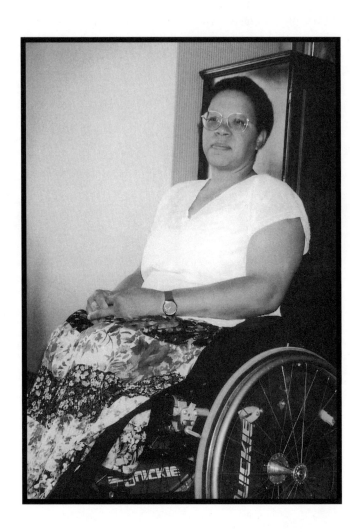

JENNIFER JOHNSON

PARALYMPIC TABLE TENNIS

July 14, 1995
White Plains, New York

AT THE 1988 SEOUL PARALYMPICS, JENNIFER JOHNSON BECAME the first African American woman to win a gold medal in a wheelchair table tennis competition. She was stricken with polio at the age of six and began playing sports for rehabilitation and recreation when she was twenty. After emigrating from Jamaica to the United States in 1980, Johnson began representing the United States in national and international wheelchair table tennis competitions, ranking number one in the country from 1982 to 1992, and number one in the world from 1988 to 1990. Johnson has earned a number of medals at the Pan American Games, National Wheelchair Games, and U.S. Table Tennis Tournaments, among others. In addition to her accomplishments as an athlete, Johnson has been pivotal in developing administrative aspects of her sport. She was Secretary of the National Wheelchair Athletic Association, Table Tennis Section from 1984 to 1987; Vice President of the American Wheelchair Table Tennis Association (AWTTA) from 1987 to 1988; and President of the AWTTA from 1988 to the present.[1] Johnson's awards and recognitions include the Martha Dilg Award for Athletic Excellence (1982), a nomination for the prestigious James E. Sullivan Award (1987), Wheelchair Sports, USA, Athlete of the Year (1993 and 2003), and induction into the Wheelchair Sports Hall of Fame (2007).

CHILDHOOD

I was born in Manchester, Jamaica, on October 25, 1948. My mother's name is Adelaide Lewis, and my father is Cleton Lewis. He was born in Manchester and my mother was born in Cuba, but she was of Jamaican parents. She moved to Jamaica when she was twelve. My father was a dental technician; he made dentures.

As a child I was pretty antisocial. At that time I had no interest in sports, none at all. I didn't like to play, because I did not like to get hurt. I just liked to sit and watch the other kids playing, jumping rope, and doing this and that. The first day I went to school I was told to wait for a girl who was supposed to accompany me home. She was late, so I walked through town and showed up at my dad's place. After that I didn't wait for the girl, I just walked by myself. One evening I decided to wait with some other children and we played a game with bird peppers. The object was to bite the pepper and not get burned, and one girl tricked me by giving me a pepper she had already bitten. When I bit into it, oh my goodness! I took off like a jet. I ran all the way home to find my mother, because she was the person who fixed everything, but she had gone to town. I was so furious at that girl! After that experience I said, "No more friends," and I became a loner.

I was diagnosed with polio in 1954, when I was about six years old. At first no one knew what was wrong with me, because polio was so new in that part of the country. My mother seemed to think I got it from the vaccinations I received at school, because I became sick with a fever afterward. After I got polio I went into the hospital. At first just my neck was affected. I don't know why, but my head was stuck all the way back, and I couldn't eat anything. That night I had such a bad fever, it drove me crazy. I could only drink, and everything I drank would come right back up. I had the worst headache and a fever as well. I remember on the way to the doctor I kept saying, "The sky is so blue. This sky is blue, blue." In those days in Jamaica, the sky was always clear and very, very blue, and I could hear the birds chirping in my mind. There was nothing else I could see. The doctor kept me at the hospital overnight because they thought I might have meningitis. They gave me an X-ray, which I hated. I could not stand that hospital. My mother sought out a prayer group, because that's what mothers do. Fathers are good, but mothers always go the extra, extra, extra bit—and then still go extra! In Jamaica they have these women who pray for the recovery of the sick, and predict outcomes. One prayer lady told my mother, "She is going to live, but it will be bad."

When I went back home I had trouble getting to school because we didn't have a car. We had a neighbor, Mr. Peart, who was a politician. He used to take me to school with his three children, but when he moved away I had to stay home. Although I couldn't go to school, I taught myself to read. My father worked with a dentist who was a Jehovah's Witness and he had some *Watchtowers* and books around. My father would bring these nice big hardcover books home and my sister and I would read them and try to pronounce the words. By the time I went back to school, I was pretty good. When the teacher asked me to read, I just breezed through the book. She said, "Who taught you to read? You read very well," and promptly had me skip a grade.

After elementary school, I needed more education before I could enter Kingston Technical School. My mother wanted me to go, but because she had no way to take me she went to see a man named Professor Golding, who was from the University of the West Indies. Dr. Golding would drive around Jamaica to see how people with illnesses like mine were doing, and she asked him to help me. One look and he took me to Kingston that night. He put me in the Princess Alice of Athlone School, which was a boarding school. People from other Caribbean countries also went there for treatment. Princess Alice of Great Britain visited us regularly, because Dr. Golding was from England and the Queen had made him a KCMG.[2] We always had to dress nicely and line up to meet her.

When I left Princess Alice School, I was given a scholarship to Kingston Technical School. I was twelve when I started there. I went to Technical for about four years and lived in a boarding house, and went home for vacations. I majored in commercial subjects, Spanish, typing, and accounting. I ended up as a secretary with the Jamaican government. I worked for the government for fourteen years before I left Jamaica.

At that time, I still didn't have a wheelchair. I had gone all through elementary school without one, because we never used them in Jamaica. We used crutches and braces, and that was how I got around. Even when I started working, I used to walk to the bus stop on crutches. I didn't use a wheelchair until I started playing sports.

PROFESSIONAL LIFE

I worked at the Department of Public Works, Public Utilities, and I moved up right through the secretarial ranks. I hated shorthand and typing, but

I figured that while I was in this job, I was going to do the best I could. I learned to write with speed, I learned to type, and I learned to do the letters the way they wanted them. Every time they had tests for promotions, I passed the examinations, but I couldn't get anywhere. The last straw was when I interviewed for a job and I didn't get it, and I knew it was because I was handicapped.

While all this was going on, I got into sports. I was almost twenty years old. There was a detective who was shot while attempting to arrest a suspect and he became a paraplegic. While rehabilitating in England, he saw some paraplegic guys playing sports and learned to play them as well. When he came back to Jamaica, he introduced sports to us. I was shy before I got polio, and it was even worse afterward because I became more self-conscious. But sports helped to boost my self-confidence. I did archery, track, and basketball. In those days, they encouraged you to play everything. Now we just play one sport, but in the past when we went to competitions we would have to do field, then I would do basketball and table tennis. I tried everything. I still didn't like the attention even though I had a lot of fun and really enjoyed myself.

I remember my first trip. I think it was in 1968. That was a real eye-opener for me. The Olympics were in Mexico that year, but we had our own Olympic competition, which we called the Paralympics, in Tel Aviv, Israel. Three years later, we Paralympians went to the Pan American Games in Cali, Columbia. We lost in the basketball finals to Argentina by one point. The score was twelve to thirteen. I remember the Argentineans, they were good-looking girls. They were little, but they were fast, and they had more experience than we did.

In 1972, the year the Olympics were in Munich, we went to Heidelberg, Germany. I think we stayed at the university there. I remember that year, because we came to America and stayed out in Queens at the Bulova School of Watchmaking, which had a sports program. From there we went to England and crossed the English Channel by Hovercraft. I was a good table tennis player, but I couldn't win at Heidelberg. We came in second to Argentina in basketball again. Somebody said we were on TV, but we were crying so much they couldn't see our faces.

In 1973, I had a son. I thought, "Well, that's it for sports, I have a baby now." But the girls kept telling me, "You've got to let him fit with your lifestyle." I went back to work and in September 1973 my coach came to see me. He wanted me to go on a trip to New Zealand. When I think of it now,

I shouldn't have gone, but when you are young you make bad decisions. I went, but I had to leave my baby, who was about four months old, with my relatives. He almost died because they didn't take good care of him. I was so upset because when I left him, he was my nice, fat, good baby, and when I came back he was sick and scrawny. I took him with me everywhere I went after that.

The next Paralympics were in Montreal, Canada, in 1976. That was the year our team disintegrated. We had trained pretty well, we had a good basketball team, we had a coach from England, and we were ready that year. We went to New York to practice, and then we went to Canada. But before the competition began, the Jamaican government decided to boycott the Games because of the presence of South Africa. We didn't compete, but Canada allowed us to remain and enjoy the festivities.

In 1978 the Pan American Games were in Rio de Janeiro, Brazil. I think only ten of us went, while in the past we had sent twenty-five people plus escorts. We didn't have a coach and were basically on our own. Nevertheless we did pretty well. We had the best team in the Caribbean, and probably the South American countries. We had good chairs and we were well-dressed. We had everything going for us, but we still didn't win.

In 1980 we had what they then called the World Games, which were comparable to the Paralympics. They used to have the World Games every year. In Paralympic years, they would try to have both competitions in the same country. The Olympic committee was against it in 1980, when the Olympics were held in Russia. The Russians claimed they didn't have any handicapped people so they didn't want the Paralympics in their country. They didn't want the World Games either, so they were held in Holland. That year I made friends with a couple of Americans, Tyler, a fellow from Westchester, New York, and a girl named Ruth. I met Ruth when I accidentally went into her room.

"Who are you?" she asked.

"I am Jennifer."

"Oh, my dog's name is Jennifer."

"Oh, great."

She thought she was paying me a compliment. We talked and I told her I was moving to Westchester, because by then I had decided to move to America.

My mother had emigrated from Jamaica in 1968, and she sponsored me. I moved to the United States when I was thirty-two or thirty-three years old. Once here I thought, "I am retired from table tennis, and I am here to make money," but my friend Tyler called me up and asked me to participate in a tournament at the Burke Rehabilitation Center, which was just down the road. It was a table tennis team from Burke Rehab against Bulova.

"I am retired and I don't want to play," I said.

"It's just for fun, just for today," he said.

"I don't have a car."

"Well, can't you get a ride?"

"No, I can't get a ride." But he was very persistent, so finally I said, "Okay, I will see if my sister can take me over there. But I don't have a wheelchair."

"We have wheelchairs."

I went and played table tennis. For some reason, everyone was impressed and they thought I was very good. Tyler got me back into competing. I started doing track again, and I even tried swimming. I'll never forget that day; I almost drowned! Swimming was the one thing I didn't do in Jamaica.

Competing again was like a new burst of life. I wanted to do it. In table tennis I was still a slammer. Tyler was also pretty good. He looked at me and said, "Jennifer, you're good, but I can make you better. You just have to learn control and how to push in."[3] He would make time for me every time we went to the gym. We would play push games where I could not hit the ball; I had to win the points on pushing. That's how I learned to push. First I started antispin[4] and I then went to pips-out[5] with no sponge. It was like hitting woods, and it worked out. Then they brought in different kinds of rubber. One side of the racquet had one kind of rubber, and the other side had a different kind. There was a coach, who some say taught a deceptive game, because he started us out with a funny rubber. At that time, there wasn't a rule about playing with two different colors on your racquet. You could have a funny rubber on one side and a smooth rubber on the other. Your opponent wouldn't know which side they were playing against, because they were both the same color. He was the one who taught me to play this funky game, which I still play to this day, and we loved it.

When I decided to start competing again, I had to rely on other people for transportation because I didn't have a car when I first came to the United States. Whenever I worked my sister would take me to work and my brother would pick me up, so I was restricted and I couldn't go to practice as often as I should have. When I started driving, I started work about 8:30 a.m. I would take my son to school and, when he could, he would get himself home. At that time I was working in Greenwich, Connecticut, which made it much easier. I would leave work at 4:30 or 5:00 p.m., drive home to Port Chester, which was quite a way, make dinner and feed my son, and take him with me to White Plains where I would play table tennis and he would do his homework. He would also go to Burke Rehab, where I would practice, with me. When I had swimming he would go with me and we would get home about 9:00 or 9:30 p.m.

I was winning competitions nationally, but not internationally. I moved to the United States in 1980, and in 1982 the World Table Tennis Championships were at Stoke in England. America didn't select me, even though I was the best woman, because I was on a green card. And Jamaica didn't want to pay for me even though I was willing to play for them. In fact, I played for them at the Pan Am Games in Halifax in 1982. To get there, my husband and I drove eight hours to Bar Harbor, Maine, and took the ferry to Halifax, Nova Scotia. We were both sick on that ferry. After we got off, we had to drive four more hours to our destination. I paid all the expenses. I don't remember the outcome, but I think my partner and I won the doubles.

In 1983, we went to Hawaii for the national games. There was a petition to try and get me on the U.S. team, and finally the international body in England said I could play for America. The year of the Los Angeles Olympics (1984), we were supposed to have the World Games here but, of course, the United States couldn't raise the money. We still have trouble supporting disabled events. Three months before we were supposed to host the World Games, the organizers said they couldn't do it. That was a big embarrassment. Instead, we went to the Stoke Mandeville Games in England.

That trip was a nightmare. We got the worst rooms. I remember they said, "We don't have beds for you Americans," and they put us in an old hospital. I was on a bunk bed so low that I would hit the board above me if I lifted my head. I had to take the mattress off and put it on the floor. They didn't care; they said; "It is your fault you are here."

In December 1986, I played in the World Table Tennis Championships in Brisbane, Australia. I placed second and a German girl named Christiana Wenninger, who had beaten me once before, beat me again! I was pretty fed up. I said, "I want to be a championship player. I want to win."

After 1987 I stopped doing other things. I said, "No more field, none of this and that, I'm concentrating on table tennis." My friend Tyler looked at me and I said, "I want to win." I was training for that German girl. The Germans have good players because they start teaching them in elementary school. They have schools for disabled kids. The Germans dominated the world ranks.

I knew that in order to beat Christiana, I would have to find an excellent coach. Henry, a friend from Burke Rehab, called me in January 1987. I was in the dumps because I was frustrated at not being able to find anyone to help me with my game. He said, "Jen, I have someone for you. I'm bringing her up. Her name is Pei Zhen Shao, and she's from Shanghai." He came up with this Chinese lady, who was dressed in a navy blue warm-up and could not speak one word of English. I was told she was a three-time Chinese national champion and had played at the banquet when President Nixon went to China. She also had a scholarship to MIT and was studying electrical engineering. When she came, we were in the gym where they had all the physical therapy equipment and about four tables set up. She just stood there and watched us. Henry said, "Jen, you need to hold onto her. She is good. She will never leave us." I wanted to train with her, so I asked the lady running the program if I could hire her as a coach. She asked, "How much time you want to hire her for?" I said, "Can you give us four hours a week? Maybe on a Saturday?" She said, "Fine." She paid her $15.00 an hour for the four hours, and a group of us chipped in and we paid her to come twice during the week.

While all this was going on, I became President of the American Wheelchair Table Tennis Association (AWTTA) in 1988. My job at that time only required that I work one week out of the month as long as I did the necessary work. The rest of the month I would be free. I run the national organization and it takes up a lot of my time to make phone calls and organize events for them. The AWTTA, a member organization of Wheelchair Sports, USA, is trying to launch a national fundraising campaign. We are in conflict with Wheelchair Sports, USA, because we are a member of that organization, and a part of their fundraising profile. It is very complicated because everybody forms organizations, and we all compete for dollars. These positions take up a lot of time and, of course, I'm also training and competing.

I prepared myself well for the 1988 Seoul Games. The first event we had was the team competition where you play singles and doubles. There were two of us on the team and I was having terrible back problems. My coach always said, "Jen, when the team is in a deuce match, I want you on the table," because at that time I was winning all deuce matches. A deuce match is when the score is 20-20, and you have to win by two points. It's the best of three games. In the third game, we were 20-20. Team play was the first event, and I reached the finals with my friend Jackie. My back was killing me and she said, "Jennifer, don't do anything, I'll take care of you," and she rubbed me down that night. "I got a gold medal riding on you," she said. She wanted a gold medal badly and would get one if we won our matches. I'll never forget it. She took care of me, we played hard, and we won! That was our first gold medal. We beat the Germans in the finals. We were not supposed to win, but we did.

We went on to the singles competitions in which we were grouped in classes according to our disability. In my group I was playing my nemesis, Christiana Wenninger. I started my first game badly, because I had a problem with the crowd. There were people on all sides. But what really bothered me was that her coach was giving her signals, which is against the rules. In the final match I didn't go down easy. The match went three games; the first game I played badly, the second game I beat her, and the third game I started off badly again. I got to fifteen and, if she hadn't won there, I would have beaten her because I started coming back. But it was too late and I got the silver.

While we were in Korea they had student unrest, and I didn't get the chance to sightsee much because I played every day. My husband was working for Longines at that time, and they gave him a limousine and a driver during the day to take him around, because they had offices there. I couldn't go with him because I was playing in the finals, but one night we used the limousine to go to Itaewon. It was a famous strip where you could buy leather items cheaply. We were sitting in a restaurant, I think it was Kentucky Fried Chicken, and this guy rushes up to the table and asks, "Which country are you from?" I looked at him and thought, "Why is he asking me what country am I from?" I said, "Jamaica." He was only giving us a religious tract, but he was very aggressive, and I thought, "I don't know what he wants, but I am not saying U.S.A., I am saying Jamaica."

I was very upset when I came back from the Seoul Paralympics, but I had to calm down because the Open Championship was coming up, and I intended to play well there. The first girl I played at the Open had won the year before, so she was the top seed. I beat her in deuce and once I eliminated her there was no stopping me. I picked up confidence. I beat that German girl, Christiana, in the semifinals. I have this great picture of that match. I got to the finals again and played an Austrian girl. They were coaching her and I could understand some of the things they were saying. They didn't realize that while they were coaching her, they were also helping me. I won the first game, she won the second, and she was up nineteen to my sixteen in the third game. She was two points from winning the gold, but it was my serve. Then I got up twenty to nineteen and it was her serve. I heard her coach tell her in German to serve me a forehand. I have always had problems with a forehand push because of my weak back and I fall on the table. As I was going for the forehand push, this little voice said, "Remember to hold your hand up, because you are going to flop." I remembered to push the ball so it made the net. I pushed the ball and I put it straight down, not across line, and the ball got on top of the net. It stood there, everybody was looking, and I thought, "Okay, what's going to happen?" If it fell back on my side, it would be deuce, and we'd still have more play. If it went over, I would be the winner. The ball gradually rolled over and dropped right at the net post on her side. I won! By that time my coach had given up on me. When I was at sixteen he had walked out because I told him, "When I am playing, Jimmy, I don't want to see you." But one of our other coaches had come and hung over the bar. I could hear her telling me, "Jennifer, you can do it." And I did it! That was my greatest tournament.

Soon after that tournament, I started having trouble with my shoulder. I think my shoulder was affected by the polio in my neck and I still have problems with it. In 1990, I went to the World Championships in Holland, but I couldn't move my arm when I got there and they gave me so much therapy and medicine that I became fatigued. I ended up with a bronze medal. My game didn't really improve and I didn't want to play after Seoul. I wanted to stop, but my coach said, "No, you can go on some more, you've got years." But I had put so much energy into it and I wasn't willing to do it again. You need to compete a lot to be sharp, especially when you go into big competitions. After that, my game got worse.

In 1991, we went on a ten-day trip to China as guests of the Shanghai Sports Federation, and we did a goodwill tour with our coach, sponsored by the athletes. We wanted to go to China and train with some of the Chinese players. I think there were seventeen of us in the group, mostly disabled athletes, but we had about three or four able-bodied people to help us, and we had a cameraman as well. We documented the trip and made a video of it called "The China Experience." Our coach, Pei Zhen Shao, was instrumental in setting it up, and she went with us. The Chinese government did not object to her leaving China, and she goes back frequently. We helped sponsor her so she could get her green card. While we were there we met with Chinese disabled athletes, visited some orphans, and met with the American consulate.

One thing I remember about Shanghai is that you had to eat lunch. You had to eat three meals a day. In America we often skip lunch, but there, you have got to eat! They had a big bowl of noodles for breakfast, and there was a lot of food at lunch and dinner, too. But I lost weight when I was there because I cannot use chopsticks. I figured if everybody else was using them I would, too. I ate with the chopsticks and when I got frustrated, I pretended I was full.

While in China, we did a small four-day trip to Beijing. The tour guys showed up with a bus, but it was not equipped for wheelchairs so they had to carry us. After they lifted thirteen wheelchairs onto the bus, they decided to switch to taxis. Our tour guide, Mr. Lee, and the others with him followed us everywhere. We could not escape them, and even when we thought we had lost them in the store, they had the store clerk watching us. They had taxis take us around and they carried us up all these steps. It didn't matter if I said, "I don't want to go," the tour guides insisted. Mr. Lee would go, "Hup, hup," to his assistants, and they would go, "Hugh, hugh." For four days they followed us and we could not do anything without them. They treated us like an army.

I'll never forget the morning we went to the Great Wall. The people there formed a circle, a wall of human beings around us, and they just stood there staring and expressionless. There was a steep push up to where the tram cars were, and they just stood and stared, never offering to help. I went part of the way in my wheelchair using those tram cars, but it didn't go all the way to the top. You had to get off and go up a steep ramp. I crawled up the ramp and some steps, but I went to the top, and I did it on my own strength. It was summer and it was so nice up there, but the people were definitely not friendly. They were probably afraid, because at that time Beijing was very conservative. I think one of them knew some English and he said he had a daughter. Jackie said, "Oh, I have two daughters," and they had a little conversation. When we were leaving we gave him a souvenir pin, but the guards came, dragged him away, and told him to return it. Ruth said, "I don't want the pin back. I want him to have it," and she refused to take it. The guards took him away anyway.

The year after my Shanghai trip the Olympics were in Barcelona, and when I arrived there I went straight to medical services. It had been a hard trip, and I asked for an icepack and went to bed for three hours. They couldn't find a room for us and half of our luggage and wheelchairs were missing. Luggage was coming down by truck from Madrid on a nightly basis and people would sit down on the sidewalk and await its arrival. We had no clothing. They never even offered us a care package, just some toothpaste and toothbrushes. One athlete's wheelchair, which had been specially made for field events, arrived in pieces. He had to race in someone else's chair. Then a Coca-Cola truck reversed into one of the athletes and hurt him badly. He had to fly home on an air force aircraft. I tell you that trip was doomed. I didn't win and, obviously no one likes losing. I certainly don't. When I went to Barcelona and didn't win, that was very humbling. That was the first trip in my entire history that I didn't win a medal.

When I came back, I decided I needed to take a break from table tennis, although I didn't quit entirely. I still play it because I want to stay in touch with the game. In 1993, I went to the national games and I won the women's category. Then I came in fifth in the combined men and women's. After Barcelona I didn't really want to play, I didn't want to be a part of it, but I hung in there and I did my part.

In 1994 we took a goodwill trip to Jamaica. It went very well, but the reception wasn't exactly how I had foreseen it. The U.S. Information Service Officer was there when we went to Mona and had a reception. We presented a wheelchair to Professor Golding, who had helped me so many years before. They videotaped some of it. The Jamaican government had no involvement in this.

I plan to go to the Paralympics in Atlanta in 1996, and I need to prepare. The first thing I have to do is go to Austria and improve my world ranking. Right now I am about sixth in my class. Ideally I want to be in the top four. When I was in Austria, after the doubles match, I came in second in the Open, another official event, and of course the Austrian girl beat me again. Now she has me cooked. When I go back home I may burn her a little bit. I am now trying to go to another tournament in Germany, because the Germans did not come to Austria. The German girl that I finally beat, Christiana, is number one now. There is another German girl, whose first showing was in 1992, and I hear she is even better than

Christiana. It is all a matter of style, because they haven't played me, but they play each other all the time. That's why I want to go to Germany in September. I don't have access to many videos of other matches, but I have watched a few tapes, and their game is basically a push and attack.

I think some people thought I was washed up. In Austria, people were surprised when they saw me play. Even my coach said, "I haven't seen you playing so well in a long time. That's the way I like to see you." I used to be too passive, but now I am more aggressive. I really get into it. My serve still needs work. I do a higher toss and I can shorten it. I am going deep, but I make a short serve, and all of that takes practice. When you don't practice your serve, and I have seen it happen to people, you go into a game and it doesn't work. You get all panicky, that's the downfall, and it just gets worse. This year is very, very critical because this is the year they are going to look at the performance of the players as the criteria to secure an invite to the Paralympics.

There are a lot of disabled people who are not aware of the recreational and rehabilitational possibilities associated with sports and competition. The Special Olympics caters to the intellectually disabled and they have no problem raising money. There are forty-three to forty-eight million physically handicapped people in the United States, so I don't know why people don't know about our competitions. I think it depends on where in the country you live. Some areas of the country are completely unaware of our organization. The only way people become aware of it is if they are motivated to find out about us. Media coverage has always been a problem with disabled athletes, because they don't come to us, we have to seek them out. It's the people who can go there and sell themselves who generally get the media's attention.

It is not just a problem for us, but for Olympic track and field events generally. Michael Johnson said recently that track and field is a dying sport in America, possibly because of the lack of television and media coverage. I remember we used to see track and field all the time on television and it was exciting, but you don't see these events on TV much anymore. The foreign wheelchair athletes are improving greatly. We used to dominate in wheelchair track and field, but we don't any more. Table tennis is even worse. We don't have any players, even in the able-bodied rankings that are world caliber. But in general they don't televise disabled or wheelchair sporting events. Even the New York American Wheelchair Race is not televised. I think part of the disregard for wheelchair sports can be attributed to the obsession with youth and beauty in this country. To get media coverage you have to be willing to do something outrageous that attracts their attention.

Sports have become a media spectacle and those athletes who are on TV are the ones kids watch and emulate. That's why it is important to do positive things if you are in the limelight and want to influence people. Whether you like it or not, if you're in the public eye, you are a role model. You don't have to say, "Here I am, Jennifer Johnson, I am your role model," but you should be aware that children are going to adopt you as a one, because of your prominence and status. I guess I am conscious of my position as a role model. At times I wish I wasn't, because sometimes people aggravate me and if I react negatively it doesn't look good. But overall I consider it to be a good thing because it puts that positive restraint on you. As a role model you can be a good influence on children, and it can make you a better person as well.

I think the reason that black people dominate in certain sports is because we are fighters. We are survivors. When hardship hits us, we don't fold, we find other ways and means to accomplish our goals. Given an equal chance, we excel. You don't find black men playing hockey even though it takes strength, but perhaps it is because hockey is more like tennis and other sports that are played in a club. You have to have money to join the clubs; the equipment is expensive, and you have to pay for time on the ice. Track is a cheap sport. You can go to any school or park and run around in sneakers. You don't have to be part of any elite class for that. But for tennis, you have to join a club and have somewhere to play. I think if black people were able to join the country clubs and tennis clubs, they would excel at golf and tennis just like they do in basketball and football and track, because we are proud and we always want to achieve. It is important for us to demonstrate that we can excel, precisely because we are too often told that we can't.

NOTES

1 For more on the American Wheelchair Table Tennis Association, visit the official Web site at http://www.awtta.org.
2 A KCMG is a Knight Commander of St. Michael and St. George.
3 A push is a backspin return of a backspin and it is usually a defensive move.
4 Antispin is a slick inverted rubber sheet usually with a very dead sponge beneath. Used mostly for defensive shots, the smooth surface of the rubber does not allow spin (rotation of the ball) to occur.
5 Pips-out is a type of racquet covering with a sheet of pips-out rubber over a layer of sponge.

NIKKI FRANKE, ED.D.

FENCING

April 22, 1994
Philadelphia, Pennsylvania

NIKKI FRANKE FOUNDED THE WOMEN'S FENCING PROGRAM AT
Temple University in 1972 and is the first and only African American
woman to coach fencing at a Division I university. Franke was a four-
year letter winner and National Intercollegiate Women's Fencing Association All-American while attending Brooklyn College, 1968–1972. She
earned her master's and doctorate degrees from Temple while coaching,
and continued to compete nationally and internationally until retiring in
1980. She was an Olympian in 1976, was selected for the Olympic team
in 1980, medaled in two Pan American Games (1975 and 1979), and was
the U.S. Fencing Association National Foil Champion in 1975 and 1980.
The Temple women's fencing team has qualified for the NCAA National
Championships in thirty-four of the past thirty-five years, and won the
NCAA National Women's Foil Championship in 1992. Franke celebrated
her five hundredth coaching victory in 2006, and has been named the
U.S. Fencing Coaches Association Coach of the Year four times (1983,
1987, 1988, and 1991). She was inducted into the Brooklyn College Hall
of Fame (1979), the Temple University Athletics Hall of Fame (1996),
the U.S. Fencing Association Hall of Fame (1998), and the International
Sports Hall of Fame (2002). She is currently Temple University's director
of women's fencing, women's foil coach, and associate professor in the
department of public health, teaching a full course load every semester
and coaching four to five hours a day. Franke is secretary of the Black
Women in Sport Foundation, a nonprofit organization founded in 1992

to facilitate the participation of black women in sports, both in the U.S. and internationally.[1]

CHILDHOOD

I was born March 13, 1951, in New York City. I grew up in Harlem, on the West Side, out by City College on 143rd Street. My father passed away when I was five, and my brother and I were raised by my mother and grandmother. My grandmother was from St. Vincent, West Indies, and had a fourth-grade education. She had three children and raised them through the Depression by herself. They all finished high school.

As far back as I can remember I was involved in sports. A girl named Peanut and I were the only two girls on the block that the guys would play stickball with, and being asked to play with the boys was a source of great pride. I was good at stickball. I had to be for them to let me play. It was a real fun time. You had those little pink twenty-five cent rubber balls and a broomstick, and you made the bases where the cars were parked. That's really one of my earliest memories of sport. That was probably before I was nine years old.

When I was nine or ten, the doctors discovered that I had scoliosis. My neighbor noticed it and my mother immediately sought help. After a great deal of exercise and therapy, the doctors decided to perform surgery, because my spine wasn't going to straighten out, and if it kept growing it would puncture my lung. I had two back surgeries when I was ten. They took a bone out of my hip and fused it to my spine to keep it straight. They did two bone fusions, an upper fusion and a lower fusion. I tease people that I have perfect posture, because my back does not bend at all. I can only bend from the waist. For a year after my surgeries I wore a body cast from my hips all the way up to the back of my head and up to my chin. I could not go to school and I had a home instructor, Mrs. Friedman. The school district provided home instructors to students who couldn't go to school. That was probably very influential in what happened to me academically.

At that point, I was living with my grandmother while my mother worked. My mother was a house cleaner, but she stopped working so she could take care of me after my operations. My love of sports never diminished, so when no one was looking, I would still go out and play stickball. The body cast was very heavy, so the kids would let me hit and somebody would run for me. One day, my grandmother was looking out of the window and saw me playing stickball. I will never forget hearing her screech. I thought the lady would fall out of the window. Within a week, the doctor put me in a convalescent home in upstate New York for the rest of the summer. He took me off the streets, totally.

After I got the body cast off, instead of going to the neighborhood junior high school, my home teacher got me into a junior high school up in Washington Heights. It was a predominantly white school. I really don't remember a lot about it, but I do remember walking into my advisor's office one day and saying, "I want to be a doctor." He told me, "Well, what about a nurse?" I do remember those kinds of things.

In my senior year there was a new program that the Board of Education was starting called College Discovery. The purpose of College Discovery was to take children who were culturally deprived and supposed "underachievers" and send them to a high school where they worked together in this program. There was one high school designated for College Discovery in each borough, and this was the first year of the program. My advisor called me in and said, "Well, you can put your name in for this. We were thinking about you as well as some other students." I was an honor roll student, so my mother's thought was, "Why are they putting you in this program that's supposedly for underachievers?" And the response of the advisor when my mother pursued it was, "Well, even though we're putting underachievers in here, we also want to put in some very successful students to make sure it succeeds." So I ended up going to Seward Park High School in the College Discovery program.

College Discovery also had a summer program, where they used to give us five dollars a week. They took us to all kinds of cultural events because, of course, we were "culturally deprived." They took us to the theater, the opera, and that sort of thing. Seward Park itself was a very diverse school, as opposed to my junior high school, because being on the Lower East Side you had middle- and upper-middle-class Jews, Latinos, Asians from Chinatown, as well as a few blacks. But being in this College Discovery group, we were kind of in a little world of our own. I probably felt that as a black person, I wasn't going to let anyone outdo me in class, but excellence was always expected of me by my family anyway. You studied, did your work, and you got good report cards, otherwise you had to deal with Mom. In my family you had to excel academically. I can remember bringing home a test and saying, "Mom, I got a ninety-nine," and she would reply, "Why didn't you get a hundred?" It was her typical response. Only the best was acceptable. Being in the College Discovery program, we had support services, and there were personal contacts. There were advisors. It was a small group, you knew the advisors and they were there to help you succeed. We had very good, supportive people involved in that program. I was in an atmosphere to succeed, at home as well as at school. I wasn't getting lost on either side.

At Seward Park High School we had something called the Leaders Club, and all the girls who were good in gym got to be "leaders," and the Leaders had their own gym class. You didn't have gym with the regular student body. The Leaders were assigned a gym class, and during your free period you would assist the physical education teacher. I was in this club, and I was on various teams, one of which was tennis. The chair of the athletic department was the tennis coach. We had a very good relationship. Leaders had officers and, during my senior year, I was president. I didn't think I would ever be president, though, because there weren't very many black girls in Leaders. They had a big award ceremony every year, and they gave you a trophy. In my senior year I went to pick up the trophy and happened to see my name on it and I was trying to act as if I hadn't seen it. But there was this other girl, Helen, and I remember her saying, "Well, the only reason you got it is because I didn't want it." I remember believing that, and saying to myself, "Well, she is popular and all the girls like her," and "Why did they vote for me?" I remember sitting in the car feeling extremely dejected, and feeling very much a token.

I wanted to get out of playing tennis, but I didn't know how to tell the chair of the department, who was a supporter of mine, that I didn't want to play on her team. There was nothing wrong with tennis, I was just tired of doing it and it wasn't fun anymore. We had no courts, so you had to walk all the way down to East River Drive, where we played on the public courts along the river. In my senior year of high school, a new gym teacher came, Mrs. Ho. She was an Asian woman, and she started a fencing club. Fencing just happened to meet at the same time on Wednesdays as tennis, so I went, "A-ha! Here's how I can get out of tennis! I'll say I want to do fencing!" I went to the chair and she asked, "Well, why don't you want to play tennis?" I said, "This fencing sounds really interesting, and I just want to try something new." That is how I started fencing. It's amazing, but that was my entire motivation.

I didn't feel odd as a black person going out for fencing. There were a couple of us, and it was a club, and we had fun. Mrs. Ho's daughter was on the team. I don't know how conscious I was of how many blacks there were, but there were people I knew from Leaders, so we were friends. For the first couple of months it was just fun and something new to do. She took us to a couple of tournaments and I had fairly good success. So now I thought I was big stuff. I thought, "I'm a really great fencer." My mother didn't know a thing about fencing. But she said, "Well, if that's what you want to do and it's part of your school, you can go." She was probably just thinking it'd keep me off the streets and keep me busy, so it was fine. I was still doing other sports, too. I played basketball, softball, and volleyball. But once I got into fencing, I started doing it even outside of school.

I graduated from high school in 1968. The political situation in the United States in the late sixties affected the way I looked at the world. Being from a good old West Indian family, there was very much a feeling of community. We lived in Harlem, and no one locked the door. If you did something wrong the news of it got home before you did. Everyone was everyone's child, and everyone looked after everyone else. My grand-mother was a very loving, giving person, and there was always this trust of people that we had been brought up with. That was the atmosphere in our household. We were never brought up with, "All white people are bad, and all black people are good." We were brought up with all kinds of people so there wasn't that racial dichotomy in our house. The assassinations during the late sixties changed my view. I can vividly remember when Dr. King was assassinated. I was on the subway when I heard that Dr. King had been killed. That really changed the perspective I had grown up with, that you could trust people. Now all of a sudden I learned that not everyone was good.

Growing up there was always an assumption that I would go to college. The only question was, "Which one will you go to?" It wasn't something my mother and grandmother beat into our heads; we just knew that's what we were going to do. In my senior year of fencing in high school, I met a girl, Ellen Jacobs, at some of the tournaments. She was a Jewish girl who went to Brooklyn College, and she said to me, "You know, you're pretty good. You should join our team and come to Brooklyn College." I just assumed I was going to City College because I grew up three blocks from the campus, and that's where my brother went, but they didn't have fenc-ing. She talked me into choosing Brooklyn College. That was the first decision in my life that fencing actually helped me to make.

COLLEGE

I attended Brooklyn College from 1968 to 1972. When I went there it cost about fifty-three dollars a semester for student fees. That was it, for fifty-three dollars you could get an excellent education. At that time there were Social Security benefits for children of veterans. Since my father had been a veteran, my mother was able to keep my brother and me in school, and not have us go out and work. That really helped when I got involved in sports.

The fencing coach at Brooklyn College, Denise O'Connor, was a wonderful lady. She has a very tough, abrupt manner, but when you get beyond all that, she's a very caring person. Brooklyn College had no scholarships for fencing. There were no such things as scholarships for women back then. My first year of fencing went well. Denise tells a story of how she saw me on the basketball court, which was next to the fencing gym. I had come out for fencing, but I was also trying out for basketball, and I couldn't quite decide what I wanted to do. She saw me on the basketball court and yelled at me, and made me come in the fencing gym. She locked the door behind me so I couldn't leave.

Denise really made that team. We worked together, we respected each other, and I thank her for that. To this day, she's still a supportive mentor. She has stopped coaching, but she's still involved with fencing. As a matter of fact on the 1976 Olympic team, which was my first Olympic team, I was the youngest player and she was the oldest. She was forty at that time, and she had also been on the 1968 Olympic team. It was really strange, the two of us on the same team.

When I was at Brooklyn College, the school had 35,000 students. There were very few blacks. If you had another person of color in your class, it was quite phenomenal. It was an occasion to celebrate. There was a lot of turmoil on campus. There were sit-ins, and I was involved in all of them. One of my strongest memories is protesting something, and standing in front of a building. A large number of the white students were screaming at us, "Get them off the campus! Get them off the campus!" I remember looking and seeing some of my other physical education majors standing there yelling, too. I can remember how much it really hurt. It didn't matter who I was, it was what I represented.

I was the only black person on the fencing team. I thought about that. In that atmosphere, you had to think about it. But fencing was something I really liked, and Denise never made me feel different. In that atmosphere and at that time, it could've been very, very different, but it wasn't. She included me in everything the team did, both on campus and off. My teammates treated me fine. As best as I can remember, there were never any major incidents within the team.

When I fenced in high school, I thought I was great stuff. Then I went to college and realized I didn't know half of what I thought I knew. I learned how to play at fencing in high school; I learned how to fence in college, and that's primarily because of the excellent coaching, and the team there. Denise was an excellent coach. She took my natural ability and talent, and fine-tuned and adapted it. She always took care of us. She was like a mother hen, and we were under her wing. People respected her, and therefore they didn't mess with her kids.

The first year we had several meets. We had a good team. I was actually a starter my first year, and I received a varsity letter. I felt very proud of that, because there were not a lot of freshman starters. I won more than I lost. Otherwise, Denise would've certainly yanked me out of there. I could always remember having a winning record, a winning season. I'm a competitive person by nature, and so the idea of competition was fun, but I refused to let it become a central part of my life. It wasn't until I was out of college that I really started thinking, "What do you want out of this?" It was fun, I enjoyed it, and that's why I continued, because I didn't put that pressure on myself. I fenced as long as it was fun, and when it stopped being fun, I retired.

I graduated with honors in 1972, and fencing had a big influence on my next step. Denise had a string of students who had graduated and gone to Temple University as graduate assistants, because Temple taught fencing classes in its P.E. program. My friend Sharon had gone to Temple, and was about to graduate with her master's. She told me they were looking for a new graduate assistant. Denise looked at who she had graduating, and said to me, "Why don't you go to graduate school?" I said, "Because I can't." She said, "Why not?" I said, "Because I'm going to teach school." My goal, my whole life, was always to be a school teacher. My life's dream was to go to college, get my teaching certification, teach school in New York, and live happily ever after. I had never thought about graduate school, or moving out of New York. Everyone was in New York. I thought, "I can't teach college, I just graduated from college." I was scared to death at the thought. Denise said, "Well, they need somebody down there. You have to get your master's anyway if you want to teach. Here's an opportunity." I don't even know when the final decision was made, but I ended up at Temple as a grad assistant, straight out of Brooklyn College.

My mother saw this as an opportunity for me to get my master's for free. I was going to get a stipend through the school. It was three thousand dollars a year at that time, which only lasted half the year. This was when the money she had been saving was put to good use. I remember taking that money out and using it to furnish my first apartment. That money really came in handy. My mother had put my brother's and my money away for all those years because our education was sacred to her.

The only thing that I had full confidence in was fencing. They wanted me to teach two fencing classes. That I could do, but I couldn't teach college students, I thought, because they were as old as I was. Some of them were older! The only reason I felt I could do it was because fencing was something I knew and enjoyed. That was the only thing that gave me some assurance. When I came to Temple, I had to deal with some issues. I had to rush to take the MATs. When I received my scores, the responses were, "My God, she did well!" Shock! So I was accepted at Temple into the graduate program.

PROFESSIONAL LIFE

My first international trip was to a meet in Moscow in 1973. Our team came in sixth. I don't remember who was ahead of us. The strong teams were from the eastern European countries in the Soviet bloc, as well as the French and the Italians. I was the only black woman on the United States team. I knew Ed Ballinger, who was on the men's foil team. It was really funny because Ed and I had never been close or good friends, but I knew Ed. I had always thought he was very brash, loud, and full of himself. He was from New York. I was naïve when I made that team, and Ed really took care of me. I was like his little sister, and rather than leave me to flounder, he would say, "Okay, I'm going over here, come on," or "Come on, do this," or "Okay, this is what you need to do." He took care of me. He really was my big brother at that first meet, because he had been on teams before, and knew the ropes. I learned what a really kind person he was. He really made sure no one messed with me, and kept me straight. He was a good fencer.

The trip to Moscow was very interesting. I observed such a different culture and saw how athletes were treated there. They were very good to us. It made you feel that you were really special, because you were an athlete. It didn't matter whether you were white or black, you were an athlete, and that was the way people treated you. Transportation was free; you just had to show your athlete's pass, and you could go anywhere in Moscow. They gave you respect because you were an athlete, and that was something I had never experienced in this country, especially with fencing, because there's no money to be made in it. In fact, it costs you a ton of money to be a fencer and to go on these trips. The Olympic committee, at that time, was not very interested in developing fencers. It seemed as though their attitude was, "You make it somehow, and when you do, we'll take credit." I had never gotten anything from the fencing association or the Olympic committee because I was a good athlete. Now in the United States, all we heard about the Soviet Union was how bad it was, how terrible these people were, and how they hate Americans. We were brought up with all that stuff, but we went there and they treated us like royalty. It was just, "My God, you can't believe everything you hear! Or everything you read!"

In 1973, I started on my doctorate. I was going to school, taking classes at night, and I was coaching. I was still teaching a course over in the health department. I wanted to keep my hand in that and, in 1974, I was still training and going to competitions. I made the team in '73 as the fifth person. In 1973–1974, I was the person on the bubble. Sometimes I was sixth, sometimes I was fifth, and they only took the top five. For most of the time I was sixth, so I was always fighting to get over to the good spot. It's the alternate spot, actually. Then in 1975 I won the national championship, which was my first championship.

In 1975, my husband Norman and I both got full-time jobs. We got married in June. One of the things I had learned from Denise, and a lot of other fencers, was that they did a lot of camping. I had never camped. I came from Harlem, where do you camp? Fencers camp at all their meets, because it's a cheap way of traveling to the different competitions, rather than staying in a hotel. I had gotten Norman into camping and, for our honeymoon, we camped cross-country. The national championships were also in June, and that year they were held in Los Angeles, California. We got married on June 14, and the nationals were the next week, so we used that week as our honeymoon and drove across the country. The campgrounds cost about three or four bucks a night. Here I was a newlywed going to nationals, and I won! First time I made the finals, never mind winning. That became the big joke, "Ah, see what marriage can do for someone!" It was great.

Ruth White had won the 1974 national championship. She was not only the first black woman to win the national championship, she was also the youngest woman. She was seventeen. She came out of the Baltimore area. She had learned how to fence at a Y in Baltimore, and then she went to New York University. I watched her win that championship. She went to NYU, as had Peter Westbrook. She ended up going to medical school, and she's now a physician. She used to read books and study between the fencing bouts.

Arthur Ashe won Wimbledon in 1975. We thought, "Oh my God, Arthur Ashe won!" We were just so excited, my husband and I, because we heard it in the car as we were driving. It was a wonderful time. That year we had a black man win the men's foil for the first time, I think it was Ed Ballinger. Peter Westbrook also won. He's won so many championships. For the first time, two out of the three men's events were won by blacks. Then I won the women's, and we had three black national fencing champions. Seeing Arthur Ashe and the other guys win, I said, "You know, Norm, this is the year, this is the year." And I won my first national championship in a year when there were two other black national champions. What a year! Everyone at Temple was very supportive, very excited. It was a real plus for the school, because it was good publicity for them.

As a result of having won the nationals in 1975, I made the '75 Pan American team for the first time, and I ended up taking second in the individual championship. A girl from Cuba was the winner. The team took third. I had the best finish of any American. That year was great, I was in heaven. At that point, I was very competitive. I was now one of the top athletes, and the goal was to go for it. Peter Westbrook had been talking to me, along with my coach, and everyone else. I was starting to train seriously, but still trying to keep fencing, from my point of view, in perspective. I still had an academic career, and I still had a family. Fencing was just a piece of the puzzle.

I had done my thesis, but I was still going to school. I was taking classes, I was teaching classes, and I was coaching, so training was just a part of my life. The U.S. Fencing Association had started a training program for the top twenty-four fencers, so one weekend every month we had to go to Princeton for this training. They made us run, and all these crazy things that we had never really done before. I started lifting weights, and started getting much more serious. I guess after '74 going into '75, fencing became more important. Then I started thinking about goals and I thought, "Hey, you know, I could make an Olympic team."

I started training more seriously. We started a national or at least a regional training program. I don't know if I had dreams of doing well or was more worried about not doing well. No one expected us to win. I was the United States national champion, but American fencing, on the ladder of international fencing was very, very low. That was the reality for us. The joy was making the team. The black members of the 1976 team were Peter Westbrook, Ed Ballinger, and me. There were never any black épée fencers, so it was only sabre and men's foil. I was the only woman. And that's the funny thing about fencing. As long as I've been doing it, there were never many blacks, but the ones that were there were near the top.

When I graduated in 1975, the university offered me a full-time coaching position, because they knew I was good. They were getting publicity because of me and they were enjoying and appreciating my accomplishments. They saw that as a reason to keep me at Temple, and to keep this team going.

The 1976 Olympics took place in Montreal, and it was great because my whole family was there, and that was neat. Being on an Olympic team was an amazing experience. It really was the joy of being there, because we did not have the expectation of winning a medal. It was fascinating, and I met some great people and had a really good time. It was a great honor. These are things you don't forget. The Pan Am Games were my first big international multi-sport meet, besides the University Games. I was on the world championship fencing team, but that was just fencing. The Olympics were just phenomenal. Meeting people, trading uniforms and T-shirts, and collecting pins; it was a lot of fun. The fencing was great but, it was funny, because I walked away from it thinking these Europeans weren't as great as everyone said they were. I knew we could do better than that. And I really came away from the '76 Olympics determined to train and to have a good result in 1980. I did the best of the Americans, but we still didn't do that well.

As a black woman participating in fencing, I would say that people were thrown by my presence. The first thing that always struck me was whenever I was on a team like that, the first question people asked was, "What do you run?" That was the question, "What do you run?" because they made an assumption. They knew I wasn't tall enough to be a basketball player, and there weren't that many black female basketball players at that time anyway. I always had to start out by saying, "I don't run." There's nothing wrong with being in track, but it was just assumed that that must be what I did. Then when I'd tell them I'm a fencer, they looked at me like I'm crazy. "You're a *what?* How did you get into that?" That was the typical response.

After 1976, I kept training. At the national championships, I was sometimes second, sometimes third, but I didn't win another one until 1980. I went to Europe for several training trips and for the 1978 world championships. I continued working very hard. It was one of my priorities, not the only one, but one of them. The 1979 Pan Am Games were held in Puerto Rico, and that was the next team to make. I made that team, and I went. I took third in the individuals, and the team took third in team competition, again. The number one foilist was a Cuban, again. Cubans are very strong. They were always our nemesis in the Pan American Games. At that time they had Russian coaches and they were supported by their government. All they did was train. In American sports in general, you have this vast number of people to draw from, but we have such poor organization in grassroots and development. In a country like Cuba, although it's a small country, they bring in top quality coaches, and they pick certain people, "You come be in the army, we'll train you." That is all they do. And then we compete against them, and everyone wants to know why we don't win medals.

When I returned home I kept training. My goal was to make the 1980 Olympic team. We were having international results, we had now gone to Europe quite a bit to train and to compete in different competitions, and the team was primarily the same group of people. My coach from college, Denise O'Conner, had retired, but there were three of us from the '76 team, and there were going to be two younger people that had really come a long way and were very strong. We all were working very hard to get ready and make that team. At that point, I knew that 1980 was going to be it for me.

After I won the bronze at the Pan Ams, there was a lot of expectation, and I think that's part of what made the Carter administration's 1980 boycott so devastating for me personally; knowing this was the end and knowing how hard I had worked for those last four years. I had put my academic work on hold, I had taken a leave from school, and I was still teaching and coaching. Then it was gone with one press conference. That was very difficult, and very frustrating. But that was that, and I knew people who had given up everything for their training, and it was probably more devastating for them than it was for me. At least I could still go home, and I still had a husband. I hadn't lost my family, and I knew people that had.

My feelings regarding President Carter's boycott of the 1980 Olympics in Moscow are mixed. I was very angry, because I was on the team and

I thought it might be my year. I understood the political statement that Carter was trying to make, but on the other side, I thought, "How dare you do this to me?" At that point I knew that after 1980 I was retiring, that that was going to be my last year. I had trained, I had sacrificed, I had put out money (at that time the U.S. Olympic Committee was just beginning to support some of the training for athletes, but most of it was on your own). After making the 1976 team, I had made a conscious decision, "I'm going to train, I'm going to do what I need to do because I want to go in '80." That was probably one of the first conscious decisions I made, as far as setting a goal. When that was taken away, it was a very frustrating time. I was very, very angry. I thought, "I understand what you're doing, but you know it's not going to make any difference, and I know it's not going to make any difference." The athletes became the pawns in a political game. Yet the Olympic ideal was supposed to be above politics.

People had put their life on hold for four years to train, and it seemed very unfair to have one person, one day, decide, "Well, you're not going to do it." I could not resolve my anger about someone controlling my destiny like that. I can go to a competition, and if I bomb, it's on me. Either I do well or I don't, but I'm in control. Here was something that, after four years of work, someone took out of your control and said, "You're not going." As an athlete, whether you understood it politically or not, it hurt, because I had put school on hold, I had put a family on hold, I had put so many things on hold, and done this balancing act for four years, to then have them say, "Sorry, not this time." And I knew there was not going to be another time for me. I had a lot of mixed feelings, and I spoke out, because I was not in agreement with it.

It was big news on all the talk shows, and there were lots of interviews, and a lot of people were asking, "What do you think?" I said, "It wasn't fair. It was something we had worked so hard for, and it all was for nothing." If you compete in sports at the college level, you have an understanding of what people go through. It isn't something frivolous. You don't make an Olympic team being frivolous. All athletes are trying to do a balancing act. You do that because it's important to you, for whatever reason. It's important to people for different reasons, but for whatever the reason, it's enough for you to alter your life to do it. I knew other people on the fencing team who had made all kinds of sacrifices. I knew people who sold their cars so they could go to meets, and then just like that, it's gone, all for the sake of a political statement. I resented it.

In the fall of 1980, the team visited China. It was my most interesting trip. The Chinese see Africans, but very rarely see African Americans. They would just come up and stare at me. They'd touch me or they'd touch my hair. They were fascinated, because it wasn't often that a Chinese person in mainland China saw a black person.

This trip to China was the end of competition for me. That was that. I wasn't sad about it, I wasn't unhappy about it. I was ready for it to be over. At this point I was twenty-nine, almost thirty, and I think if I had been leaving fencing altogether, it would've been different. But I wasn't leaving fencing, I was coming back to coach my team. Fencing was still very much a part of my life, as it is today. I don't think I could have a life that didn't involve fencing. It gets in your blood and it's just part of you. When I came back from China I felt a sense of relief. It was all over. The pressure to do well, to perform, was over. It was tough, and it was a sigh of relief after that last tournament. If we had gone to the Olympics, I think we would've had a significant result. I'm not saying a medal, but I think we would at least have gotten to the semifinals, which would've been great. But I came back, and the job was here. I got back into the rhythm of teaching and coaching the team.

I have always been very demanding of my team. I don't think I could get more demanding. The expectation was always there, and I'm a firm believer in hard work, in spite of what I did. I laugh and tell people, "You know, if I had been on my team, I would've quit." There's no way I would have done everything I make my girls do, but I think our success as a team has been a result of how hard the girls work. I really look at work ethic when I am recruiting girls. We've gotten into recruiting and scholarships and that whole bit. We've had a program for fourteen years now, since the NCAA started women's fencing in 1981, and we have been in the final four for twelve out of those fourteen years.

Up until 1980 my teams had mixed success. They were not final four teams. We did not really start getting kids with high school experience until we offered scholarships in the late 1970s. That was about the same time that I began to have my own personal success. We had our first winning record in '76. Things started to get better each year, because of my added experience, as well as the quality of the fencers that were now coming into the program. This also enabled the walk-ons to improve, because they were practicing with stronger people. I try to tell the girls, "You're going to learn more from each other than you're going to learn from me." I depend a lot on the girls working with each other, helping each other, and giving feedback to each other. As we got some experienced girls, it really helped to raise the level of the entire team, and we became more and more successful. Consequently, we began getting better and better recruits. It's a nice circle.

I think my approach to the sport has been instrumental to our team's success. You can't have success without a good skill level. The girls have a certain skill level when they come in, and there's not one fencer, I think, who would say that when they exited the program they weren't at a higher level. But the approach to the game, the mental toughness that you need to succeed, is the piece I added. Very few high school coaches will deal with that. Some kids have a natural personality for this sport, because you have to be pretty level-headed, you have to be a quick thinker, and be able to think really fast on your feet. Some come in and are able to do that very easily and are really easygoing. Others come in and they really have to work at it. I think the thing that I'm happiest about having done is exposing new kids to the sport, and taking kids who had been exposed to the sport to a higher level. High school fencing and collegiate fencing are very different, and collegiate fencing and fencing on a national level are very, very different. We've been able to take them to a higher level, show them the areas they need to work on, and then work on those areas with them. I think my intensity, my true belief in the work ethic, probably comes from my grandmother. Making them put out, in many cases, more than they ever thought they could, seeing them realize that and seeing them just run with it, in the gym, in the classroom, and in life, is truly rewarding.

I think the notion that black people are gifted or superior physically reflects a certain mindset, and one of the things that we're trying to do with the Black Women in Sport Foundation is to break down some of those mental barriers that we have, because I think we see domination in sports where we've been allowed to participate, but we also see domination in sports where there is a large grassroots development. I hear my daughter, who is now running track, saying, "Well, I don't want to run distance, I'm gonna run the hundred." We see a domination of blacks in sports in certain track events, and African athletes are coming in and doing distance events, but we don't see American blacks running in those events. On the other hand, I hear whites saying, "Well, I can't run as fast in the hundred, so I'll go to the mile," and we still have that dichotomy.

I don't think we stretch ourselves as much and broaden our own perspective. I think it's a matter of exposure. If I hadn't been in a place and time where I was exposed to fencing, I would never have grown up saying, "I want to be a fencer." I think the more opportunities we give our youngsters, the more things they are going to excel at, because everyone has strengths and weaknesses, and what our society does is limit the opportunities for young black kids to be exposed to different things at an early age.

I think there's a lot of growth and a lot of things that are a by-product of competing in sports. I think that when one is involved in sports there are so many transferable skills that you learn. Sport teaches you how to deal with frustration and disappointment. It teaches you how to set a goal and come up with a plan to achieve that goal. It teaches you how to imagine a path and to see yourself on that path. All of those things relate both inside and outside the gym. If the first time you go for a job interview and you get turned down, you might find that totally devastating, and that can affect how you approach the next job interview. Whereas if you've been in sports, you know you lose sometimes, and you think, "Oh well, there's tomorrow's game, and I'm gonna come back and kick your butt." I think that sport gives your personality a certain resilience that is very, very important for success in life. It helps a person realize they can succeed. Even if it's a small goal, there are ways to succeed. Sport gives you a competitiveness that allows you to go into that office and win.

There was a time when black people were allowed or disallowed to do certain things based on the opportunities made available to us. More than that, our society reinforces its own stereotypes by what it promotes through the media. They will pay Michael Jordan millions of dollars to dunk, and that will be highlighted in the media, while people never see Dr. so-and-so in an academic area. The images that our kids are allowed to see, and who our society puts on that media pedestal, has a lot to do with what people think is within the realm of possibility. Society perpetuates the sense that this is what you're good at and so this is what you should do. Kids grow up saying, "Well, that's what I see, and he's making all that money. Look at that car, and look at that house. I'm gonna do that," because they don't see Dr. Walter over there writing books and writing articles. They only ask, "Can he dunk a basketball?" I'm not ready to buy into this natural ability thing. What I do buy into is the idea that the images that are portrayed have a great influence on what people feel are their strengths or capabilities. We have people succeeding in all types of areas, but you don't hear about it.

The double whammy of being black and female certainly exists in sport. There's no field more gender-conscious and sexist than athletics. Even within the black community, there was a time you couldn't be a female in sports. Then the other side of that is that to be involved in sports you had to be a great athlete. I think that the future of black women in sport is mixed. I think there are still stereotypes that all women have to deal with, but black women especially. I think it's tough to be that superstar, to get any recognition, to get that college scholarship, or to get that professional opportunity. I think that many black women who are involved in sports on various levels are very cognizant of the importance of being a role model, because there weren't as many out there when I was growing up. Women are declining in the coaching roles, because coaching is becoming big-time and very time consuming. You have to give up so much to do it, and not everyone has an understanding husband, or partner, like I do to say that it's okay to spend all these hours away. It's expected that a wife would do that for her male husband coach, but to reverse that we have to deal with some of those personal issues and relationship issues that are very different.

One of the frustrations of my life is not being able to bring fencing to more black communities. That's why I got involved with the Black Women in Sport Foundation. We're going to start a mentoring program. There's more I would like to do, but there's just a point where you have to decide what you need to do and make the time for it. You have to decide what your priorities are. What Peter Westbrook has done is fabulous, and I feel that I am doing similar work to some degree. I've brought a lot of black women into fencing here at the university who never would've been exposed to it. I feel good about that. I think my presence was what attracted them to try fencing, whereas if there had been a white coach, they probably wouldn't have tried, because they wouldn't have seen it as something black women do. People think black folks don't fence, they don't play golf, and they don't play ice hockey. But once they see someone doing it, it's now within their realm and their frame of reference. I think I've made some small steps in exposing young people to nontraditional sports through the Foundation and helping them broaden their horizons and alter their mindset and belief in their own abilities. The key is exposure to new and different opportunities and positive role models.

NOTES

1   For more on the Black Women in Sport Foundation, visit the official Web site at http://www.blackwomeninsport.org.

PETER WESTBROOK

FENCING

December 5, 1990
New York, New York

PETER WESTBROOK IS ARGUABLY THE BEST SABRE FENCER THE United States has ever produced, breaking a number of barriers in his ascension to the top of his sport. As a child growing up in the projects of Newark, New Jersey, Westbrook began his career when his mother paid him to take up fencing as a means of keeping him off the streets. He soon excelled, and in high school caught the eye of recruiters from a number of colleges, including New York University, which he attended on a full scholarship from 1971 to 1975. While Uriah Johns, ranked fourth in the world in 1964, became the first African American to win a United States Fencing Championship in 1971, Westbrook is the first African American to win the NCAA Fencing Championship (1973). He is also the first African American to medal in Olympic fencing, taking home the bronze at the 1984 Los Angeles Games. Throughout his illustrious career, he has won three Pan American Games gold medals and competed in six Olympics between 1976 and 1996. He was national champion in men's sabre from 1974–1975, 1979–1986, 1988–1989, and in 1995. Inducted into the United States Fencing Association Hall of Fame in 1993, he is now retired and coaches fencers through the Peter Westbrook Foundation, which he established in 1991.[1] Since its inception, this organization has produced Keeth Smart, the first American and African American fencer ever to rank number one in the world, as well as four of the fourteen members of the 2004 U.S. Olympic fencing team.[2]

CHILDHOOD

I was born April 16, 1952, in St. Louis, Missouri. When I was nine months old my parents moved to Newark, New Jersey. I have an African American father and a Japanese mother. They met during the Korean Crisis and he brought her to America. My parents split up when I was about four or five years old. I grew up in a single-parent home and lived with my mother and sister in the Hayes Homes Projects. In Newark there were projects everywhere, brick buildings, twelve stories tall, and overcrowded. Someone once gave me the analogy that the projects were like Indian reservations because they were so overcrowded.

I went to grammar school at Queen of Angels Catholic School. My mother is a Catholic, a very committed Catholic. She thought I could get a better education at a Catholic school, and back in those days I think you did get a little better education, although I'm not so sure how it is now. What was nice about it was that I was taught mostly by African American sisters. There were a lot of black children; it was 60 percent white and 40 percent black. There were a lot of white priests there, but I think I related more to the black nuns. After I reached the sixth grade, the student population became 80 or 90 percent black, but I was still being taught by black sisters and white priests. Being brought up by these African American sisters, I had good role models as to how I should feel and behave in my environment. If you live in an overcrowded area, the way you look at things, the way you view things, is not always socially correct. The ways you relate and express yourself to other people, in many instances, does not fit in with the social mainstream. I didn't realize until later that my way of thinking was "a little warped" as this Indian guy once told me. And something was wrong, because I found myself, at times, not as happy as I could have been.

The Catholic connection has been very significant in my life. The white priests at Queen of Angels were very unusual, because they really wanted to help us little African American kids. They really gave of themselves. I always like to give back to my people, give back to my God, so when I'm at the church I currently attend, I give what's in my pocket, but I give my true solid, hearty donations to Queen of Angels because of what the priests and nuns there tried to do for us.

What got me in the white world was fencing. At first I felt uncomfortable because all I was used to was the environment I grew up in. I have always looked at myself as a black person, but by being half Japanese and African American, the blacks in my neighborhood would tease me every day. I had to fight my way through it because I didn't fit in at all. When you have a Japanese mother and no African American father, it made life hard. But I am glad I was in that situation, because it gave me a certain character and strength that a lot of my friends don't have. I wouldn't trade that for the world.

Queen of Angels had grades one through eight. After eighth grade it was straight to high school. I entered high school in 1967. As do most children of African American descent, I lived in my own world. We have our own customs and our own habits. We have our own way of talking and our own way of relating to one another emotionally.

I started getting into the mainstream of society when I got to high school. I had to adapt, because I just wasn't used to all this. What a culture shock! It was much different in high school because at Queen of Angels most of the people were African American, and I was living in a black neighborhood. When I went out into the white world, I couldn't relate to white people the way I related to blacks. Even with the people I used to fight all the time, there was still some kind of bond I didn't have with even friendly Euro Americans. I didn't know what it was. I couldn't put my finger on it, but I can tell you now, what a void! Because of this, I felt empty as I started to enter mainstream society.

The more I got involved in fencing the more this loneliness started to intensify, because fencing was a very elite, European sport. If you grow up in a poor neighborhood, a lot of times that instills in you what I call an extra, super strength. For me, that easily translated into my work for white corporations, and my years in a white sport. It gave me a certain strength of character that a lot of people in fencing don't have. I can see now what I have gained from my African American background, and I tell my younger "brothers" that we all share such a special strength and special drive. I see this in sports and corporations; when the chips are really down most people will fall by the wayside. Most people will just give up, if it is hard to go forward. Because of our background we learned never to give up, to keep on fighting. All of us from that kind of background have this super strength.

My mother talked me into trying fencing. I didn't want to fence. I used to do a lot of boxing, and I was pretty good at it, although I never really took any lessons. All the kids in the neighborhood went to boxing clubs. My mother tried to keep me away from all that, because she thought, "Oh no, I don't want my kid to be terrible." My mother is of a Japanese mind.

She said, "Peter, I'd like you to try fencing." I said, "Fencing? I don't want to fence!" Her brother in Japan used to do Kendo, Japanese fencing, so she said to herself, "If I get Peter involved in some kind of unconventional sport, he may meet a kind of clientele that he would not normally meet living in these projects." That was her thinking. My thinking was, "This is not for me!"

My mother gave me five dollars to try it. The next day at home I said, "I'm quitting this." She said, "I'll give you ten more dollars," so I stayed with it. I used to watch those movies like "Zorro." Those male TV characters were my heroes. I said to myself, "Hummm, this is pretty good! This is great! It's like fighting with swords," so I stopped taking money from her, and just tried it. On one occasion, my mother went to my high school and inquired about their fencing program. This was at Essex Catholic High School in Newark. She pleaded, "Can you please let my son in the program? I know it has started, but please let him in." She practically got on her knees and said, "Please, please let him in, just for two weeks." She pleaded and pleaded. The next thing I know they came to me and told me, "We would like you to come and start in this program." Within one month of starting out, I was beating up on everyone, even people who had been fencing for about a year. If it wasn't for my mother I would not be involved in fencing, and I wouldn't be sitting here, with this white shirt and suit on either.

The coach who got me started was Dr. Samuel D'ambola.[3] He's a physician in New Jersey. Dr. D'ambola helped me out of the goodness of his heart. He wasn't getting paid for it. I worked with him for three hours every day after I got out of school, for about four years. Fencing was pretty much year round, except for summer vacation. It started in September and ended in May.

The summers were when I got into trouble. Summer, with nothing to do, just idle time. I started hanging with people from the neighborhood, seeing what kind of ruckus we could start up. I got into fights all the time, although I was always one of the good boys in the neighborhood. My mother made sure of that.

One thing I grew up with was definitely a lot of discipline. Japanese people are so disciplined, and my mother was like that. She was highly disciplined and very clean. Too clean! I had to take my shoes off when I came into the house and wash my hands every ten minutes!

When I graduated from high school, I didn't really think I wanted to go to college. You don't really think like that until your parents or your peers start putting that idea into your head. Otherwise, you think like everyone else where I lived: you get out of high school, try to have some fun, and just get a job. That's it. Not high paying, just any kind of job. I just wanted to get out of high school. Since I seemed to be good in fencing, my only goal in life was to one day win a fencing tournament or some kind of national championship. But then colleges started to contact me, including NYU (New York University), Seton Hall, and St. John's University. NYU offered me a full scholarship.

First of all, I was glad I was accepted into college, because I never thought that I was even going. But I was also scared, because I would be going to a university with all these strange people. And my social skills? You have to understand that social skills are acquired and learned from your parents and your environment. Living in the projects all my life, my social skills were limited to fighting. I didn't know what going to NYU with all these Caucasian people was going to be like. I thought, "Oh my God. I'm going to be in some serious trouble. This isn't going to be fun; it's going to be a painful experience." It's funny how things fall into place. I got the scholarship through fencing and that's when I really started learning my social skills.

I remember my mother "the discipliner" saying, "Someone gives you a full scholarship to go to college, you better go!" I had people contacting me and speaking to me about college as though it was a normal thing, and to me it was very unnatural. A lot of people started calling and asking, "What college are you going to?" What college am I going to? I didn't even know I was going! I thought, "If I don't go, there must be something wrong with me." But I didn't think that until it was communicated to me that, "Well, you've got to go to college or there's something wrong." Really? I'd never heard that. After just a few telephone calls I realized, "I'm going to college. I'm really weird if I don't go." That's how I got there. There were recruiters and coaches calling my house, telling me, "Come to this school, you've got to come here. You'll fit right in." They were recruiting for fencing, but they also made me feel that if I didn't go to some college, I was a misfit. Just by my mother's logic, I realized, "I don't want to go, but it's the right thing to do." I picked NYU because it was one of the biggest schools offering me a scholarship, and it was in New York, which seemed closer to Newark than Seton Hall or St. Johns, which were in the boonies. NYU was right in the Village. I thought, "Well, it might not be totally bad, just 80 percent."

COLLEGE

I went to New York in 1971. I had a full scholarship, including room and board. I was a pretty good fencer, so they also gave me a stipend for some pocket money. I didn't do well in my courses when I got to NYU. You need someone to sit down with you and counsel and guide you; you need a good role model to tell you exactly what to do. Since I didn't have that, it really affected me. First time I'm on my own with no rules and no restrictions. I could do as I pleased, and that's exactly what I did. My grades fell below average, but that didn't really bother me because I didn't know if I belonged there anyway. My instincts and the discipline my mother instilled in me kept me going. I thought to myself, "Well, Pete, it looks like you got two Ds and two Cs." Now that was fine with me, but my mother was going to be displeased. I thought, "I'm not really trying to my full capacity. Let me try harder." The following semester I did a little better. I got all Cs, and maybe one D.

After the first year my coach told me, "Pete, maybe you can make the Olympic team." I said, "What?" Then somebody else said, "Pete, maybe you could make the Olympic team someday. You're that talented." I said, "Really?" They said, "Oh, yeah! You could win a National Championship!" I thought, "I'm really that good? God, if I can just win a U.S. title, I'll be happy for the rest of my life. I don't care if I don't graduate from college. I don't care if I never make the Olympic team. That's all I want." And it's funny, after I got a whiff of that, it had a snowball effect. It got big fast.

When I started going to NYU, my coach was Hugo Costello. Because I had worked with D'ambola in high school, Costello decided to take a look at me and he recruited me. After taking lessons and working with Hugo, other guys on the team said, "Pete, you gotta go to Csaba Elthes. He's an Olympic coach, and you've got the skills and talent to go to the Olympics. You gotta go to him." Elthes wasn't connected to the university. In the summer of 1972 I introduced myself to him, and the first thing he did was look at me and say, "I don't know if you have what it takes. If you want to stick around, I can give you everything you need, I can make you great. But it depends on how weak you are." His method is strong, fierce, negative teaching. He became another disciplinarian in my life, rough, hard, regimented, unyielding, and with no emotion. His methodology is, "I will teach you and every time you make a mistake, I'm going to beat you with this blade. I'm not going to communicate it to you. Communication is a waste of time in combat. I must show you where you make errors." So he would hit you, whack you with his blade. That's how he trains. If you can take it fine, if not, get out.

For one semester, I got out. I thought, "This is not for me." But again, my mother's discipline started to get to me. I was getting better grades in school, all Cs, and something kept telling me, "The right thing to do is to go back. You can make the Olympic team with him, you can win the national championship." I thought, "This is going to be very painful." But because of my roots, because of that little extra strength I gained from where I was raised, I got over another hard hurdle. I went back to Coach Elthes and asked, "May I come back again and train with you, sir?" He said, "Absolutely," and that's when I decided to stick with it. He charged everybody at the club, but he knew I didn't have any money, so he said, "You don't live in this town, so you can come for free." That made me realize again how special and blessed I was. Here was this great coach, who must really see something in me for him to do this for free. I thought to myself, "For free? I must persevere." I started seeing him during my sophomore year of college, and he is still my coach now.

When I began training with Coach Elthes, I started being around nothing but white people, because those were the only people in fencing. I joined a club, and it had doctors, lawyers, and businessmen, and then me, this little black kid. That was a big culture shock, but I had already made up my mind that I was seeing this through. I didn't know how far I was going, but I was going to carry it through.

In 1973, my junior year, I won the NCAA Championship in men's sabre. That was a big achievement. I got my NCAA ring. When I came back to campus I was a hero, because I had won an NCAA Championship for the school. I had not only won it individually, but I carried my team. I was totally undefeated, so we won in two areas. Anything I wanted, I could have. "Do you need a stipend? Is it enough? Are you sure Pete? How are your grades? Are you doing okay?" I got the red carpet and it was a very comforting experience. The next year, I won the U.S. Men's Championship! The men's national team was made up of all the people in the country trying out for the 1976 Olympic team. When I won that event, I realized, "My God, I'm the best in the country now. The best one in college, the best one in the country, and the number one candidate for the Olympic team! My gosh, I'm sticking with this." I was still the only black person on the team, and the first black man to accomplish this.

By now, my goals were starting to change a little. Before, just winning a title was my whole dream, but after I won the collegiate title, that was no longer enough. Now my goals in life were to graduate from college, and to make the Olympic team. I had learned to make Bs, and even received a few As. I still had Cs, though, Cs always follow me around. I thought to myself, "Hey, I'm happy."

My mother could not believe her dream had come true, that this seed she had planted was now flourishing. But even though I was doing well, the way I looked at things in those days was still a little "warped," not the way I see things now. I was perhaps a little arrogant and my views, by normal standards, were still a little "different." In those days most black people were involved in sports like basketball, football, baseball, and boxing in particular. Not too many people were into fencing. How did my people react when I won? First of all they asked, "What is it?" Black people were not familiar with fencing, so how could they say, "Wow, that's great! That's bad, man!" I get that now, but even that is more because of me as a celebrity than because of their knowledge of the sport. I received more positive reactions from the white community because it's a white sport, but I still didn't get much feedback, except from the people at colleges and universities. After I began to win these championships in college, other blacks began to say, "Oh my God, who is this young Muhammad Ali in the white community?" That made me feel pretty good.

My coach, who was a member of the New York Athletic Club's fencing club, had talked to the people there. I was the first black kid they allowed in. They didn't make me a member, but in 1974–75 they wanted me to come to the club. They gave me a card, and whenever this black kid walked into the club, everybody looked up, like they were thinking, "What do you want?" I just said politely, "I'm here to fence, here's my card." I wasn't really a member, but they gave me a locker, so everybody thought I was. Nobody knew what was going on. Every time I walked into the club, every time I took a shower, they would always talk. Always! For years and years, when I walked into the club I always got that face, but when I went upstairs to the showers and the fencing room, everybody said, "Hey, Pete!" After a while, it wasn't just the fencers, everybody started talking to me: the wrestlers, the judo people, the karate people, everybody knew me now. In fact, they asked me recently to become a member, but I represent my club in New York, the United Fencing Club, where I persuaded a lot of African American brothers to participate. They are my teammates now, and I couldn't abandon them. I couldn't bring myself to join, because of what the club represents. There are two ways of thinking about that. I could have joined this club and been the first black member, and then tried to get a lot of other blacks to join me. Be the first to break the doors down. If I did that, I would be abandoning all my brothers here at the Fencer's Club. Even if I joined the New York Athletic Club, it wasn't going to let many more African Americans in. It wasn't as though I was going to be the first and open doors for other blacks. I would have been the first and perhaps the only for quite awhile. I thought of that possibility and said no.

I graduated from NYU in January 1975. I couldn't believe it, I got a degree! That hadn't even been in my dreams when I was growing up. But after I had been in the fencing world for a while, I absorbed a lot, and what all these white doctors and businessmen were telling me was, "Pete, you want to make sure you get a degree." I had wanted to be a teacher, but everyone in my neighborhood said, "No. Get a marketing, business, or economics degree. It will be more useful to you." I didn't know if I wanted to take all those statistics and accounting courses, but everybody said, "Pete, that's the way to go." So I graduated in marketing and economics. After that things really started to unfold in very positive ways.

PROFESSIONAL LIFE

In 1975 I won another men's U.S. National Title. I didn't have a job then, because after I graduated I decided to work for the university. I had just made the Pan American team, which was a big thing. You have to take three or four weeks off for the Pan American Games, so I thought, "Maybe I should keep this bursar's job." Then the university said, "If you stay here Pete, we'll pay for your graduate education." Now I began thinking about graduate school. A seed can grow into a tree! I went to the Pan American games for the first time in 1975, and I won the bronze. I was just so happy to be there. I was asked to fence in individuals and team. I was really pumped. I said to myself, "I think I can really do it now."

After all my training, I got to the Olympics in 1976. I'm proud and I'm training. I'm young, fast, strong, and ready to take on the world. People began to hear about me internationally, because everyone thought black Americans weren't good at fencing. At that time, there were maybe two of us who could win a medal, maybe three. I went to tournaments prior to the Olympics and defeated a lot of world champions. Everybody I was fencing was a professional, and I was an amateur. I had a job, and I was training two to three times a week after work. These professional fencers didn't work. I was competing against Russians and Hungarians, whose only job was to fence. They trained in the morning, took a nap at lunch, and came back to train in the evening. I was competing against those kinds of athletes, and they had still heard about me. I fenced and beat them.

When I was in Montreal training for the Olympics, the Italian world champion came over to me. He said, "Westbrook, let's go on the side and do some sparring." I thought, "Wow, what an honor," but I knew he wanted to check me out. I said, "Sure, fine." There was no room, so he suggested we spar on the wrestling mats, which are kind of soft and spongy. I began sparring with him, not giving up too many of my secrets, and my right foot got stuck in a soft part of the mat and turned my ankle—riiiiip! It was the most painful thing I've ever experienced in my entire life. I tore two ligaments in my ankle! I couldn't walk into the opening ceremonies. I was on crutches and finally they put me in a wheelchair, but I said, "Well, if there is any way possible, I'm going to stand up, just to do something." They had doctors and specialists there giving me treatments. Four days, that's all I had, then it was my event. They asked me, "What do you want to do? You could shoot cortisone." I said, "No, I don't want to do that. No, I don't even like the sound of that." They put on some kind of brace, and I went on and competed. I came in thirteenth, but I did better than any other American. I felt so devastated, like I had let myself and everyone else down. But once the Games were over, I didn't feel so bad, because I had done better than all the other Americans. After a while, I felt good. When I came home, it was three months before I could return to practice. I was still working for the university, but after the Olympics, I decided to look for a new job.

At this point I felt I had nerves of steel. No one believes me when I say this now, but one day I just walked in off the street into the IBM Corporation and said, "Good morning, sir, my name is Peter Westbrook. I would like to speak to someone in charge of personnel." The person at the desk said, "Fill out an application sir, leave it here, and we'll call you." By that time I thought my articulation skills were getting better, and I said, "Well, I could leave an application the way most people do, but that's not going to be good enough. I want to ask the director of personnel a question. I'm really not interested in a job. I don't want to take too much of his time, I just want to ask him one question." I walked into his office and said, "First of all, I want to thank you very much for the time you're giving me." I had immediately begun looking around the room to find out what I could say to catch his attention. I saw some trophies, so obviously, I started to talk about fencing.

"I see you're an advocator of sports. I went into sports myself." I also saw a psychology book, so I commented, "I see you read psychology books."

"What makes you say that?" he asked.

"Well, I read that book you have on the shelf also."

I impressed him right away. I spent two hours talking to him. By the end, he just wanted to know what on earth I wanted.

"I gave you a minute of my time sonny, now do you want a job or not?" he said.

"Absolutely sir, but I was just trying to get to know you, sir."

They had me come back two weeks later to meet two or three other people. Next thing I know, I got a letter and a job offer in the mail from the IBM Corporation, after walking in off the street.

Large corporations are not threatened by an employee's participation in the Olympics. They know if they have an Olympian, they have a winner. He or she might have to take off a couple of weeks once in a while, but they will bring in revenue and they know how to deal with people when the pressure gets rough. When the times get tough, they just get tougher! This is how they equate Olympians. When I told him I had to take off time, it wasn't even an issue.

IBM was the first corporation I had ever worked for. When you work for large corporations, you realize, "Holy cow, what a cruel, cold, racist world it is." It still didn't really hit me. When you grow up in a certain environment, around your people, you think the world is like that. You get a little whiff of reality when you go to college, but you don't get a glimpse of what the racist world is really about until you start working for a large corporation, especially when, as an African American, you are competing against white people in an area like sales and marketing. But I got an education in another sense, because I realized, "Ah-ha! There are different types of white people; the kind I see in the fencing world, in the sports arena, and the kind I see in the business world."

I went through training at IBM for one year. I got the best training of my life, better than what I learned in my whole four years of college. I mean, truly, you're talking about high-tech, high-powered individuals coming in to teach you how to speak, about business applications, about your mannerisms, everything. The skills I learned will be with me for the rest of my life. After I had been there a while I said to myself, "It's been two years, but

I still want to stay and put more under my belt. I don't want to be a quitter, or a loser, or a cop-out." I stayed there for three years, and after that I realized, "This job is just not for me. Let me get out of here." That's when I went to Pitney Bowes.

My experience at IBM allowed me to go to any corporation and get a job, so when I went to the Pitney Bowes Corporation they welcomed me with open arms. "You came from IBM? Please come here." I went to their training course and graduated number one in the class. There was only one other African American in the group. After working for Pitney Bowes, I came here to North American, and I've been here for eleven years. They permit me to take off all the time I want for fencing, with pay, and that has allowed me to continue competing. Right now I have twelve national championships.[4]

When I look back on my life so far, fencing has saved me from sharing the fate of most of the people I grew up with in the projects. One of the few avenues that have been open to African Americans is sports, so I definitely think it makes for social change. We excel in sports, so sports are a viable vehicle for African Americans to use as a springboard into other areas. You do not have to be great, and you certainly do not have to be a medalist. If you're just exposed to a sport, you will learn that when the times get tough, you need to get a little tougher. There are basic things in sports that are transferable to other areas of life, like work and relationships. You don't have to be a world champion fencer, because you will be a world champion in relationships, in social skills, and in the corporate environment.

I've been around the world, and I've been around a lot of great white athletes, and my personal opinion about that is, yes, African Americans are a little bit more athletic. But I don't think that's because we have been blessed with "special genes" or "special blood," I think it's because that is one of the only avenues that has been open to us. I've seen some white Europeans that are just as gifted, but they also have opportunities in universities, colleges, major corporations, and trades that they can pursue. African Americans, however, have not been able to get into all of those areas, so our energies are geared to sports. That makes it appear as if African Americans are supermen and superwomen in athletics. If there were opportunities for African Americans to get into the mainstream corporate environment, university environment, and trade specialties, I guarantee you would find a lot of us in those areas, saturating those fields also.

Sports have not made a great contribution toward progress in the past, but they're starting to. There are a lot of African American people who now want to join fencing. I want to start the Peter Westbrook Foundation as a nonprofit organization to teach inner city youth fencing for free, no charge. Bring this sport into these communities, with people like Mike Lofton and some of my other teammates. I want to expose these children, not just to fencing, but also to the discipline the sport requires, and share some of our life experiences with them. Most of all, we want to give them good role models. This idea is all new to me. I just got the paperwork done. What gave me the idea was another African American guy I'm very impressed with, who isn't in the papers too often. My fiancée Susan Miles has a son and we got him involved in taking karate. His sensei Sam McGee teaches karate, and he is taking all these inner city youths and adults, and he's teaching them for free. I'm talking about two hundred people. I've watched and seen what he's done for a lot of them who have been down in the dumps with no role models and on alcohol. They have a lot of integrity and self-esteem now. When I saw that, I told myself, "That is something I have to do."

I can understand the perspective of black athletes who do not participate in the community, because ten years ago, I would not have been doing it either. Everything in life is an evolution of emotions and realizations. I guarantee that when you're coming up in the fast lane, sometimes you can't even see the forest for the trees. Never mind helping other people, you can't even help yourself. You're just trying to stay abreast, even with all that money. When you get a little more mature, then you learn how to give. You ask any person, including white people, and it's more than likely 99.9% percent of them were not giving people in their youth. All they wanted was, "Give me, give me, give me." People are just people. It's not until we get a little older, a little more mature, that you'll find a lot of us giving back. That's what I'm doing now. I wouldn't have been doing it five years ago. I wasn't saying, "Give me, give me, give me," but I definitely wasn't out there trying to start a foundation to help inner-city kids. As I said, I'm maturing now and I don't want to get myself in trouble. I want to give back to people, my people. These African American people who are on top now, when they come to the realization and get mature, they can't help but want to give back. Look at people like Muhammad Ali, Larry Holmes, and Arthur Ashe, they're all trying to give back to their community.

I've come to the conclusion, and this is something that I'm pretty adamant about, that we're not athletic because of physicality, but we've socially evolved that way because it is the only free path historically open to us. I definitely feel that African American people are a little more honed into sports for this reason. As a kid in an inner-city African American environment, physical competition determined how people looked at you. You're raised all your life not to consider who's the smartest, not who has the best grades in school, but who's the baddest, who's the strongest, and who's the fastest. That attitude remains as you grow up and develop into an adult, and it is instilled in you. It was so instilled in me that I took it for granted. Now many of us feel instinctively, "Hey, I take pride in my physical ability, I want to do my best. I never give up." We just love to use our physical prowess.

There's a guy I work with, a white guy who holds the national championship in karate. He's also from the inner city, and he has the same drive that I'm speaking of. It's not really a person's color that determines whether you have that initiative, it's just being exposed to that mentality at an early age, and most white people are more exposed to the academic experience. My message is, "Hey, we have a lot of special gifts and talents we acquire in the inner city and in African American communities, and a lot of times people don't look on those talents and gifts favorably because it doesn't compare to what mainstream Caucasians have done. We have something so special, that will, that drive and determination can also transfer into other areas of life. Never forget that."

NOTES

1 For more on the Peter Westbrook Foundation, visit the official Web site at http://www.peterwestbrook.org.

2 For more on Peter Westbrook, see his autobiography, *Harnessing Anger: The Inner Discipline of Athletic Excellence.*

3 Dr. Samuel D'ambola is a member of the United States Fencing Hall of Fame, and is famous for producing superb high school fencers.

4 Since 1990, Peter Westbrook has won one silver (1991) and two gold (1995) medals at the Pan American Games. He was national champion in men's sabre (1995), and was a member of two U.S. Olympic teams (1992 and 1996) and two U.S. World Championship teams (1990 and 1991).

MAURICE SMITH

MARTIAL ARTS

May 17, 1995
Seattle, Washington

A WORLD-RENOWNED PROFESSIONAL MARTIAL ARTS COMPETITOR
for over twenty years, Maurice Smith won the World Kickboxing Council
(WKC) Light-Heavyweight Championship in 1983. That same year, he also
won the World Kickboxing Association (WKA) World Heavyweight Championship, becoming the first African American to achieve those feats. He
successfully defended the latter title for nearly a decade. Later, Smith
became the first black fighter to hold the titles of Battlecade Extreme
Combat World Heavyweight Champion (1996 and 1997), International
Sport Karate Association (ISKA) World Heavyweight Champion (1996),
and Ultimate Fighting Championship (UFC) World Heavyweight Champion (1997). His other titles include World Martial Arts Council (WMAC)
World Heavyweight Champion (1992) and K-1 USA Champion (2001).
Smith, the first black head coach in the International Fight League since
2006, rarely competes anymore, but as a true pioneer in a newly devel-
oping American sport, he has set a superb example for aspiring African
American martial artists.

CHILDHOOD

I was born in Seattle, Washington, on December 13, 1961. I had two fathers,
a biological father, and a father that took care of me. My father, who took
care of me, was Ernest Michael White, and he was killed in a fight during
a card game when I was nine. I saw it happen. Soon after that my mother,

my brother, and I all left for Pasadena, California. We lived there for about a year, and then we moved back to West Seattle in 1971.

Before I went to California, I was aware of race, but not to any major degree. I was mostly among blacks and Latinos, so there was little interaction with whites. I didn't experience racism, and I didn't understand it in the way that I do now. I was aware that I was black, and different from other ethnicities. When I got back from California, my grammar was a little different, my slang was different. My friends back on the southside of Seattle noticed and occasionally made fun of me, but my personality overruled most of that. They would say, "You sound white," or they would ask, "Are you oriental or Asian?" It was a joke, but nevertheless it was said. It wasn't really a problem, but I did think about it.

I went to Schmitz Park Elementary, which was in an all-white area. I then attended Sharples Junior High, which was back on the southside of Seattle, in a black area. At age thirteen, I became interested in the martial arts because of a Bruce Lee movie. I was thoroughly fascinated. Tae kwon do was my first martial art. My initial instruction was not provided by a traditional martial arts school. My friends were involved in martial arts, as well as other things, and they invited me to meet an instructor, who was a home teaching kind of guy. At that time a lot of Samoans were moving to Seattle, and there was tension between them and blacks. That also encouraged me to learn martial arts.

Although I developed an interest in martial arts, I still played other sports. I played football for the Rainier Recreational Center when I was in junior high. In high school I did football and gymnastics. There were two or three other blacks on the gymnastics team. In football I didn't think much about race, but when I played baseball back in grade school, I was the only black person on the team. But even though I became a good football and baseball player, I continued training in martial arts because I liked the idea knowing I could defend myself.

When I graduated from junior high in 1977, I decided to attend West Seattle High School because I'd heard Garfield High didn't have a good reputation, but it turned out to be a bad decision. This was during the busing era. I played tackle in football for West Seattle High and running back in my junior year. I was an okay player. I lettered, but school wasn't a big interest to me anymore. In my junior year I started having problems; I began to feel that going to school was a waste of time. I was always late because I couldn't get up in time for the bus, so I decided to quit. I was eighteen, and I had just started fighting in full-contact karate, which is called PKA karate.

I quit high school after the eleventh grade, because it had reached the point where I was going to school, standing in the halls, and nothing was happening for me. In eleventh grade I learned I would have to repeat the grade or go to summer school. My grades had faltered because I was being bused from the Central District to West Seattle, and waking up very early for the bus made it hard for me to get to school on time and stay awake in school. I decided to quit school and go to work. I don't remember all that was said when I told my mother I was quitting school, but I think she asked, "Is it your grades?" I said, "I don't think that my grades are good enough." By this time I had a job, which I kept until I was twenty-three. I have always worked. I worked in junior high and high school. I worked for McDonald's; I worked in a barbecue restaurant; I was a janitor at the community college in West Seattle; I worked summer jobs; I did paper routes. I worked a lot. When I made the decision to quit school, I wasn't a tremendous headache to my family, so they didn't mind. I still lived at home until I was about nineteen or twenty, but I was not a burden. I have never regretted quitting high school. I think I made the right decision.

When I was eighteen I began taking lessons from Leon Preston, an instructor who is still teaching at the Hec Edmundson Pavilion at the University of Washington. We would have sparring practices, not to win or lose, but just because we could. I still didn't know how good I was until some of the guys began to say, "You're tough," or "You're fast," or "You're tricky." I was trying to determine whether I was a fighter, a form (kata) competitor, or a weapons competitor. I eventually went for fighting. I began getting involved in traditional martial arts competitions, but I wasn't very good at that because it was more, "point contact," which basically means it was tag. I competed once with this old guy, and when I lost to him, I said, "This is not for me!"

After I quit high school, I knew that I needed a skill to make money. I had worked different jobs, but after high school I decided to move on. I worked for Easterners Leather Goods and then detailing cars at a car dealership for a time. That is when I started getting into martial arts competitions. I decided to go into full-contact PKA karate. Everybody at the time was involved with PKA karate, which is sanctioned by the professional karate associations. It was the most popular style, so we fought under their guidelines even in amateur competitions.

PROFESSIONAL LIFE

Getting into professional martial arts competition in the 1980s was not an orderly progression. As an amateur I would hear about an event, find out who the promoter was, approach him, and say, "Hey, this is who I am. This is what my weight is. When can I get on your next card?" Then the promoter would decide if I was any good. It didn't take me long to get on a card. My first competition as a PKA full-contact karate fighter was in Hec Edmundson Pavilion in September of 1980. Here I am out of high school, working, and now I am trying to do this karate stuff. I won that bout with a TKO. In my amateur time, I competed about every two or three months. I fought in Seattle; Tacoma; Vancouver, Washington; and in Portland, Oregon.

I didn't have my driver's license at the time, so I couldn't drive myself to these events. Let's say the Canadian promoter wanted me to come up there for a fight. My friends and I would all meet up and drive there together as a group. Since I was working and fighting, it was hard. I didn't have a special diet; all I did was train hard. I didn't have a trainer at that time either, even though a trainer was necessary. All the guys who were into martial arts back then, including me, Leon Preston, and Marcus Reed, would hook up at the IMA (Intramural Activities Building) at the University of Washington, and train together. Keith Hirabayashi, who is now doing movies under the name Keith Cooke, would occasionally meet with us and train as well.

I had my first taste of international competition when I went up to Canada in 1980 to fight Kelly Worden. I won, and that encouraged me to continue. The next year I had six fights and I won all of them. My record convinced me I was a good amateur, so I decided to turn professional. I was now at the point where a promoter asked, "Can Maurice fight this pro fighter?" and we said, "Sure." When we found out who I would be fighting, I said, "What do I have to lose?" The WKC World Light Heavyweight Champion then was Tony Morelli, a formidable fighter, but this was an opportunity of a lifetime. If I lost to the World Champ, it was no big deal. If I beat him, I'd become famous. We relied on the fact that at the World WPK Council Championship, he had looked terrible.

In our fight he didn't beat me, but I didn't win. I gassed out. At the time I had only had seven fights, and he had had twenty overall. He beat me because I lacked experience, but I had gone seven rounds with the world champion, so I knew I had what it took to be in this business. Even though I lost my first professional fight, it was a good learning experience for me. It was held in Canada, in the Royal Towers Hotel in Surrey. I had been paid about $500 for my fights as an amateur. For my first professional fight I was paid only a little more, even though the fight was on Canadian television.

Even though I was fighting as a professional, I had other jobs, too. But the fights were on the weekends so they didn't interfere with my work. In fact, my bosses were very good to me. They were Chinese and owned Mr. Rags, which is a retail chain that sells clothing. They were very supportive. They let me go away whenever I had to. They were very proud of me; they sort of adopted me. I worked for them from about 1980 to 1985.

My second professional fight was in Las Vegas and it was televised as well, but I was still on the undercard. I fought Don Neilson. He is half Japanese, half white American. At that time he had a great reputation, but I beat him. The money for this fight was about the same as before but, to me, it was more of an opportunity because it was going to be on TV. Money wasn't an issue until later on. After this fight I felt that I was good, even though my training regimen was not the best. I fought Don Zaleska before the year was out and won, so now I was ready for 1983.

I fought Tony Morelli again for the World Karate Cruiser Weight title in 1983, this time in Hawai'i. I had lost to him in Canada in 1982, but this time the result was different. I knocked him out. I was the first African American champion in that weight class sanctioned by the World Karate Council. The people that I used to hang around with were very proud of me. They were proud of me for what I had achieved.

After I fought Tony in Hawai'i, I came home to a "Welcome Home, Champ!" reception. My friends congratulated me, but I knew that the heavyweight title was there to try for. I prepared myself with three fights before I went to Mexico City to fight Travis Everett for the World Kickboxing Association (WKA) Heavyweight title. I won two of those three fights, losing only to Don Wilson in the second fight.

I lost the fight against Wilson in Japan because I got tired, so I felt I needed to train harder. When I fought Wilson, I had only five professional fights on record, but I was good for a beginner. After that loss, I changed my regimen. I started running the stairs at Hec Edmundson, I started sprinting, I lifted weights, and I swam. I did a lot more bag work, and shadowboxing. I went to work at eleven a.m. and got off at six p.m. Then I would drive from work to the gym, and train from six-thirty until ten-thirty or eleven, sometimes midnight. I would play basketball and swim, all in that four-hour span. I was young, so I could do that. That was my life, that and work. I felt a little pressure there, but seeing my name in the magazines helped, and being paid a little more was encouraging. I worked hard to prepare myself for the heavyweight fight. If I won that title, the money would come later. Winning the heavyweight title meant a lot to me, everything considered.

The weight divisions in kickboxing are the same as in boxing. Karate has one extra division called the super heavyweight, and it depends on your associations, but basically it is the same as boxing. There are various organizations in the sport of kickboxing. At the time, there was PKA karate, which is kickboxing; the World Karate Association (WKA), now the World Kickboxing Association; the World Karate Council; and the ISKA, the International Sport Karate Association. There are a lot of karate sanctioning organizations, but the main ones right now are the WKA and the ISKA, and then the Muay Thai Federation. We are just like boxing except for the money.

The heavyweight championship fight in Mexico City was held in a disco. I was confident because even though I had lost earlier in the year to Don Wilson, I had subsequently beaten Craig Kingle and my professional record at that time stood at 5–2. If I included all my fights, then my record was 12–2. I won that fight, beating Travis Everett and becoming the World Kickboxing Association Heavyweight Champion. Even though the fight was televised, there was no money from television rights. The promoters did, however, pay my expenses and prize money. After winning the heavyweight championship in 1983, I did not lose again until late 1984 when I lost to Jimmy Walker, only to beat him before the year ended.

My fights are typically knockouts, TKOs, and decisions. Some decisions are knockouts, which is when your opponent just quits. I have about thirty to forty knockouts out of fifty fights. When we say "knockout" in my sport, it is the same as in boxing. A TKO is when a fighter suffers a cut and can't continue. It is also called when a fighter is counted out while standing up. A knockout typically means a fighter is down on the ground and he can't move. He may be conscious, but he can't get up. If he is up, and he can't continue, then it is a TKO. Typically I have a lot of knockouts, when they can't get up or won't continue.

When I first went to Japan with Don Neilson back in 1982, he was a star and I was a nobody. But with my win I became a star. These fights are held at night, or around five o'clock. After a fight you're taken to a lavish dinner by the promoter. You get a dinner as a nobody, too, you just are not with the leading crowd. At present I am with the elite crowd. More with the bosses and business people, so now they sit at the same table with me. This is a big deal with the crowds. I will say it till the day I die, the Japanese are the most appreciative fans one can ever meet.

Although I was a star in Japan, when I came home there was no recognition. My sport originated in Thailand, and its origins are in Muay Thai. Now the Thais have a stranglehold on it. Thais have the best fighters, pound for pound in Muay Thai, than anybody in the world. The next country behind them is Holland, then Japan, followed by a lot of European countries, but America doesn't necessarily have top fighters. In America it is strictly baseball, basketball, football, tennis, golf, and that's it. Seattle is not a fight city, so you get no publicity unless you win at the Olympics.

When I came back from Japan I still had a job, but I was mentally making the transition to leave. I worked for a person who detailed cars. I didn't like it, but it was a job. I still had to fight, and I still had to work, but in 1983 I had a child. I continued kickboxing without a loss. In 1985, I came home from the fights, and my professional record was 14–4–2. This was a great record, but now I had to think about how to make money. A friend of mine who worked at Phil Smart Mercedes suggested I try for a job at Barrier Motors in Bellevue. I applied and got a job there as a porter, which means you wash the cars, and then you transport your customers from here to there. I did that for a while. I told them I fought a little bit, and they said, "As long as you do your work here, that is the most important thing." After Thanksgiving though, I was laid off. I asked myself, "What am I going to do now?" Finally, I decided I to go to school for welding.

The welding course I took was supposed to finish in about a year, but it ended up being a little longer because the school closed. When I finished I felt good. I went to work for Coca-Cola for a while, and then I ended up at Alaska Fisheries as a welder on their ships. While welding, I occasionally asked myself, "Here I am, Maurice Smith, World Champion. What is there for a black man like me?" I said, "Well, at least I have a skill." It was something to fall back on.

In 1984, I fought Marcel Schwank in Holland and I knocked him out in the first round. In Holland there are plenty of black people, from Surinam, and being black is not an issue with the Dutch. They are like the Japanese, they like the home boy to win, their own fighter. They feel annoyed when you knock down their champ. If they feel the fight was not called right, they will whistle, which means boo. But the Dutch fight in 1984 was important in the sense that it helped me to win in many later fights.

After that fight the Dutch treated me royally. I fought them quite a few times, and I generally won, until recently. We went on a tour and took a boat through the canal, and went through the cheese country and the tulip farms. It was a great trip. Now I'm making a bit more money. At that time it was about three thousand dollars per fight. I didn't have any training expenses, other than the gas for my car, because I trained myself.

My next title fight, after I came back from Holland, was against Raymond Horsey in Atlanta, Georgia, in '86. There were about six other fights on that card, and we were the main event. Typically each card has about six fights. The maximum for a good promotion is no more than eight or nine fights. The people you import can fight all night. The Atlanta fight was televised, but I have never seen it. I knocked Raymond out, but when it was over they didn't like me, because I low kicked him. The low kicking game was not popular in America, yet, so they did not understand it. Honestly, I would rather get a kick in the leg than in the head any day. Kicking someone in the head is more damaging than kicking them in the leg. You can always recover from kicks to the leg after a couple of days, or a week or so. I won, but the crowd didn't understand or appreciate the game, and they were angry. They thought I was cheating. But everything was fine later.

In 1987, I went back to Japan. On that trip I fought a Canadian guy named Steve Tremble, and I won. In Japan there are usually six to eight different fights in one night. I had become a star now, and I fought in Japan at least five or six times a year. The people I fought in Japan were mostly non-Japanese. They came from Holland, Canada, and elsewhere. But now I am not fighting any more Canadians. I am fighting strictly Dutch, or Japanese if they are big enough. I have fought one of their Japanese stars. The fans don't care. They just love the two competitors, as long as they fight well. By 1986, the fans would hang out after the fight and get my autograph, touch me, and want pictures. By 1987, when I walked on the street, they would recognize me and go, "Oh, oh," and tried to pronounce my name.

In 1988, 1989, and 1991, I won all my fights. When I started going to Japan and beating all the competition, regardless of where they came from, that took my career to another level. I began competing in what they called mixed matches, which consist of a kickboxer versus a karate fighter, or a kickboxer versus a wrestler. When I finally fought their top Japanese star, we had a mixed match, where the first round was kickboxing, the second round was karate, the third round was kickboxing, and the fourth round was karate. They called it a draw, because I didn't knock him out.

In the nineties I got into other style of fighting, wrestling. I fought a Japanese fighter in 1990, and I beat him in the third round. I was uncomfortable doing this kind of fighting. I don't like to wrestle, but I knocked him out in front of a crowd of about 60,000 people in the Tokyo Dome, where they play baseball. I was the draw, but there were wrestling fans there, too, a mixed crowd. I have my kickboxing fans, my karate fans, and now my wrestling fans. All for Maurice!

By this time the money had increased. It had been steadily increasing, but now it took a big jump. The increase in my pay was not substantial for my lifestyle. In my sport there are no endorsements of any kind. Even in boxing, aside from people like Foreman, Ali, and Frazier, how many other world champion boxers have gotten a lot of endorsements? So my not having endorsements is not unusual. In 1989–90 I was given an opportunity to do a movie called *Blood Fist II*, which was filmed in the Philippines and shown here. Being in the movie didn't pay a lot of money; it wouldn't have bought a new car in the nineties. At the time I received the offer I was working at Boeing. I applied for a leave of absence and they asked me why I wanted it. I explained to them that I had this opportunity to be in a movie, but they did not approve a leave, so I had to quit my job.

After the film, I fought some more in Japan. I've fought in America only three or four times in the last five years. I fought in Florida once, but my last few fights have been in Las Vegas, and I will fight in Los Angeles in June or July.

After the Tokyo Dome fight, I fought Stan Longindis, a Greek Australian, in Australia in 1991. That year I won all five of my fights. Stan's the first true heavyweight out of Australia, and he's the one who brought me there. We're friends, but when we were doing our press conference, he said, "Maurice, I'm going to beat you." I thought, "This isn't Stan!" He was trying to convince himself that he could beat me. Stan and I fought a twelve-round kickboxing championship fight for my heavyweight title. In the first round, he got a knockdown, although it was not a true knockdown. In the second round, he got me with a right hand and put me in a corner. After that the fight turned around completely. Stan's strategy was different from mine. He is typically a fast burn, hard fighter. I pick the pace up slowly, round by round. By the sixth round, the fight was probably even. From that point on, I just kept kicking and kept going. I didn't knock him out, but I won.

After the fight against Stan in Australia, I fought in Japan next, and then a Dutch fighter named Audrey Mannart, in France. I had three fights in three months. Then I fought again in Japan and won. By this time, in 1991, I was well known there. I began branching out into different areas of martial arts. I had started in kickboxing, moved to mixed match fights, and then to mixed match wrestling fights. I had a lot of things going.

In 1992, I started fighting Pancrase, which is a Greek form of fighting based a lot on kickboxing and wrestling, but in which you are not allowed to use gloves. We can punch to the face with the palms, but not with the closed fist. We can use a closed fist to the body. The Pancrase rules are that you can knock a person out or make the person submit. I got involved with this because it has become popular, and I am always challenged by new forms of fighting.

I came back from Japan, and everything was still going pretty well. When I went back to Japan, I fought a guy from Holland. He broke an ankle bone. He kicked at my thigh, but I blocked him with my shin and I broke his ankle. I think the concussion of the kick caused the break. The fight only lasted about forty-five seconds, maybe a minute maximum.

After I won that fight, I went back home and, in 1992, I fought in Las Vegas in a pay-per-view event against an American opponent named Steven Kurwell. The Americans aren't very good kickboxers yet. The Dutch are superior, because they are very crafty. As a group the Dutch and the Thais are the top fighters. There are only about five Americans that are very good at any one time in kickboxing. The Dutch are typically cleverer with the low kick, and the Thais are very deliberate. My fighting style is more Dutch, and when I was fighting the Americans I would eat them up with the low kicks. It is just constant bombardment. For the pay-per-view fight we had guests: Chuck Norris, Jean-Claude Van Damme, and Elvis Presley's widow, Priscilla Presley. A lot of stars were there. The production was pretty good, but it didn't live up to its billing, and the money was no better than at a regular fight.

By 1992, I wasn't working anymore. My career became fully, 100 percent kickboxing. The fights were coming in, so they were no worries for me at this time. There was always a fight coming, but if you're not fighting then you sweat it. I have an agent now who takes care of my fights, and I am fighting regularly. Most of these fights are taking place in Japan, France, and Holland. I've fought in Japan approximately thirty times, and most of my title fights have been there.

In the summer of 1993, I got knocked out for the first time. I was fighting Peter Aerts of Holland in his home country. In the fourth round, he was winning the fight on points. We got over in the corner, and he reached out to me with his right hand, not touching me, but I kind of sensed the move and, as I sensed the move, the kick came on my left side. It hit me in the neck, and I went out. Everything up to that point I remember clearly, but from then on, there is probably an hour that I will never find again. I don't know how long I was down, probably three to five minutes, maybe even more. I don't remember getting to the locker room; I don't remember taking a shower; I don't remember doing anything. It was like a movie, you fade to black. That is about an hour or two that I cannot replace. The kick didn't hurt and there was no loss of blood. It was actually quite pleasant. If I am going to get knocked out I would rather get knocked out that way instead of in the chin or the head or whatever. It was the first time I had ever been knocked out like that. It is just part of the business, but at the time it happened, there were even rumors that I was dead, because this was the first fight that I had lost by a knockout ever. I asked myself, "What happened?" What I did first was get back in the ring again, just to make sure I was okay.

Later I fought three fights. I won two, lost one, and had to quit for a year because of a bone spur on my right ankle. After the surgery, I gained some weight. I got as high as 235. The doctor said I would be ready in six months, but that is if I wasn't doing anything. I had a contract in Japan, so I had to compete in a mixed match with a Pancrase fighter, and I lost. I had just three fights in 1994. In 1995, I fought another Pancrase match, and then I fought in the kickboxing match in April of 1995, in Japan. I fought twice in Japan in the last month. I fought a Dutch fighter named Glen. He was black, from Surinam. He actually quit in the third round, because he hurt himself kicking me and then he got tired. I was just coming back still. Then I went back and fought a Pancrase match against Bass Rutten. He is Dutch and he's white. He's a real cool guy and we got along very well. He beat me with a knee bar to submission. I was just learning Pancrase, so I needed more practice, and my friend Frank Shamrock was coming to teach me.

I have fights coming up in June, July, September, October, November, and December. That's my schedule for the rest of 1995. These fights will be either kickboxing or Pancrase. I have a kickboxing fight in June, and one in California in July. The fight in September is Pancrase. In October, I have a K-l type fight in Denver. K-l is the big kickboxing organization that was started in Japan. It has kickboxing and wrestling brackets, and the winner of each bracket fights in the end. In November, I have a kickboxing fight in Japan, and then in December I go to Russia. The fight in Russia is more of a C-class fight. Of all the different types of fighting that are referred to as kickboxing, I prefer B class, that is, kickboxing in which we can kick the legs as well as above the waist, and then the Thai boxing which is A class. In Muay Thai you are allowed to use the knees and the elbows to the body and the head. Certain organizations may not allow elbows, but they allow knees, or they allow elbows, not to the head but just to the body. There are different modifications for the different styles in different countries.

The stuff being done by Chuck Norris and Jean-Claude Van Damme is not kickboxing, that's just for the movies. It's just kicking and carrying on. Steven Seagal's style is more grappling, which is good, like jujitsu or judo. I don't know if Bruce Lee could really fight, because all I have seen him do is in movies. But Bruce Lee inspired me, and I am grateful for the example he set.

I have been in the business for about fifteen years now. My record is pretty good. I have sixty-five knockouts. Whether or not I can keep this stuff up depends, first of all, on my desire. Second, it depends on money, and third, it depends on injuries. With all that in mind, if everything is good, my goal is to fight until I am thirty-five years old, which is a year and a half away. But beyond that, if the money has increased, injuries aren't bothering me, and the desire is still there, I will go until I get tired of it. That is for the kickboxing. As far as the Pancrase, you can go awhile longer because it is a kind of wrestling. So my future is somewhat indefinite.

I am planning to open a gym in Bellevue, Washington, in a month or so, and later I plan to open one in Seattle as well. It will be a kickboxing gym with Thai boxing. Without my skills I would be stuck here working like everyone else, and paying my way to travel like everyone else. I don't regret my decision to quit school. It hasn't prevented me from doing what I want to do and it hasn't prevented me from learning. I learn more now as an adult than I did as a child. I think I can make everything that I need through gyms and promotion of fights, the promotion of fighters, and possibly more movies. I will do seminars as well. I'm not limited to my base, which is teaching people how to fight. My career is still going to be based on my knowledge of martial arts, and trying to convey that to other people.

You can have knowledge, but you must also be able to get it out. I believe I have the speaking skills to do that. I am not limited too much.

To kids who tell me, "I want to be like Maurice," I say, "Look, I thought about selling drugs, but I had a responsibility to my children, so the risk was not worth it." Doing that was not part of my moral compass. I realize that increasing numbers of young black children are not finishing high school. I tell the kids that are coming up to finish high school, because you need an education, and you must realize that since we are not the majority, or the ones in power, you have to be as good or better than your white counterparts. That's been true for a long, long time. You have to be smarter, stronger, more diligent, and more outgoing than other people. But by the same token, you can't be a token. Don't blame white people.

I want to be a role model because of who I am as a person, not because of my athletic abilities. My character is not what I achieve by my physical ability, because that is only temporary. When people call me "Champ," I say, "No, that's not who I am," because if I lose my title, I'm not a champion anymore. So, I am Maurice. That's what I want to be called; that's forever.

BLACK ATHLETES INTERVIEWED FOR THE
BLACKS IN SPORTS ORAL HISTORY PROJECT

University of Washington, Department of American Ethnic Studies, funded by The Ford Foundation

Alpha Alexander, Sports Administration
Arthur Ashe Jr., Tennis*
Nehemiah Atkinson, Tennis
Alvin Attles, Basketball
Don Benning, Wrestling*
Bernie Bickerstaff, Basketball
Peter Bynoe, Basketball Ownership
Anita DeFrantz, Rowing
Jim Ellis, Swimming
Wayne Embry, Basketball
Lee Evans, Track and Field
Mae Faggs Starr, Track and Field*
Nikki Franke, Fencing*
Tina Sloan Green, Field Hockey and Lacrosse
Larry Holliday, Figure Skating
Ken Hudson, NBA Referee*
Jennifer Johnson, Paralympic Table Tennis*
Sam Lacy, Sports Journalism*
Earl Lloyd, Basketball
Bernadette Locke Mattox, Basketball

Edith McGuire Duvall, Track and Field
Madeline Manning Mims, Track and Field
Lenda Murray, Bodybuilding
Archie Moore, Boxing
Alan Page, Football*
Robert Pipkins, Luge
Oscar Robertson, Basketball
Maurice Smith, Martial Arts*
Debi Thomas, Figure Skating
Dean Tolson, Basketball
Wyomia Tyus, Track and Field*
Peter Westbrook, Fencing*
Mal Whitfield, Track and Field*
Bill White, Baseball
Willye White, Track and Field
Lenny Wilkens, Basketball*
Reggie Williams, Football
Sidney Williams, Football

*Athletes included in this book.

SELECTED BIBLIOGRAPHY

Aaron, Hank, with Lonnie Wheeler. *I Had a Hammer: The Hank Aaron Story.* New York: Harper-Collins, 1991.

Abdul-Jabbar, Kareem, and Peter Knobler. *Giant Steps: The Autobiography of Kareem Abdul-Jabbar.* New York: Bantam, 1985.

Ali, Muhammad, with Richard Durham. *The Greatest: My Own Story.* New York: Random House, 1975.

Allen, Maury. *Jackie Robinson: A Life Remembered.* New York: Franklin Watts, 1987.

Armstrong, Henry. *Gloves, Glory, and God: An Autobiography.* Westwood, NJ: Fleming H. Revell, 1956.

Arroyo, Eduardo. *"Panama" Al Brown.* Paris: J. C. Lattès, 1982.

Ashe, Arthur, and Arnold Rampersad. *Days of Grace: A Memoir.* New York: Knopf, 1993.

Ashe, Arthur, with Frank Deford. *Portrait in Motion.* Boston: Houghton Mifflin, 1975.

Ashe, Arthur, with Neil Amdur. *Off the Court.* New York: New American Library, 1981.

Ashe, Arthur R., Jr. *A Hard Road to Glory: A History of the African American Athlete.* 3 vols. New York: Warner Books, 1988.

Astor, Gerald. *And a Credit to His Race: The Hard Life and Times of Joseph Louis Barrow.* New York: Saturday Review Press, 1974.

Axthelm, Pete. *The City Game.* New York: Harper and Row, 1970.

Aycock, Colleen, and Mark Scott. *Joe Gans: A Biography of the First African American World Boxing Champion.* Jefferson, NC: McFarland & Co., 2008.

Bak, Richard. *Joe Louis: The Great Black Hope*. New York: Taylor, 1996.

Baker, William J. *Jesse Owens: An American Life*. Urbana: University of Illinois Press, 2006.

———. *Sports in the Western World*. Urbana: University of Illinois Press, 1988.

Balf, Todd. *Major: A Black Athlete, a White Era, and the Fight to Be the World's Fastest Human Being*. New York: Crown Publishers, 2008.

Banker, Stephen. *Black Diamonds: An Oral History of Negro League Baseball*. Princeton, NJ: Visual Education Corporation, 1989.

Bankes, James. *The Pittsburgh Crawfords: The Lives and Times of Black Baseball's Most Exciting Team!* Dubuque, IA: Wm. C. Brown, 1991.

Barrow, Joe Louis, Jr., and Barbara Munder. *Joe Louis: 50 Years an American Hero*. New York: McGraw-Hill, 1988.

Bass, Amy. *Not the Triumph but the Struggle: The 1968 Olympics and the Making of the Black Athlete*. Minneapolis: University of Minnesota Press, 2002.

Behee, John. *Hail to the Victors! Black Athletes at the University of Michigan*. Ann Arbor: Swink-Tuttle Press, 1974.

Benson, Michael. *Althea Gibson: Tennis Player*. New York: Ferguson, 2006.

Berkow, Ira. *The Du Sable Panthers: The Greatest, Blackest, Saddest Team from the Meanest Street in Chicago*. New York: Athaeneum, 1978.

Betts, John R. *America's Sporting Heritage: 1850–1950*. Reading, PA: Addison-Wesley, 1974.

Billet, Bret L., and Lance J. Formwalt. *America's National Pastime: A Study of Race and Merit in Professional Baseball*. Westport, CT: Praeger, 1995.

Birrell, Susan, and Cheryl Cole, eds. *Women, Sport, and Culture*. Champaign, IL: Human Kinetics, 1993.

Bontemps, Arna. *Famous Negro Athletes*. New York: Dodd, Mead, and Co., 1964.

Borries, Betty E. *Isaac Murphy, Kentucky's Record Jockey*. Berea: Kentucky Imprints, 1988.

Brailsford, Dennis. *Bareknuckles: A Social History of Prize-Fighting*. Cambridge, MA: Lutterworth Press, 1988.

Brashler, William. *Josh Gibson: A Life in the Negro Leagues*. New York: Harper and Row, 1978.

Brill, Marlene Targ. *Marshall "Major" Taylor: World Champion Bicyclist, 1899–1901*. Minneapolis, MN: Twenty-First Century Books, 2008.

Brooks, Dana D., and Ronald C. Althouse. *The African American Athlete Resource Directory*. Morgantown, WV: Fitness Information Technology, 1996.

———. *Diversity and Social Justice in College Sports: Sport Management and the Student Athlete*. Morgantown, WV: Fitness Information Technology, 2007.

———, eds. *Racism in College Athletics: The African American Athlete's Experience*. Morgantown, WV: Fitness Information Technology, 2000.

Brooks, Scott, Charles Kenyatta Ross, and Porter L. Fortune Jr. *Race and Sport: The Struggle for Equality on and off the Field*. Jackson: University Press of Mississippi, 2004.

Brown, Jim, with Myron Cope. *Off My Chest*. New York: Doubleday, 1964.

Brown, Jim, with Steve Delsohn. *Out of Bounds*. New York: Kensington, 1989.

Bruce, Janet. *The Kansas City Monarchs: Champions of Black Baseball*. Lawrence: University Press of Kansas, 1985.

Bryant, Howard. *Shut Out: A Story of Race and Baseball in Boston*. New York: Routledge, 2002.

Carino, Peter. *Baseball / Literature / Culture: Essays, 2002–2003*. Jefferson, NC: McFarland, 2004.

Carroll, John M. *Fritz Pollard: Pioneer in Racial Advancement*. Urbana: University of Illinois Press, 1992.

Cashmore, Ernest. *Black Sportsmen*. London: Routledge and Kegan Paul, 1982.

Chadwick, Bruce. *When the Game Was Black and White: The Illustrated History of Baseball's Negro Leagues*. New York: Abbeville, 1992.

Chalberg, John C. *Rickey and Robinson: The Preacher, the Player, and America's Game*. Wheeling, IL: Harlan Davidson, 2000.

Chalk, Ocania. *Black College Sport*. New York: Dodd, Mead, and Co., 1976.

———. *Pioneers of Black Sport: The Early Days of the Black Professional Athlete in Baseball, Basketball, Boxing, and Football*. New York: Dodd, Mead, and Co., 1975.

Chambers, Ted. *The History of Athletics and Physical Education at Howard University*. Washington, D.C.: Vantage, 1986.

Coakley, Jay J. *Sport in Society: Issues and Controversies*. Boston: McGraw-Hill Higher Education, 2007.

Cottrell, Robert C. *The Best Pitcher in Baseball: The Life of Rube Foster, Negro League Giant*. New York: New York University Press, 2001.

Davies, Richard O. *America's Obsession: Sports and Society Since 1945*. New York: Harcourt Brace, 1994.

Davis, Lenwood G. *Joe Louis: A Bibliography of Articles, Books, Pamphlets, Records, and Archival Material*. Westport, CT: Greenwood, 1983.

Davis, Lenwood G., and Belinda Daniels, comps. *Black Athletes in the United States: A Bibliography of Books, Articles, Autobiographies, and Biographies on Professional Black Athletes, 1800–1981*. Westport, CT: Greenwood, 1983.

Davis, Michael D. *Black American Women in Olympic Track and Field: A Complete Illustrated Reference*. Jefferson, NC: McFarland, 1992.

Davis, O. K. *Grambling's Gridiron Glory: Eddie Robinson and the Tigers Success Story*. Ruston, LA: M&M Printing, 1983.

Dawkins, Marvin P., and Graham C. Kinloch. *African American Golfers During the Jim Crow Era*. Westport, CT: Praeger, 2000.

Dixon, Phil, and Patrick J. Hannigan. *The Negro Baseball League: A Photographic Essay*. Mattituck, NY: Amereon House, 1992.

Dorinson, Joseph, and Joram Warmund, eds. *Jackie Robinson: Race, Sports, and the American Dream*. Armonk, NY: M. E. Sharpe, 2002.

Duberman, Martin B. *Paul Robeson*. New York: Knopf, 1988.

Early, Gerald. *The Culture of Bruising: Essays on Prizefighting, Literature, and Modern American Culture*. New York: Ecco Press, 1994.

———. *The Muhammad Ali Reader*. New York: Ecco Press, 1998.

Edmonds, Anthony O. *Joe Louis*. Grand Rapids, MI: Eerdmans, 1973.

Edwards, Harry. *The Revolt of the Black Athlete*. New York: Free Press, 1969.

———. *Sociology of Sport*. Homewood, IL: Dorsey Press, 1973.

———. *The Struggle That Must Be: An Autobiography*. New York: Macmillan, 1980.

Eisen, George, and David K. Wiggins, eds. *Ethnicity and Sport in North American History and Culture*. Westport, CT: Greenwood, 1994.

Eitzen, D. Stanley, and George H. Sage. *Sociology of North American Sport*. Dubuque, IA: Brown and Benchmark, 1993.

Elias, Robert, ed. *Baseball and the American Dream: Race, Class, Gender and the National Pastime*. Armonk, NY: M. E. Sharpe, 2001.

Entine, John. *Taboo: Why Black Athletes Dominate Sports and Why We Are Afraid to Talk About It*. New York: Public Affairs Press, 2000.

Falkner, David. *Great Time Coming: The Life of Jackie Robinson from Baseball to Birmingham*. New York: Simon and Schuster, 1995.

Farr, Finis. *Black Champion: The Life and Times of Jack Johnson*. Greenwich, CT: Fawcett, 1969.

Festle, Mary Jo. *Playing Nice: Politics and Apologies in Women's Sports*. New York: Columbia University Press, 1996.

Fitzpatrick, Frank. *And the Walls Came Tumbling Down: Kentucky, Texas Western, and the Game That Changed American Sports*. New York: Simon and Schuster, 1999.

Fleischer, Nat. *Black Dynamite: The Story of the Negro in the Prize Ring from 1782 to 1938*. New York: Ring Magazine, 1947.

Fletcher, Marvin E. *The Black Soldier and Officer in the United States Army, 1891–1917*. Columbia: University of Missouri Press, 1974.

Ford, Carin T. *Jackie Robinson: Hero of Baseball*. Berkeley Heights, NJ: Enslow Publishers, 2006.

Fox, Stephen. *Big Leagues: Professional Baseball, Football, and Basketball in National Memory*. New York: Morrow, 1994.

Frey, Darcy. *The Last Shot: City Streets, Basketball Dreams*. Boston: Houghton Mifflin, 1994.

Gaddy, Charles. *An Olympic Journey: The Sage of an American Hero, Leroy T. Walker*. Glendale, CA: Griffin, 1998.

Gaines, Kevin K. *Uplifting the Race: Black Leadership, Politics, and Culture in the Twentieth Century*. Chapel Hill: University of North Carolina Press, 1996.

Gardner, Robert, and Dennis Shortelle. *The Forgotten Players: The Story of Black Baseball in America*. New York: Walker, 1993.

Gates, Henry Louis, Jr., and Cornel West. *The African-American Century: How Black Americans Have Shaped Our Country*. New York: Free Press, 2002.

George, Nelson. *Elevating the Game: Black Men and Basketball*. New York: Harper-Collins, 1992.

Gerber, Ellen, et al. *The American Woman in Sport*. Reading, PA: Addison-Wesley, 1974.

Gibson, Althea. *I Always Wanted to Be Somebody*. New York: Harper, 1958.

Gildea, William. *Where the Game Matters the Most*. Boston: Little, Brown, 1997.

Gilmore, Al-Tony. *Bad Nigger! The National Impact of Jack Johnson*. Port Washington, NY: Kennikat Press, 1975.

Gilroy, Paul. *Against Race: Imagining Political Culture Beyond the Color Line*. Cambridge, MA: Belknap, 2000.

Goldman, Robert M. *One Man Out: Curt Flood Versus Baseball*. Lawrence: University Press of Kansas, 2008.

Gorn, Elliott J. *The Manly Art: Bare-Knuckle Prize Fighting in America*. Ithaca, NY: Cornell University Press, 1986.

———, ed. *Muhammad Ali: The People's Champ*. Urbana: University of Illinois Press, 1995.

———. *Sports in Chicago*. Urbana: University of Illinois Press, 2008.

Gorn, Elliott J., and Warren Goldstein. *A Brief History of American Sports*. New York: Hill and Wang, 1993.

Gould, Stephen J. *The Mismeasure of Man*. New York: Norton, 1981.

Graves, Joseph L., Jr. *The Emperor's New Clothes: Biological Theories of Race at the Millennium*. New Brunswick, NJ: Rutgers University Press, 2001.

Greene, Bob. *Hang Time: Days and Dreams with Michael Jordan*. New York: Doubleday, 1992.

Greenfield, Eloise, and George Ford. *Paul Robeson*. New York: Lee & Low Books, 2009.

Grombach, John W. *The Saga of Sock: A Complete History of Boxing*. New York: A. S. Barnes, 1949.

Grundy, Pamela. *Learning to Win: Sports, Education, and Social Change in Twentieth-Century North Carolina*. Chapel Hill: University of North Carolina Press, 2001.

Guttmann, Allen. *The Olympics: A History of the Modern Game*. Urbana: University of Illinois, 2002.

———. *A Whole New Ball Game: An Interpretation of American Sports.* Chapel Hill: University of North Carolina Press, 1988.

Halberstam, David. *Playing for Keeps: Michael Jordan and the World He Made.* New York: Random House, 1999.

Hales, A. G. *Black Prince Peter: The Romantic Career of Peter Jackson.* London: Wright and Brown, 1931.

Harris, Cecil, and Larryette Kyle-DeBose. *Charging the Net: A History of Blacks in Tennis from Althea Gibson and Arthur Ashe to the Williams Sisters.* Chicago: Ivan R. Dee, 2007.

Harris, Reed. *King Football: The Vulgarization of the American College.* New York: Vanguard, 1932.

Hart-Davis, Duff. *Hitler's Games: The 1936 Olympics.* New York: Harper and Row, 1986.

Hartmann, Douglas. *Race, Culture, and the Revolt of the Black Athlete: The 1968 Olympic Protests and Their Aftermath.* Chicago: University of Chicago Press, 2003.

Hauser, Thomas. *The Black Lights: Inside the World of Professional Boxing.* New York: McGraw-Hill, 1986.

———. *Muhammad Ali's Life and Times.* New York: Simon and Schuster, 1991.

Hawkins, Billy. *The New Plantation: The Internal Colonization of Black Student Athletes.* Winterville, GA: Sadaki, 2000.

Heintze, Michael R. *Private Black Colleges in Texas, 1865–1954.* College Station: Texas A&M University Press, 1985.

Henderson, Edwin B. *The Black Athlete: Emergence and Arrival.* New York: Publishers Company, 1968.

———. *The Negro in Sports.* Washington, D.C.: Associated Publishers, 1939.

Hietala, Thomas R. *The Fight of the Century: Jack Johnson, Joe Louis, and the Struggle for Racial Equality.* Armonk, NY: M. E. Sharpe, 2002.

Hoberman, John. *Darwin's Athletes: How Sport Has Damaged Black America and Preserved the Myth of Race.* Boston: Houghton Mifflin, 1997.

Holway, John. *Blackball Stars: Negro League Pioneers.* Westport, CT: Meckler, 1988.

———. *Voices from the Great Negro Baseball Leagues.* New York: Dodd, Mead, 1975.

Hoose, Philip M. *Necessities: Racial Barriers in American Sports.* New York: Random House, 1989.

Hotaling, Edward. *The Great Black Jockeys: The Lives and Times of the Men Who Dominated America's First National Sport.* Rocklin, CA: Forum / Prima Publishing, 1999.

Hurd, Michael. *Black College Football, 1892–1992: One Hundred Years of History, Education, and Pride.* Virginia Beach, VA: Donning Co., 1993.

Jackson, Donald Maurice. *Fourth Down and Twenty Five Years to Go: The African American Athlete and the Justice System*. New York: iUniverse, 2007.

Jarvie, Grant, ed. *Sport, Racism and Ethnicity*. London: Falmer Press, 1991.

Jay, Kathryn. *More Than Just a Game: Sports in American Life Since 1945*. New York: Columbia University Press, 2004.

Johnson, Jack A. *Jack Johnson Is a Dandy: An Autobiography*. New York: Chelsea House, 1969.

Johnson, Rafer, with Philip Goldberg. *The Best That I Can Be: An Autobiography*. New York: Random House, 1998.

Jones, Wally, and Jim Washington. *Black Champions Challenge in American Sports*. New York: David McKay, 1972.

Jones, William H. *Recreation and Amusement Among Negroes in Washington: A Sociological Analysis of the Negro in an Urban Environment*. Westport, CT: Greenwood, 1970.

Joravsky, Ben. *Hoop Dreams: A True Story of Hardships and Triumph*. New York: Harper Perennial, 1996.

Jordan, Pat. *Black Coach*. New York: Dodd, Mead, 1971.

Joyner-Kersee, Jackie, and Sonja Steptoe. *A Kind of Grace: The Autobiography of the World's Greatest Female Athlete*. New York: Warner Books, 1997.

Kennedy, John H. *A Course of Their Own: A History of African American Golfers*. Kansas City: Andrews McMeel, 2000.

Keown, Tim. *Skyline: One Season, One Team, One City*. New York: Macmillan, 1994.

Kershner, Jim. *Carl Maxey: A Fighting Life*. Seattle: University of Washington Press, 2008.

King, C. Richard, and Charles Fruehling Springwood. *Beyond the Cheers: Race as Spectacle in College Sport*. Albany: State University of New York Press, 2001.

King, C. Richard, and David J. Leonard. *Visual Economies of / in Motion: Sport and Film*. New York: Peter Lang, 2006.

Kirsch, George B. *The Creation of American Team Sports: Baseball and Cricket, 1838–72*. Urbana: University of Illinois Press, 1989.

Kirwin, Bill. *Out of the Shadows: African American Baseball from the Cuban Giants to Jackie Robinson*. Lincoln: University of Nebraska Press, 2005.

Krugel, Mitchell. *Jordan: The Man, His Words and His Life*. New York: St. Martin's, 1994.

Lacy, Sam, with Moses J. Newson. *Fighting for Fairness: The Life Story of Hall of Fame Sportswriter Sam Lacy*. Centreville, MD: Tidewater, 1998.

LaFeber, Walter. *Michael Jordan and the New Global Capitalism*. New York: Norton, 2000.

Lanctot, Neil. *Fair Dealing and Clean Playing: The Hilldale Club and the Devel-*

opment of Black Professional Baseball, 1910–1932. Jefferson, NC: McFarland, 1994.

Lapchick, Richard E. *Broken Promises: Racism in American Sports.* New York: St Martin's, 1984.

———. *Five Minutes to Midnight: Race and Sport in the 1990s.* Lanham, MD: Madison Books, 1991.

———. *100 Pioneers: African-Americans Who Broke Color Barriers in Sport.* Morgantown, WV: Fitness Information Technology, 2008.

———. *The Politics of Race and International Sport: The Case of South Africa.* Westport, CT: Greenwood, 1975.

———. *Smashing Barriers: Race and Sport in the New Millennium.* New York: Madison Books, 2001.

Leckie, William H. *The Buffalo Soldiers: A Narrative of the Negro Cavalry in the West.* Norman: University of Oklahoma Press, 1967.

Lee, George L. *Interesting Athletes: Black American Sports Heroes.* New York: Ballantine, 1976.

Lemon Meadowlark, with Jerry B. Jenkins. *Meadowlark.* Nashville, TN: Nelson, 1987.

Leonard, Wilbert M., II. *A Sociological Perspective of Sport.* New York: Macmillan, 1993.

Lewis, James, La'Tonya Rease Miles, and University of California, Los Angeles. *Baseball, Race and Los Angeles: An Oral History of Negro Leaguers of Southern California.* Los Angeles: University of California Press, 2006.

Lind, Rebecca Ann. *Race, Gender, Media: Considering Diversity Across Audiences, Content, and Producers.* Boston: Pearson, Allyn and Bacon, 2004.

Lipsyte, Robert, and Peter Levine. *Idols of the Game: A Sporting History of the American Century.* Atlanta: Turning Publishing, 1995.

Lloyd, Craig. *Eugene Bullard: Black Expatriate in Jazz-Age Paris.* Athens: University of Georgia Press, 2000.

Lomax, Michael E. *Operating by Any Means Necessary: Black Baseball and Black Entrepreneurship in the National Pastime, 1860–1901.* Syracuse, NY: Syracuse University Press, 2003.

———. *Sports and the Racial Divide: African American and Latino Experience in an Era of Change.* Jackson: University Press of Mississippi, 2008.

Londino, Lawrence J. *Tiger Woods: A Biography.* Westport, CT: Greenwood Press, 2006.

Louis, Joe, with Edna and Art Rust Jr. *Joe Louis: My Life.* New York: Harcourt Brace Jovanovich, 1978.

Lowry, Philip J. *Green Cathedrals: The Ultimate Celebration of Major League and Negro League Ballparks.* New York: Walker and Co., 2006.

Lucas, John A., and Ronald A. Smith. *Saga of American Sport.* Philadelphia:

Lea and Febiger, 1978.

Luke, Bob. *The Baltimore Elite Giants: Sport and Society in the Age of Negro League Baseball*. Baltimore, MD: Johns Hopkins University Press, 2009.

Malloy, Jerry, comp. *Sol White's History of Colored Base Ball with Other Documents on the Early Black Game, 1886–1936*. Lincoln: University of Nebraska Press, 1995.

Mandell, Richard D. *The Nazi Olympics*. Urbana: University of Illinois Press, 1986.

Matthews, Vincent, with Neil Amdur. *My Race Be Won*. New York: Charterhouse, 1974.

McDaniel, Pete. *Uneven Lies: The Heroic Story of African-Americans in Golf*. Greenwich, CT: American Golfer, 2000.

Mead, Chris. *Champion: Joe Louis, Black Hero in White America*. New York: Scribner's, 1985.

Mergen, Bernard. *Play and Playthings: A Reference Guide*. Westport, CT: Greenwood, 1982.

Messner, Michael A., and Donald F. Sabo, eds. *Sports, Men, and the Gender Order: Critical Perspectives*. Champaign, IL: Human Kinetics, 1990.

Miller, Patrick B., ed. *The Sporting World of the Modern South*. Urbana: University of Illinois Press, 2002.

Miller, Patrick B., and David Kenneth Wiggins. *Sport and the Color Line: Black Athletes and Race Relations in Twentieth-Century America*. New York: Routledge, 2004.

Moore, Joseph T. *Pride Against Prejudice: The Biography of Larry Doby*. Westport, CT: Greenwood, 1988.

Morris, Willie. *The Courting of Marcus Dupree*. Garden City, NY: Doubleday, 1983.

Nalty, Bernard C. *Strength for the Fight: A History of Black Americans in the Military*. New York: Free Press, 1986.

Novak, Michael. *The Joy of Sports*. New York: Basic Books, 1976.

Noverr, Douglas A., and Lawrence E. Ziewacz. *The Games They Played: Sports in American History, 1865–1980*. Chicago: Nelson-Hall, 1988.

Olsen, Jack. *The Black Athlete: A Shameful Story*. New York: Time-Life Books, 1968.

O'Neil, Buck, with Steve Wulf and David Conrads. *I Was Right on Time*. New York: Simon and Schuster, 1996.

Oriard, Michael. *King Football: Sport and Spectacle in the Golden Age of Radio and Newsreel, Movies and Magazines, the Weekly and Daily Press*. Chapel Hill: University of North Carolina Press, 2001.

———. *Reading Football: How the Popular Press Created an American Spectacle*. Chapel Hill: University of North Carolina Press, 1993.

Orr, Jack. *The Black Athlete: His Story in American History.* New York: Lion Books, 1969.

O'Toole, Andrew. *The Best Man Plays: Major League Baseball and the Black Athlete, 1901–2002.* Jefferson, NC: McFarland, 2003.

Overmyer, James. *Queen of the Negro Leagues: Effa Manley and the Newark Eagles.* Lanham, MD: Scarecrow Press, 1998.

Owens, Jesse, with Paul Neimark. *Blackthink: My Life as a Black Man and White Man.* New York: Morrow.

Page, James A. *Black Olympian Medalists.* Englewood, CO: Libraries Unlimited, Inc., 1991.

Paige, Leroy (Satchel), as told to David Lipman. *Maybe I'll Pitch Forever: A Great Baseball Player Tells the Hilarious Story Behind the Legend.* Garden City, NY: Doubleday, 1962.

Pennington, Richard. *Breaking the Ice: The Racial Integration of Southwest Conference Football.* Jefferson, NC: McFarland, 1987.

Peterson, Robert W. *Cages to Jump Shots: Pro Basketball's Early Years.* New York: Oxford University Press, 1990.

———. *Only the Ball Was White: A History of Legendary Black Players and All-Black Professional Teams.* Englewood Cliffs, NJ: Prentice-Hall, 1970.

Phillips, Murray G. *Deconstructing Sport History: A Postmodern Analysis.* Albany: State University of New York Press, 2006.

Platt, Anthony M. *E. Franklin Frazier Reconsidered.* New Brunswick, NJ: Rutgers University Press, 1991.

Porter, David L., ed. *African American Sports Greats: A Biographical Dictionary.* Westport, CT: Greenwood, 1995.

Powell, Shaun. *Souled Out? How Blacks Are Winning and Losing in Sports.* Champaign, IL: Human Kinetics, 2008.

Quercetani, Roberto L. *A World History of Track and Field, 1864–1964.* London: Oxford University Press, 1964.

Rader, Benjamin G. *American Sports: From the Age of Folk Games to the Age of Spectators.* Englewood Cliffs, NJ: Prentice-Hall, 1983.

———. *Baseball: A History of America's Game.* Urbana: University of Illinois Press, 2002.

Rampersad, Arnold. *Jackie Robinson: A Biography.* New York: Knopf, 1997.

Reed, Adolph L., Jr. *The Jesse Jackson Phenomenon: The Crisis of Purpose in Afro-American Politics.* New Haven, CT: Yale University Press, 1986.

Reese, Renford. *American Paradox: Young Black Men.* Durham, NC: Carolina Academic Press, 2004.

Reisler, Jim. *Black Writers / Black Baseball: An Anthology of Articles from Black Sportswriters Who Covered the Negro Leagues.* Jefferson, NC: McFarland, 1994.

Remnick, David. *King of the World: Muhammad Ali and the Rise of a Hero.* New York: Random House, 1998.

Rhoden, William C. *$40 Million Slaves: The Rise, Fall, and Redemption of the Black Athlete.* New York: Crown Publishers, 2006.

Ribowsky, Mark. *A Complete History of the Negro Leagues, 1884 to 1955.* New York: Birch Lane Press, 1995.

———. *Don't Look Back: Satchel Paige in the Shadows of Baseball.* New York: Simon and Schuster, 1994.

———. *The Power and the Darkness: The Life of Josh Gibson in the Shadows of the Game.* New York: Simon and Schuster, 1996.

Riess, Steven A. *Major Problems in American Sport History.* New York: Houghton Mifflin, 1997.

Riley, James A. *The Biographical Encyclopedia of the Negro Baseball Leagues.* New York: Carroll and Graf, 1994.

Ritchie, Andrew. *Major Taylor: The Extraordinary Career of a Champion Bicycle Racer.* San Francisco: Bicycle Books, 1988.

Roberts, Randy. *But They Can't Beat Us! Oscar Robertson's Crispus Attucks Tigers.* Champaign, IL: Sports Publishing, 1999.

———. *Papa Jack: Jack Johnson and the Era of White Hopes.* New York: Free Press, 1983.

Roberts, Randy, and James Olson. *Winning Is the Only Thing: Sports in America Since 1945.* Baltimore, MD: Johns Hopkins University Press, 1989.

Robinson, Frazier, with Paul Bauer. *Catching Dreams: My Life in the Negro Baseball Leagues.* Syracuse, NY: Syracuse University Press, 2000.

Robinson, Jackie, with Alfred Duckett. *I Never Had It Made.* New York: Putnam, 1972.

Rodman, Dennis, with Tim Keown. *Bad as I Wanna Be.* New York: Delacorte, 1996.

Rogosin, Donn. *Invisible Men: Life in Baseball's Negro Leagues.* New York: Athenaeum, 1987.

Rosaforte, Tim. *Raising the Bar: The Championship Years of Tiger Woods.* New York: St. Martin's, 2000.

Ross, Charles K. *Outside the Lines: African Americans and the Integration of the National Football League.* New York: New York University Press, 1999.

Ruck, Rob. *Sandlot Seasons: Sport in Black Pittsburgh.* Urbana: University of Illinois Press, 1987.

Rudolph, Wilma. *Wilma.* New York: New American Library, 1977.

Russell, Bill, as told to William McSweeney. *Go Up for Glory.* New York: Conrad-McCann, 1966.

Russell, Bill, and Taylor Branch. *Second Wind: The Memoirs of an Opinionated Man.* New York: Random House, 1974.

Rust, Art, and Edna Rust. *Art Rust's Illustrated History of the Black Athlete.*
Garden City, NY: Doubleday, 1985.

Rutkoff, Peter M., ed. *The Cooperstown Symposium on Baseball and American
Culture, 1997 (Jackie Robinson).* Jefferson, NC: McFarland, 1997.

Sage, George H. *Power and Ideology in American Sport: A Critical Perspective.*
Champaign, IL: Human Kinetics, 1988.

Sailes, Gary. *African Americans in Sport.* New Brunswick, NJ: Transaction, 1998.

Salzberg, Charles. *From Set Shot to Slam Dunk: The Glory Days of Basketball in
the Words of Those Who Played It.* New York: Dutton, 1987.

Sammons, Jeffrey. T. *Beyond the Ring: The Role of Boxing in American Society.*
Urbana: University of Illinois Press, 1988.

Sanchez, Ray. *Basketball's Biggest Upset.* New York: Authors Choice Press, 2006.

Savage, Howard J., Harold W. Bentley, John T. McGovern, and Dean F. Smiley.
American College Athletics. Carnegie Foundation for the Advancement
of Teaching, 23. New York: Carnegie Foundation for the Advancement of
Teaching, 1929.

Schaap, Jeremy. *Triumph: The Untold Story of Jesse Owens and Hitler's Olympics.*
Boston: Houghton Mifflin, 2007.

Scott, Jack. *The Athletic Revolution.* New York: Free Press, 1971.

Shouler, Kenneth A. *Total Basketball: The Ultimate Basketball Encyclopedia.*
Wilmington, DE: Sport Classic Books, 2003.

Shropshire, Kenneth L. *Being Sugar Ray: The Life of Sugar Ray Robinson, America's Greatest Boxer and First Celebrity Athlete.* New York: BasicCivitas, 2007.

———. *In Black and White: Race and Sports in America.* New York: New York
University Press, 1996.

Sifford, Charlie, with James Gallo. *Just Let Me Play: The Story of Charlie Sifford, the First Black PGA Golfer.* Latham, NY: British American Publishing,
1992.

Sinnette, Calvin H. *Forbidden Fairways: African Americans and the Game of
Golf.* Chelsea, MI: Sleeping Bear Press, 1998.

Slade, Suzanne, and Tom Spence. *Jackie Robinson: Hero and Athlete.* Minneapolis, MN: Picture Window Books, 2008.

Sloan-Green, Tina, et al. *Black Women in Sport.* Reston, VA: American Alliance
for Health, Physical Education, Recreation, and Dance, 1981.

Smith, Earl. *Race, Sport, and the American Dream.* Durham, NC: Carolina
Academic Press, 2007.

Smith, Sam. *The Jordan Rules.* New York: Simon and Schuster, 1992.

Smith, Thomas A. *Sport and Freedom: The Rise of Big-Time College Athletics.*
New York: Oxford University Press, 1988.

———, ed. *Big-Time Football at Harvard 1905: The Diary of Coach Bill Reid.*
Urbana: University of Illinois Press, 1994.

Somers, Dale. *The Rise of Sports in New Orleans*. Baton Rouge: Louisiana State University Press, 1972.

Sperber, Murray. *Onward to Victory: The Crises That Shaped College Sports*. New York: Holt, 1998.

Strode, Woody, and Sam Young. *Goal Dust: The Warm and Candid Memoirs of a Pioneer Black Athlete and Actor*. New York: Madison Books, 1990.

Telander, Rick. *Heaven Is a Playground*. Lincoln: University of Nebraska Press, 1995.

Thompson, Richard. *Race and Sport*. London: Oxford University Press, 1964.

Torres, Jose. *Sting Like a Bee: The Muhammad Ali Story*. New York: Abelard-Schuman, 1971.

Tunis, John R. *Sports: Heroics and Hysterics*. New York: John Day Company, 1928.

Tygiel, Jules. *Baseball's Great Experiment: Jackie Robinson and His Legacy*. New York: Oxford University Press, 1983.

———. *Extra Bases: Reflections on Jackie Robinson, Race, and Baseball History*. Lincoln: University of Nebraska Press, 2002.

———, ed. *The Jackie Robinson Reader: Perspectives on an American Hero*. New York: Penguin Dutton, 1997.

Wade, Harold, Jr. *Black Men of Amherst*. Amherst, MA: Amherst College Press, 1976.

Walker, Chet, with Chris Messenger. *Long Time Coming: A Black Athlete's Coming-of-Age in America*. New York: Grove Press, 1995.

Wallechinsky, David. *The Complete Book of the Olympics*. New York: Viking, 1984.

Watterson, John S. *College Football: History, Spectacle, Controversy*. Baltimore, MD: Johns Hopkins University Press, 2000.

Wertheim, L. Jon. *Venus Envy: A Sensational Season Inside the Women's Tennis Tour*. New York: Harper-Collins, 2001.

Whitaker, Matthew C. *African American Icons of Sport: Triumph, Courage, and Excellence*. Westport, CT: Greenwood Press, 2008.

White, G. Edwards. *Creating the National Pastime: Baseball Transforms Itself, 1903–1953*. Princeton, NJ: Princeton University Press, 1996.

Wideman, John E. *Hoop Roots: Basketball, Race, and Love*. New York: Houghton Mifflin, 2001.

Wiggins, David K. *Glory Bound: Black Athletes in a White America*. Syracuse, NY: Syracuse University Press, 1997.

———. *Out of the Shadows: A Biographical History of African American Athletes*. Fayetteville: University of Arkansas Press, 2006.

Wiggins, David K, and Patrick B. Miller. *The Unlevel Playing Field: A Documentary of the African American Experience in Sport*. Urbana: University of Illinois Press, 2003.

Wigginton, Russell Thomas. *The Strange Career of the Black Athlete: African Americans and Sports.* Westport, CT: Praeger, 2006.

Williams, Pat, and Mike Sielski. *How to Be Like Jackie Robinson: Life Lessons from Baseball's Greatest Hero.* Deerfield Beach, FL: Health Communications, 2004.

Winfield, Dave, and Michael Graubart Levin. *Making the Play: How to Get the Best of Baseball Back.* New York: Scribner, 2008.

Winters, Manque. *Professional Sports: The Community College Connection.* Los Angeles: Winmar Press, 1984.

Woods, Earl. *Playing Through: Straight Talk on Hard Work, Big Dreams and Adventures with Tiger Woods.* New York: Harper-Collins, 1998.

Young, Andrews S. *Great Negro Baseball Stars and How They Made the Major Leagues.* New York: A. S. Barnes, 1953.

——. *Negro Firsts in Sports.* Chicago: Johnson Publishing, 1963.

Zang, David W. *Fleet Walker's Divided Heart: The Life of Baseball's First Black Major Leaguer.* Lincoln: University of Nebraska Press, 1995.

Zimbalist, Andrew. *Unpaid Professionals: Commercialism and Conflict in Big-Time College Sports.* Princeton, NJ: Princeton University Press, 1999.

Zinkoff, David. *Go Man Go!: Around the World with the Harlem Globetrotters.* New York: Pyramid Books, 1958.

INDEX

A

Aaron, Hank, 16, 237
ABC, xxx, xxxi
ABC's Wide World of Sports, xxx
Ackerley, Barry, 95
Aerts, Peter, 231
African American Ethnic Sports Hall
 of Fame, 99
Afro-American Newspapers, xx, 3, 6,
 8, 10, 18
Alaska Fisheries, 227
Albritton, Dave, 35
Alcorn A&M, 146
Alexander's Ragtime Band, 9
All-Africa High Jump Championship,
 34
All-African Games, 37
All-American Football Conference,
 xviii
Al Lang Field, 15
All-Pro defensive tackle, 151
All Souls Presbyterian, 116
All-Star game (basketball), 79, 87, 89,
 92, 158
All-Star team (basketball), 89

Amateur Athletic Union, xxii, 28, 133
The Amateur Wrestler News, 71
American Association (baseball), 11
American Bowling Congress, xxi
American Football League (AFL), 157
American League (baseball), 8, 10–11
American Racing Cyclists Union, xv
American Stud Book, xv
American Tennis Association (ATA),
 122
American Wheelchair Table Tennis
 Association (AWTTA), 171, 178, 185
antispin, 176, 185
Arkansas AM&N, xiii
Arledge, Roone, xxx
Armstrong High School, 6
Arthur Ashe Stadium, 115
Aryan race, xix, xxvi
Ashe, Arthur, xxiv, xxvi, xxxii, xxxiv,
 114–31, 149, 196, 217, 235, 242
Atlanta Journal, xix
Atlanta Technical College Presiden-
 tial Award, 99
Atlantic Hotel, 13–14

C

California Club, 126
California State Legislature, xxx
Campanella, Roy, 15, 18
Campanis, Al, xxxi
Camp Lejeune, North Carolina, 85
Canadian Football League, xiv
Carlos, John, xxvii, xxix
Carnera, Primo, xviii
Carter, Art, 11
Carter, Jimmy, xxx
Cascade Company, 105
CBS, 93–94
Central Catholic High School, 152
Central High School, xii, 59, 73
Central State University, 103, 113
Charleston, Oscar, 12
Chase Park Plaza Hotel, 15–16
Chicago Cubs, 11
Chicago Bears, xviii, 151, 157, 161, 169
Chicago Daily News, 35
Chicago Defender, 9–11
Chicago Public Schools, 68
Chicago White Sox, 15
Children's Orthopedic Hospital, 88
City College, 188, 191
Civil Rights Act of 1964, xxiv–xxvi
Civil Rights Commission, xxii
Civil Rights movement, xxix
"Civil Rights Revolution," xxiv
Cleveland Browns, xviii, 157
Cleveland Cavaliers, 79
Clifton, Nathaniel, xxi
Coachman, Alice, 44
Coach of the Year, 71, 79, 187
Coca-Cola Company, xxix. *See also*
    New England Coke
Cole, Nat King, 13
Coleman, Jerry, 15
College Discovery program, 189–90
College Football Hall of Fame, 151
College Opportunity Program, 56
Compton, Oklahoma, 46
Congress of Racial Equality (CORE),
    xxix
Connor, Bull, 124
Considine, Bob, 9
Cooke, Keith, 224
Cooper, Chuck, xxi
Cosby, Bill, 51
Costello, Hugo, 210
Cousins, Tom, 87
Crazylegs, ix
Creve Coeur, 119
Cultural Exchange Program, 23, 28
Cunningham, Sam "Bam," xxiii

D

D'ambola, Samuel, 208, 219
Dana, Charles A., xvi
Dana College, 65
Daniel, Marcella, 147
Daniels, Isabel, 53–54
Davis, Willie, 17
Davis Cup, xxx
DeFrantz, Anita, xxx
de Gaulle, Charles, 126, 131
Democratic Farm Labor (DFL), 165
the Depression, xxvi, 8, 25, 60, 100,
    188
Detroit Pistons, 89
Devaney, Bob, 71
de Varona, Donna, 148
DeVos Sport Business Management
    Program, xxxvi
Dickson, Paul, 158
Didrikson, Babe, 44
Dihigo, Martin, 12
Dillard, Harrison, 29

Robeson, Paul, 10–11, 240
Robinson, Jackie, xx, 3, 12, 16, 63, 130, 237, 240, 243, 246, 248–50
Robinson, Mack, xxvi
Roche, Tony, 129
Rockefeller, Nelson, xxix
Roeder, Bill, 16
Rose Bowl, 131
ROTC, 84
Royal Towers Hotel, 224
Royce Hall, 125
Rudolph, Wilma, 45, 53–54, 136–37
Russell, Bill, xxix, 86, 89–91, 94, 97, 106, 109, 113
Ruth, Babe, 130
Rutten, Bass, 231
Ryan, Buddy, 163

S

"Sacred Six," 117–18
Sanford, Florida, 13
San Francisco Giants, 14
San Jose State University, 131
Saskowsky, Herman, 92–93
Schenley Hotel, 15
Schmeling, Max, xviii
Schmitz Park Elementary, 222
Schulman, Sam, 89–90, 93, 95
Schwank, Marcel, 227
Scott, Bill, 10
Seagal, Steven, 232
Seattle Seahawks, xiv, 93
Seattle SuperSonics/Sonics, 79, 88–89, 91–95
"separate but equal," 8, 21
Seton Hall University, 99
Seward Park High School, 190
Seymour, Paul, 87
Shamrock, Frank, 231

Shanghai Sports Federation, 180
Sharples Junior High, 222
Shelley v. Kraemer, xx
Shelton, Lonnie, 95
Sheraton-Jefferson Hotel, 83
Sherman Elementary School, 60, 62
Shinnecock Indian, 3–4
Shoreham Hotel, 14
Short, Bob, 90
Sikma, Jack, 94–95
Simpson, O. J., 128, 168
Sissler, George, 12
sit-ins, xxiv, 123, 192
Smart, Keeth, 205
Smith, Kenny, 17
Smith, Maurice, xxxii, 220–33
Smith, Tommie, xxvii, xxix, 145–46
Smith, Wendell, xx, 3, 12, 18
Smith v. Allwright, xx
Snyder, Dick, 95
"Southern Strategy," xxvi, xxix
Southwest YMCA, 99
Special Olympics, 88, 183
"Spook Wafflers," 26
Sports Illustrated Award of Merit, 59
"stacking," xiv, xxv
State Legion Baseball Tournament, 65
States' Rights Party, xxii
State Supreme Court, 165
St. Johns African American Episcopal Church, 61
St. John's University, 209
St. Louis Cardinals, 15
St. Louis Hawks, 79, 82–83
St. Louis University, 83
St. Mary's clinic, 88
Stoke Mandeville Games, 177
Stokes, Louise, xxvi
Stoneham, Horace, 14
St. Philip Hospital, 115

University of Nigeria, 31
University of Notre Dame, xxv, 154
University of Oklahoma, xxiii
University of Omaha, xxiv, 65
University of Pennsylvania, xxxvi, 11, 149
University of Southern California, xxiii, 121
University of Texas, El Paso, xxiv, 160
University of the West Indies, 173
University of Toledo, 154
University of Washington, xiv, 223–24
U.S.A. Track and Field Hall of Fame, 23, 39, 133
U.S. Department of Justice, xvii
U.S. Fencing Association, xxxii, 187, 196
U.S. Fencing Association Hall of Fame, 187
U.S. Foreign Service, 23–24, 32
U.S. Information Service, 28, 182
U.S. Men's Championship (fencing), 211
U.S. Olympic Committee, 199
U.S. Olympic Hall of Fame, 23, 133
U.S. Olympic Wrestling Committee, 59
U.S. Open (tennis), 115
U.S. State Department (Cultural Exchange Program), 28
U.S. Supreme Court, xx, xxvi, 164, 166
U.S. Table Tennis Tournaments, 171

V

Van Damme, Jean-Claude, 230, 232
Vero Beach, Florida, 13
Vertlieb, Dick, 88–89, 91
Viking of Distinction Award, 59
Virginia Beach, Virginia, 119, 242

Virginia Public School System, 118
Virginia Union University, 116

W

Waldorf Astoria, 35
Walker, Jimmy, 226
Walker, Mel, 35
Walker, Wally, 95
Wallace, George, 124
Walton, Bill, 93
Warren, Earl, xxvi
Washington, Kenny, xviii
Washington Capitols, xxi
Washington Heights, 189
Washington Homestead Grays, 12
Washington Nationals, 7
Washington Redskins, 17
Washington Senators, 5, 15
Washington Times-Herald, 9
Washington Tribune, 6–9
Waterbury, Tom, 160
Watergate, xxx
Watts, California, 24
WBAL-TV, 19
Webster, Marvin, 94
Weinberg, Larry, 93
Wenninger, Christiana, 177, 179
Wesley, Dr., 103
West, Jerry, 87, 90
Westbrook, Peter, xxxi–xxxii, 196–97, 203, 204–219
Westchester, New York, 175
Western Conference (basketball), 90
Westinghouse High School, 102
West Seattle High School, 222
West Side Tennis Club, 123
Westwood Baptist Church, 116
Wheaties, 131
Wheelchair Sports, USA, 171, 178